UGLY

UGLY

A Letter to My Daughter

Stephanie Fairyington

PANTHEON BOOKS

NEW YORK

FIRST HARDCOVER EDITION
PUBLISHED BY PANTHEON BOOKS 2026

Published by Pantheon Books, a division of Penguin Random House LLC,
1745 Broadway, New York, NY 10019.

Pantheon Books and the colophon are registered trademarks of
Penguin Random House LLC.

Credit to Anne Mathiasz and Daria Pushka for illustrations appearing on page 47.

Library of Congress Cataloging-in-Publication Data
Name: Fairyington, Stephanie, [date] author.
Title: Ugly : a letter to my daughter / Stephanie Fairyington.
Description: First hardcover edition. | New York : Pantheon Books, 2026. |
Includes bibliographical references.
Identifiers: LCCN 2025038956 (print) | LCCN 2025038957 (ebook) |
ISBN 9780593701881 (hardcover) | ISBN 9780593701898 (ebook)
Subjects: LCSH: Women—Social conditions. | Ugliness. | Feminine beauty
(Aesthetics)—Public opinion. | Mothers and daughters.
Classification: LCC HQ1155 .F348 2026 (print) | LCC HQ1155 (ebook) |
DDC 305.42—dc23/eng/20260112
LC record available at https://lccn.loc.gov/2025038956
LC ebook record available at https://lccn.loc.gov/2025038957

penguinrandomhouse.com | pantheonbooks.com

Printed in the United States of America

1st Printing

The authorized representative in the EU for product safety and compliance is Penguin Random House Ireland, Morrison Chambers, 32 Nassau Street, Dublin D02 YH68, Ireland, https://eu-contact.penguin.ie.

IN MEMORY OF MY FATHER, H.A.K.

Dedicated to

My Mother
Sabrina
Our Daughter
& You.

May you resist, overcome, and transcend
the ugliness of this world.

Contents

In certain instances, the names and anecdotes represented in this text have been changed to ensure the anonymity of the people rendered herein.

UGLY

Prologue

Letter to My Daughter

I am an ugly woman. I was an ugly child, too. Not in a way that would elicit mouth-gaping stares—it's a perfectly normal face; all the parts sit in their proper place—but it's bland, offensively so, like a person who's given up or doesn't try.

My type of ugly is the most off-putting kind because it's *not* garish enough to entertain like Medusa with her snake hair. Instead, it looks like an active and hostile repudiation of what I, as a woman, am called upon, daily, to do: please the gaze of others, especially men (but women, too), a message that's already worked its way through your young consciousness, like an insidious snake.

I already see you—and so many other young girls—walking the tightrope, carefully moving through each moment of your life, trying to sidestep ugly like a body with restricted motion, a limited range of possibilities.

Unlike you with your soulful brown eyes and the sweet delicate features of your birth mother, I didn't win the genetic lottery. I've traveled most of my days unnoticed, like a specimen only visible under a microscope, but when someone, man or woman, looks into the eyepiece and sees my face in close proximity, maybe on a crowded subway or a bus, and I suddenly become highly visible, I see contempt in their eyes for what they perceive as a brazen refusal to try, and I'd fall short even if I did.

Mine's a face that refuses to lie back and get fucked, which is, perhaps, the ultimate definition of an ugly woman.

Ugly, a word with fangs that can kill a woman's self-esteem in one bite, has followed me from childhood to womanhood. To this day, anytime I hear the word *ugly,* I wince. "Yo, ugly," I'll hear a teenager sneer on a New York City subway, and I'll look up. I'm so aligned with the perception that I am ugly, an epithet hurled at me one too many times over the course of my forty-nine years, it feels like I'm being addressed, like it's my name.

So I understand the impulse to carefully craft and maintain this manufactured conception of beauty.

To defy the pretty imperative is to become invisible, which is a kind of death. I know that all too well.

Edicts about how we should look, behave, and think are the psychological violence through which we are made—not born—women.

And even if we could evade those violent blows, we'd render ourselves culturally unintelligible. Undefined shapes of nothingness. Outside rationality. Madwomen. Witches.

When you were in second grade, you met a pale-faced ethereal-looking third grader clothed in a long Victorian dress in the park. She said she was a witch and invited you to a coven—which she pronounced "coben"—and became your obsession. Soon after, you decided you, too, were a witch and would be needing an assortment of witchy accessories like a wand—the Harry Potter one would do—a spell book and all-black dresses so you could hide in the night, you said, "like a black cat."

In your witchiness, I saw a future you living life in happy communion with the ineffable and mystical, rejecting all the forces converging to knock you down and cut you up.

You're too little to know it yet, but when you open your grimoire and chant under the full moon from a window in our small living room—"I smell a child tender and mild . . . I smell a child windy and wild"—it could have gotten you killed in ages past.

Witches—those wonderful heretics, outlaws, sorcerers who defy easy categorization and occupy a state of unpredictability, capable of unimaginable things, good, bad, and benign—have been persecuted throughout history for the ways they fail to fit and conform. From the fourteenth to the seventeenth centuries, tens of thousands thought to have been witches were executed across Europe; twenty others were put to death during the Salem Witch Trials in Massachusetts in the 1690s.

Misogyny underlay the hysteria—they were unilaterally women who bucked convention by remaining unwed and celibate, eschewing motherhood and aging into a deeply wrinkled season of life. They were, in sum, ugly.

By situating yourself in a history of women who refused to acquiesce and obey imperatives about how they should be, I'm hopeful that a voice within you is forming that will override the toxic messages you're trying to adapt to now.

And yet, I also know that living in opposition to societal norms is not a real refuge or liberation: We are defined as much by what we are for as by what we are against. Feminists of the Third Wave believe our liberation is in our active resistance—that we can subvert the patriarchy in our own individual micro-orbits of transgression or defiant self-celebration in the face of cultural contempt and degradation. But I'm not convinced it's fully possible to fly free of the layers and layers of cultural "fuck you" in some academic fantasy or theoretical promise of our ability, our agentic power, to overcome the indignities of being on the outside of the inside, of existing in a matrix of meaning that subsists on our exploitation and subjugation.

Real liberation lies somewhere in that part of you that knows, with unutterable certainty, that your value—and the value of every life around you—is vaster and more meaningful than the ways it's been constructed by earthlings.

In these pages, I will go thread by thread with you to tease out how I came to see myself as ugly—and weave those threads anew, into something as yet unknown, something transcendent, something that will always be here for you, a place in which you can remember how to love yourself through every iteration of being, each day, moment to moment, when the world makes it exceedingly hard.

This is for us, for you, when you're old enough to know the ugly truth.

Chapter 1

Blood

We were preoccupied with your aesthetics—your material condition—just as you've been trained to be, even before you were conceived, when you were just an idea, a hope.

On a trip to Chicago to meet your newly born cousin Mari, I began to long for the impossible: to fuse my bloodline with Sabrina's—your biological mother whom you call Mama Sabby, the love of my life for the past seventeen years—through you. I wanted to concretize our love, an unquantifiable, abstract thing, in material form.

There was irony—perversity, really—in this longing. At one time, I would have found such a desire unimaginative and lazy, counter to the goals of creating nonbiological forms of kinship and community and new ways of being and relating in the world in accordance with my queer ethos.

Biology, for most of my life, has felt more like a problem—even a punishment—than a solution. I never felt quite right in this body in which I live—like I'm an imposter walking through rooms, sitting on couches, sleeping on beds in a house that doesn't belong to me. It wasn't just the creeping sense that my gender and sex were out of sync or the undeniable desire and longing I felt for other girls; it was the poverty of my genetic inheritance visible in my face, a face that wouldn't have registered as anything spectacularly unattractive if it wasn't abutting the beauty of my mother and handsome older brother. Where they had full lips, I had thin ones; where they had silky straight hair, mine was thick and wiry; where they had aquiline noses, I had a bulbous red one; where they had perfectly shaped almond eyes—my mother's blue, my brother's green—mine were big and buggy and slightly mismatched. I could always see the quiet disbelief—disdain, even—in the faces of strangers when they realized we were related. Their biology visually cohered; mine did not, leaving me outside their pretty dyad and full of dysmorphia.

The unease I felt about my appearance was amplified by the creeping awareness that I was queer, that I was socially disfigured, a biological aberration, ugly on the inside, too, in the eyes of the world. When my politics became more radical—more self-affirming and defiant at Berkeley in the late 1990s—biology troubled me in a whole new way. The mainstream LGBTQ movement has historically sought to secure our civil rights by appealing to a "born this way" politic or a "politic of pity." This strategy, an effective one in the short term but a limiting one in the long run, goes like this: *I'm gay through no fault of my own, through some mysterious congenital defect, as sexologists all the way back to the nineteenth century argued in our defense, so it's unjust to discriminate against me and deny me equal rights.* It's meant to generate sympathy and rally people to our cause, but subtextually it communicates the self-disparaging message that no right-minded person would willingly submit to such a loathsome and miserable condition.

What kind of acceptance have we truly gained if it's contingent upon people thinking that we're genetic mistakes? How does it really help us to take choice out of the equation when we all know that essentialist arguments, those rooted in a fixed and biological understanding of identity, have historically hurt certain populations of people—women, African Americans, and Jews, for example? Isn't the elasticity of identity more empowering and self-affirming?

While holding these questions in my own mind, I, too, resorted to the expediency of bio logic when I came out to my own mother in a letter at age twenty-eight: "If there were a straight pill, I'd swallow it faster than you can say the word *gay*," I wrote idiotically. That was easier to digest because it let both of us off the hook and elicited more compassion than a radical "politic of choice" would—a politic that would lean on the argument that we deserve the freedom to self-determine, to carve out and create a life that brings us meaning and happiness or nihilism and despair, however we see fit as long as we're not hurting anyone else.

And yet, I get the impulse toward the pragmatism and accessibility of an essentialist understanding of homosexuality: When I was twelve, I witnessed my gentle-hearted dad try to defend gay people using the logic of determinism, which my Argentine grandmother, a passionate Baptist, dismissed in thundering protest. Sitting at the big brown table that occupied half of my grandparents' small kitchen, my grandmother and father were intellectually sparring about whether or not people were born gay. My father, who I believe knew I was a lesbian from an early age, argued that if our condition was congenital, if we "couldn't help it, like people born with Down syndrome," he reasoned aloud, then it was unethical and immoral to condemn us. This premise unleashed my grandmother's fury to such an unusual extent, she slammed her fist on the table hard enough to make the plates clank and their coffees spill. "My God does *not* make mistakes!" she roared with merciless certainty. "Okay, Mamá, okay," he said, visibly shrinking himself, as he often did before the overpowering women in his life.

It was the first time I'd heard my dad's thoughts on the topic of homosexuality, although it didn't at all surprise me that someone so elegant and compassionate would have a more generous viewpoint than your average American male in the conservative 1980s, even *with* all his religious training—and he could, indeed, recount every character and story in the Bible with frightening detail and exactitude. But hearing my grandmother's firm and unforgiving take on the topic, our family's highest spiritual authority, made me feel like I was awash in the devil's filth: I was the opposite of God and goodness, the essence of beauty. Even my dad's more tolerant perspective confirmed to me that I was a malformation, a genetic error. Whatever side of this argument one landed on, my material and immaterial self were troubling affronts—either to nature or to God.

My marriage and wish to materialize my love for Sabrina in you was ironic in other ways, too. As a kid, I vowed that I'd never get married and have babies, a stance reinforced at U.C. Berkeley, where I learned to question and critically disassemble all the beliefs, values, and institutions that organize our society—gender, sexuality, race, marriage, monogamy, capitalism, God—in an effort to see what could be reworked or outright annihilated for the betterment of us all, but especially for those of us on the social peripheries.

All this to say, I never wanted you; I never dreamed I *could* want you because our dreams are bound by the systems of meaning, institutions, and laws that rule our lives, and in Downey, California, in the mid-1980s, a young person awakening to her same-sex desires could not conceive of getting married and having kids. We were not represented anywhere in popular culture, and whatever one may think of the merits or demerits of the aspiration to marry and have children, neither was an option at the time.

Even acting on our queer lusts was, technically, against the law in all but twenty-one states, although rarely enforced—except in the case of Michael Hardwick, a handsome bartender in Atlanta, Georgia, in the summer of 1982, who was spied by a cop performing oral sex on a married schoolteacher in Hardwick's very own bedroom. Both were arrested on charges of sodomy and possession of pot. A lower court in the conservative state of Georgia, stunningly, ruled in Hardwick's favor, but the state appealed to the Supreme Court of the United States.

In June 1986, three months after I turned ten, emerged from puberty, and realized my same-sex attractions, the highest court in the land ruled against Hardwick, arguing that his right-to-privacy argument, inferred in the Fourteenth Amendment's due process clause, did not cover his right to engage in sodomitical acts, letting anti-sodomy statutes stand throughout the land.

When Hardwick's lover was arrested, he pleaded for the officer not to tell his wife or publicly disclose his arrest because he could lose his teaching position in North Carolina where he lived—and that was a real concern throughout the '80s and '90s, when educators "discovered or perceived to be gay," says Jennifer C. Pizer, the chief legal officer at Lambda Legal, a civil rights organization fighting for LGBTQ equality, could be dismissed from their posts on moral grounds supported by the Supreme Court's *Hardwick* decision. It wasn't until that law was overturned in 2003 that LGBTQ advocates were able to successfully win us greater civil liberties. As Pizer put it via email: "Lambda Legal's 2003 victory in *Lawrence v. Texas* marked a sea change in our ability to secure more robust legal protections for LGBTQ+ people in many more parts of the country," she explained. "It set the stage for increasing successes in our marriage equality advocacy by removing one of the persistent obstacles to achieving comprehensive family law protections for LGBTQ+ people and their families." She points out that while we had already made important strides in securing nondiscrimination protections in certain states before the *Lawrence* decision—including efforts to prevent discrimination in public employment, address bullying of LGBTQ+ students, and combat various forms of police misconduct—*Lawrence* removed a major barrier. "After that, we were able to make legal progress more quickly and effectively."

Despite decades of progress since then, we're heading back, derailingly fast, to a time of restricted freedoms for women (with the end of reproductive choice), for people of color (with the elimination of affirmative action, narrowing voting rights, and Trump's assault on diversity, equity, and inclusion initiatives), and for LGBTQ communities, especially trans people, whose very existence is under attack: Several states aim to reinstate laws similar to those formulated in the bygone era of my '80s youth. Alabama, Arkansas, Indiana, Iowa, Kentucky, North Carolina, Mississippi, Texas, and Florida, to name a few states, have ongoing campaigns against us. Florida, for one, passed HB 1557, the Parental Rights in Education bill (popularly known as "Don't Say Gay"), in 2022, largely outlawing discussions of sexual orientation and gender identity in grades K through 12. Before an agreement between proponents and opponents of the law was reached in the spring of 2024, allowing discussion of the topic as long as it is not a part of academic instruction, it was an open question as to whether queer teachers would be forced back into the closet or risk suspension or expulsion if they displayed welcoming rainbow flags or showcased pictures of their queer families in the classroom. The state's quest to limit or eliminate references to LGBTQ people extended to its many public school libraries, too, where several purged their collections of books with LGBTQ characters and themes. In northeast Florida, however, a settlement was reached with the School Board of Nassau County, resulting in the restoration of queer titles to the district's bookshelves. I told you about such wins so you could see intolerance and bigotry successfully thwarted but reminded you that we must remain vigilant and engaged, especially in the age of Trump. Just days ago from this writing, the Supreme Court ruled in favor of religious parents' request for an "opt-out" provision to excuse their children from school lessons and literature that include LGBTQ people and other curricular content that conflicts with their religious beliefs. We wondered aloud how it might make queer students feel that a schoolmate could skip class just because a book reflecting LGBTQ experiences and feelings was discussed.

If we lived in Florida, you'd asked, would *Belle of the Ball,* a story about a lesbian love triangle, or *The Girl from the Sea,* a book about an interspecies romance between a lesbian mermaid and a teenage girl, be available in your school library. You've read both graphic novels over and over, reminding us each time, "Moms, these girls are just like you guys."

"It would depend on where we lived in Florida, but in some school districts, no, those books would not be in the school library," I said.

I didn't want to admit to you that we were seen, to some, as a moral affront to the laws of nature and God, an idea too large and complex to unpack and one that might inadvertently taint your perception of us, so I just explained that sometimes people are scared of people who are different from them. "That fear brings out their ugly side," I said, reflecting on Florida's fraught LGBTQ history going all the way back to the late 1970s, when singer-turned-activist Anita Bryant fronted a vicious campaign called Save Our Children. Her gay-hating crusade aimed to remove known homosexuals from teaching posts in public schools after Dade County made it illegal to discriminate against gays and lesbians in public accommodations, hiring, and housing. Bryant, using the language in anti-sodomy statutes, told an anchorwoman at the height of the controversy: "According to the Word of God, it's an abomination to practice homosexuality. . . . Archbishop Carroll . . . took the stand that he would go to jail rather than to hire known homosexuals into their schools, and our pastor said that he would do the same and would even burn the school rather than allow them to be taught by homosexuals. . . . This county ordinance is asking us, in essence, to go against the law of Florida and to go against, even more important, what we believe is above the law of the land: God's law." She took her animus and hysteria up an even higher octave in a now-infamous quote: "God made mothers so that we could reproduce; homosexuals cannot reproduce biologically, but they have to reproduce by recruiting our children."

That kind of vitriol and ignorance lay at the heart of the *Bowers v. Hardwick* ruling, which swiftly derailed LGBTQ activists' efforts to challenge anti-sodomy laws in federal courts. These arguments had drawn on emerging Supreme Court precedents recognizing a constitutional right to sexual privacy—cases that affirmed access to abortion (*Roe v. Wade*) and contraception for married couples (*Griswold v. Connecticut*) and single people (*Eisenstadt v. Baird*). When the *Lawrence* decision finally came down from the highest tribunal in the land, protecting our right to sexual autonomy and self-determination and paving the way for marriage equality across the nation with the Supreme Court's *Obergefell v. Hodges* decision in 2015, I was twenty-seven. That's nearly twenty years after my gay awakening, when it wasn't conceivable to me to want this, to want you.

I've always loved children, but I didn't see how I could have one without committing a kind of self-transgression with the opposite sex. Only a smattering of states in the 1970s and 1980s allowed gay adoption. Back then, the law regularly denied LGBTQ mothers and fathers custody if their homosexuality surfaced during divorce proceedings. The anti-sodomy laws provided the legal justification for denying us custody of our own children, as well as the opportunity to foster or adopt kids. The beliefs underlying those laws were akin to those expressed by Bryant—that we were unfit to parent children due to our immoral and illicit behavior, our "abominable and detestable crimes against nature."

Even though I wasn't aware of gay people's legal status as a child, nor did I have a full picture of their social positioning, I amorphously understood that being gay was bad, a degenerate sort of existence, gangrenous in appearance. The historical backdrop against which my desires formed kindled my self-aversion, compelling my reflexive recoiling from my own queer face. Because I had no template for seeing myself living within societal norms and longed to express all the feelings I had to stifle, I began fantasizing about a future life as a writer in a big city, living against the status quo, reimagining the world through words, a plan I concocted at age ten on Cord Street in Downey, California, where I grew up.

Under a rotting and dried-out palm tree between my family's house and our neighbor's, I told Jimmy, one of my best childhood friends, that I wanted to be a writer. The desire formed in my mind with such certainty, it felt like a tangible body part, a new limb. In a way, it was: The dream of growing up, moving to New York City—I even did my fifth-grade research report on the state's Eastern bluebird—to become an author, helped me move through the rest of my youth on firmer footing, envisioning the freedoms I might enjoy existing outside the mainstream. I had a goal, a destination, and an identity—and I didn't have to be a wife or a mother.

The dreaming of a dream is sometimes enough to get you through the hardest parts of your life, each day, moment to moment. Even if it's intangible or unrealizable in the end, it organizes your life and gives hope, no matter how small or fragile, where there was none.

I somehow thought I could make my dream more concrete by customizing dog tags, which my father ordered for me from a weird infomercial we saw on television, with THE WRITE PURSUIT emblazoned on one side and my name on the other.

I'd just seen the movie *Top Gun* in a small theater in Downey, where I imagined kicking Tom Cruise off the screen, taking his motorcycle, and speeding down the highway in a leather bomber jacket, gold-trimmed Ray-Ban sunglasses, and a tight muscle tee with military identification tags jangling against my chest in hot pursuit of Kelly McGillis. No one would have guessed at the time that McGillis would one day come out as a lesbian, a fact that would have eclipsed her beauty and marketability in an instant had it been known back then.

I wore those tags, like a secret, inside my shirt everywhere I went. With their military connotations, they represented the most masculine masculinity, a go-to fantasy where I took to the sky in fighter jets or to the ground on battlefields in dirt-stained fatigues with a semiautomatic in my holster. It's not lost on me now that I was in a kind of combat to preserve my life in the conservative community in which I grew up, and I nebulously knew that writing—telling my story—would be a way to save myself.

You learned that lesson early, too. After your relationship with your best friend since babyhood deteriorated when you were seven, you began to carry your sadness, the weight of your feelings, in your body, in your movements; you seemed to move through the world more slowly, like wading through swampy waters. Initially you couldn't talk about it, but it grew heavier and more challenging to carry alone. We gave you a book called *Ruby Finds a Worry* by Tom Percival to encourage you to share it with us. In the book, Ruby's unspecified worry balloons to an intolerable size until she musters up the strength and courage to tell someone; the more she talks, the more it shrinks, until she can finally walk through her life with her former levity and joy.

"There is no agony like bearing an untold story inside you," American folklorist Zora Neale Hurston wrote in her autobiography *Dust Tracks on a Road.* Words, like heavy rocks, pile up, undignified mountains of unsaid things that can only take meaningful shape when they're expressed. Writers from Joan Didion to Flannery O'Connor to James Baldwin have variously said that we survive—and change the world—by the stories we tell and hear. So I'm not being playful or silly when I ask, as we walk hand in hand through Sunset Park after school, "What's your story?" It's a value and a habit of mind I hope to instill: What you have to say, and how you choose to say it, doesn't just matter to you as an individual or to me as your parent; it matters to our collective consciousness, our shared reality.

Before I landed on the dream of writing, I harbored actorly ambitions like all kids who grow up within a drive of the Hollywood sign, amid a steady stream of movie star hopefuls. But it passed fleetingly and derived from a more pathological impulse: a desire to *not* be myself and paradoxically to become hypervisible as this other, more desirable self. I wanted to be seen in all the ways I contrived in my imagination—a muscly man with boyish good looks like Tom Cruise—but that wasn't possible while inhabiting the body I did or with the face I had. In the foyer of a crowded restaurant that smelled like fried food and greasy floors, my childhood friend Dee announced to her father, a cop with actor aspirations, that I harbored the same dream. The hulk-like man with blond hair and defeated blue eyes scanned the restaurant with misdirected disdain and, without looking down, said, "She'll never make it." He dismissed my dream because he'd lost his own. I know that now, but as a child, I attributed it to the ever-growing sense that I was not attractive enough for center stage—that I was not, in fact, attractive enough for real life.

Maybe I supplanted my thespian aspirations for writerly ones as a defense, but a part of me had a vague reckoning that real power lay behind the camera, not in front of it, and I began stalking bookstores and libraries with my dad, who also loved to read, to get books about screenwriting (Syd Field) and filmmaking (James Monaco). He also got me a subscription to *Premiere,* a new magazine about the film industry, from which I learned about Hollywood heavyweights like movie producers Richard and Lili Zanuck and Scott Rudin and talent agent Michael Ovitz.

I sent them stories I'd been working on and asked Mr. Ovitz if I could work in the mailroom at Creative Artists Agency (CAA) on the weekends if my dad would drive me there. They all wrote back with words of encouragement—I still have the letters—and Mr. Ovitz invited me and my dad to Beverly Hills to tour CAA. A lovely woman named Arlene Newman showed us the beautiful theater where they screened their clients' movies, and it was magical to know that one day I, too, could bring my inner world, my black-and-white life, into Technicolor vibrancy.

I couldn't know then that the movie of my life, the one I created with you and Sabrina—the life I could never imagine for myself in my early youth—would be the real stuff of dreams and magic.

On that trip to Chicago to meet baby Mari, all the sweet comments everyone was making about her resemblance to various family members, like your late grandfather for whom you are named, made me reflect on the baby Sabrina and I couldn't create together. "She looks just like Daddy!" Grandma Elizabeth gushed in her thick Bronx accent.

"Why do you think she looks like Dad, Mom? Because she's bald and gassy," Sabrina joked. "She's definitely got your mouth, Joanne," Sabrina added.

"And Jamie's eyes," I said.

Heading back to New York City, Sabrina and I discussed all the possibilities—and difficulties—of how to make a baby as a same-sex couple, including the emotional challenges it might pose for you in not knowing your father and half your DNA.

As a queer person making a family, I knew I should be antagonistic toward and cautious about biologizing identity and kinship. I knew I should take pride in the ways our ties help reconfigure and expand the concept of family or shatter it altogether. And I do, especially when I think about a lesson family historian Stephanie Coontz once imparted to me.

Coontz, who wrote the pioneering family history book *The Way We Never Were: American Families and the Nostalgia Trap* and *For Better and Worse: The Complicated Past and Challenging Future of Marriage,* told me that the insight we, as a society, should take from same-sex families is the reclamation of our "evolutionary heritage" and the understanding that biology is not enough to secure our personal and collective welfare: "LGBTQ families are helping us *recover* the idea that intimate connections and obligations are not confined to biology." Foregrounding the work of anthropologist Sarah Blaffer Hrdy, author of *Mother Nature: A History of Mothers, Infants, and Natural Selection* and *Father Time: A Natural History of Men and Babies,* Coontz explained to me that "biological relatedness is not the most important thing when you look back at how our Stone Age ancestors organized social cooperation, food sharing, and child-rearing." In many of the contemporary foraging societies closest to our earliest ancestors, infants are held and even nursed by someone other than his or her own mother for much of the day; childcare is shared freely throughout the camp; and meat from big game hunts is distributed to all members of the group, regardless of whose family member made the kill, Coontz explained. Putting my concerns about your paternal absence in perspective, she said: "In matrilineal societies, children are much closer to their uncles instead of their biological fathers because descent and obligations inherent to the female line position your mother's brother above your biological father, and it is he you'll have the most intense relationship with and who will take the most interest in you."

Reiterating her point that biology does not necessarily offer the strongest links between people, nor the right nourishment for our personal growth and well-being, she cited a study out of Michigan State University showing that strong friendship networks are a better predictor of happiness than biological ties for the elderly. In fact, in her view, married people ought to behave more like single people, as she once argued in *The New York Times.* Unlike couples who often isolate in domesticity, singles tend to enjoy greater social integration, prioritize hobbies, cultivate interests, participate in activities (i.e., sports, book clubs, etc.), and provide more support to extended kin and friends: "When I look back at the evolution of human beings, what stands out, absolutely, in all the historical and anthropological research is that people had to get beyond the nuclear family in order to organize social cooperation. And the way they did that was by creating obligations in new ways, between people who had no biological connection. Marriage, for example, was less about creating the biological child than it was about creating obligations between people on both sides of that relationship."

Knowing that our kind of home honors our prehistory and reveals the fault lines beneath the foundation of the nuclear family is satisfying on the one hand but cold comfort on the other; our world is a long way off from that ancestral one, and the biological connections tethering traditional kinship units continue to assert dominion over every other familial configuration.

Psychologist and host of Showtime's *Couples Therapy* Orna Guralnik once explained to *Oprah Daily* that the centrality of the nuclear family, and the overwhelming pressures placed on it, rests on the fact that it has had to absorb all the obligations and responsibilities that our neoliberal late-stage capitalist society fails to offer us in the way of governmental social services and supports. That's why progressive queer thinkers like scholar Lisa Duggan of New York University and journalist Richard Kim chafed at the shortsightedness of the mainstream LGBTQ movement's preoccupation with securing our right to wed. As they argued in an impassioned article for the *Nation* back in 2005, "Beyond Gay Marriage," the fight for marriage equality would undo all the progress made toward creating other forms of family ties via civil contracts or domestic partnerships between friends or lovers of the same or opposite gender. A more ambitious goal might have been to untether the benefits and privileges of matrimonial coupledom (i.e., social security, healthcare, tax breaks, retirement perks, etc.) from the institution of marriage itself to ensure other pairings of people or single individuals would not be coerced into marriage and could, in fact, reap the same protections and advantages of their married counterparts. Instead, we won the right to marry, keeping the nuclear family and the emphasis on bloodlines intact—to our detriment and to yours.

I knew our relationship would represent a disruption in the cohesive flow of familial bloodlines—that we might feel the sting of our biological asymmetry. Thinking about the language people use to mark the distinction between full-blood relations (which go unmarked, like white people vis-à-vis people of color) and "half" siblings or "step" parents or "adopted" children is a case in point: Such linguistic constructions position us lower in the family hierarchy and might amplify your ancestral yearnings or fraught feelings about our bloodless connection. With more than twenty-seven million people registered on Ancestry.com, fifteen million on 23andMe, and the enduring popularity of *Finding Your Roots,* which is going strong in its eleventh season, I can't help but think that the biological organization of family and our longing to know from whom we materially descend is primal, not just cultural. I once put the question to Alice Ruby, the executive director of the Sperm Bank of California, who thinks deeply about such issues given her leadership role in a nonprofit that caters to biologically discordant families.

"Well, I like to say that genetics mean *something*. Denying that genetics means anything doesn't help anybody. It just doesn't mean *everything*, and it doesn't mean the same things to everyone. It's one way to make a family, but it's not the *only* way," she said. Personally, she said, she knows several adopted and donor-conceived people who aren't interested in their biological families of origin. In fact, 65 percent of the children conceived by donors in the Identity-Release Program don't request their donor's contact information when they turn eighteen. Of the one-third that do, the experiences are varied with many, but not all, choosing to contact the donor. She also pointed out that the desires around learning one's biological ancestry can change at different stages of a person's life.

The affirming research and theories and anecdotes were all well and good, but you weren't an intellectual experiment; you were going to be a flesh-and-blood human being, a baby, my baby, living in the material world within structures of meaning and relationality that might make you feel a profound lacking, so I wanted to fully confront and weigh all the possibilities of what your lived reality might be without a complete genetic profile or father.

Of course, I couldn't know in advance how the question of your unknown ancestry and paternity would affect you. Despite being well versed in the academic literature demonstrating that children raised in two-mom families were as well-adjusted as children in opposite-sex families—in some studies even *better* adjusted—I couldn't shake the feeling that built into our family would be an absence, that I was standing in that absence, that I was the asymmetry, the queer rupture destabilizing the conventional order and clarity you might long for.

I tried to imagine my life without my own father, a man whose dark brown eyes, small button mouth, and ample nose were shaped just like mine; whose dorky disposition and quickness to tears when overcome by anything even remotely moving mirrored my own; and whose limitless curiosity and orientation toward intellectual and spiritual pursuits made him feel like my twin on a like-minded quest to understand—or sit in awe of—the mystery and meaning of our existence.

If I never knew him, I imagine he'd take center stage in my daydreams. I'd wonder: *Do we look alike? Do we share the same sense of humor and interests? Does he have an affinity for the same foods, books, art, or movies I do? Does he feel touched by the same things?*

Or I'd wonder what it would feel like to nestle under his arm or against his scruffy chin while he read me a bedtime story in a low octave.

To ensure that you'd know your biological father and to fuse our bloodlines, we decided to ask my brother, Uncle Andreas, to be our donor. As a newly divorced dad of two who also happens to be a staunch Republican, we had little hope he'd say yes, but he surprised us: "I love you both very much . . . and I'd be honored to help you guys," he said.

We didn't think through all the implications, the messiness, of the decision. As unprocessed as our mission to create a biologically unified family was, we were nonetheless excited and grateful that he agreed. Your grandmothers, as well, were thrilled—too thrilled—at the beautiful child their good-looking eldest children would bear: "What a gorgeous baby they'll make together," they both said in different ways from opposite coasts.

That made me pause.

Chapter 2

History of Difference

—

In their youths, your grandmothers succeeded where I've always failed: Sabrina's mother—Grandma Elizabeth—was a proverbial bombshell, a dead ringer for Valerie Perrine, the glamorous movie star from the 1970s, with her golden tresses, ocean-green eyes, and radiant smile.

My mom—*Yia Yia* to you, which is Greek for grandma—was similarly situated. My earliest memories of her from the 1980s include a big wave of feathered hair, brightly hued makeup, cable-knit sweaters by Ralph Lauren, and cardigans by Calvin Klein over polo shirts she tucked into knee-length golf shorts and tapered slacks. To me, she looked like an ad, a place I was meant to aspire to go but knew I never could.

In her adolescence, her natural charisma and irreverence—along with her long blond hair, fierce blue eyes, and high cheekbones—earned her a number of teen distinctions that placed her in the upper reaches of her high school's social ranks back in the 1960s: "Biggest Flirt," "Best Sense of Humor," runner-up for prom queen in 1968—and "Best Figure" in middle school.

If I'd gone to school with *Yia Yia,* we would not have been friends. I stood outside the social pecking order, watching life unfold from the sidelines. I wasn't a cool girl hip to the latest trend or pretty enough for popularity. If beauty is balance and order, I was the exact opposite, asymmetry itself: My teeth were buck, unforgettably so, my face was zit-filled and shaped like a pinball—and my wardrobe would have made my gender indeterminate if not for my long hair and boobs.

As a child, I'd study my mother's face when she was putting on makeup in her powder blue bathroom or in the rearview mirror as she drove down Firestone Boulevard or while dragging me through department stores at the Stonewood shopping center in the heart of downtown Downey. I'd scrutinize her features, hoping to see myself in them somewhere, anywhere, but I never did; I only saw how different I was from her. I was completely absent from her visage, so much so that I once snuck into her closet to sift through a security box in which she kept important documents to see if she was indeed the woman listed on my birth certificate. Impossibly, she was, but I longed to see myself where I wasn't.

"A boy once called me 'corroded nose' because it's slightly bent at the tip," she told my brother and me. "Insults like that stay with you." It was a detail I never noticed until she pointed it out because all I could see was a top-of-the-mountain perfection. The legibility of her flaw did nothing to tarnish her beauty in my eyes. What I remember most from that conversation is the story she told about an unpopular girl: "She was a big nerd to kids in the in-crowd, but she had the last laugh. She walked in a dork but walked out a doctor ten years later at our reunion," she said, urging us not to put too much stock in superficial things "because being cute and cool doesn't get you anywhere if that's all you've got. Stupid lasts forever; looks don't." I wonder if she saw a parallel between her classmate and me and wanted me to see my future well-being and success in her peer's post-high-school ascent.

As a child, I always loved it when my mom would sweep through my elementary school classroom in her carefree way, softly perfumed with her perfectly coiffed hair and shape-defining sweaters and slacks to deliver a lunch she'd forgotten to pack for me. In those moments, I felt imbued with her beauty just by virtue of being her child—and proud.

Sabrina and I have sometimes wondered if our tomboy aesthetics—a homogeneous rotation of battered jeans, printed T-shirts, flannel button-downs, and scratched-up sneakers—embarrass you when we visit your classroom on Family Fridays because you once asked if we'd wear dresses. We considered it for a second. But then we reflected on the fact that wearing dresses, an uncomfortable experience growing up under the quizzical side-eyes of our attractive mothers and society's unrealizable beauty ideals, would be a self-violation, a kind of gender transgression for both of us, and would reify the notion that there is only one way to be a woman. When you asked that we step into some girly duds, I wanted to share a quote with you from one of your favorite musicians, Bad Bunny, who's known for his flamboyant style and frocks: "What defines a man, what defines being masculine, what defines being feminine? I really can't give clothes gender. To me, a dress is a dress," he told *GQ*, suggesting, wittingly or not, that the artifice that helps set up a dichotomy between men and women is false, a cultural fiction that masquerades as an incontestable truth, as feminist theorist Judith Butler articulated in 1990 with the publication of *Gender Trouble*. In her widely impactful book, Butler argues that gender is performative, something that needs to be deliberately enacted, undertaken, and carried out and as such is always unstable and in danger of unraveling. Younger generations of women and men (boyish girls, girlish boys, and legions of others in between) who can't or don't feel comfortable strictly adhering to gender norms in behavior and presentation have found solace, self-empowerment, and a kind of liberation in Butler's slippery understanding of masculinity and femininity. Those invested in keeping the rickety distinction between men and women intact, however, find it increasingly threatening, especially today, as Butler's ideas have fully permeated the culture, leaving the very notion of what constitutes a man and a woman hotly contestable.

Take, at this moment, our über-masculine Secretary of Defense Pete Hegseth and President Donald J. Trump himself as a case in point. By trafficking in stereotypes about women and mothers, Hegseth argued that females do not belong in combat: "Dads push us to take risks. Moms put the training wheels on our bikes. We need moms. But not in the military, especially in combat units," he has said. In September 2025, he summoned military leaders across the country to Quantico, Virginia, to outline his plan for making the military more "capable" and "lethal" by calling for an end to "dudes in dresses" and "gender delusions." Intent on securing a firm border between men and women, Trump declared at his joint address to Congress in March 2025, "I signed an order making it the official policy of the United States government that there are only two genders: male and female." Both men's stances seem more about shoring up their own fragile masculinities, especially in a world of younger—and far cooler—guys like Bad Bunny, whose security doesn't rely on their success at performing Rambo-style machismo.

No, we couldn't have accommodated your wish that we slip into some dresses. Instead, we've sought to expand and diversify your narrow view of what it means to be a woman, to show you how and why beauty imperatives coalesced with femininity and how they continue to wreak both psychological and physical havoc on women. Right now, in these pages, we will travel to the four corners of the world throughout history, modern-day ghosts sweeping over skies in faraway lands, to show you an endless procession of women aspiring to impossible—sometimes ridiculous—aesthetic ideals, often at their expense or peril.

While heeding historian Umberto Eco's guiding principle in his scholarly works *On Ugliness* and *History of Beauty*—that ideas of beauty and ugliness throughout history are ever-changing, culturally contingent, and often operating in the service of a power structure that seeks to maintain a certain ordered rank—I want to take you across the globe in this discussion, to emphasize that beauty means different things to different people in different times and different settings. None of it is *essentially* true. None of it is *universal.* In highlighting what beauty means in various historical and cultural contexts, I want to dislodge these notions of beauty that you experience as biblical edicts you must obey. If you understand them as collective fictions created for specific purposes, you can start to play with them, challenge them, or reject them outright when they don't serve you.

—

Starting in Northeast Asia, during the Heian era in Japan, dating from 794 to 1185 CE, aristocratic beauty ideals demanded that women have "pale, round, plump face[s] with elongated eyes." Their paleness or whiteness indicated their leisure (non-laboring) class status, and their fuller figures showed their access to rich supplies of food and nourishment in contrast to the lower, thinner (hungrier) masses. Encased in layers and layers of expensive robes called *jūnihitoe* to connote their higher social station, they grew their hair so long, it swept the ground. In a practice called *hikimayu,* they shaved their brows to then paint them back on as black dots or smudges above their eyebrow line. Although you continue to long for hair that travels past the length of your back, I'm fairly certain locks that kiss the floor like a broom would not register as particularly pretty, nor would shearing your brows. But nothing, perhaps, would surprise—or unsettle—you as much as the ancient Japanese custom of blackening one's teeth to fully embody the culture's ideals. "One theory is that nonblackened teeth seen in dim indoor settings appeared like animal fangs," Laura Miller, a Japanese studies and history professor at the University of Missouri–St. Louis, explained. From a remove of more than twelve hundred years, all that comes to mind when I conjure the image of these so-called aristocratic beauties with their dark chompers reminiscent of decay and floor-sweeping tresses is brain-eating zombies. Where they see beauty, we see ugly; and conversely, where we see beauty, they'd likely see ugly—especially our preference for white teeth.

Heading westward from Japan to China, a different conception of beauty was taking shape . . . in women's feet: Chinese women of the tenth century on through the middle of the twentieth century went to chilling lengths to attain a three-inch foot called the "Golden Lotus," misshapening their feet, starting at the age of five or six, in an agonizing process that could result in paralysis, gangrene, ulceration, and even death. As historian Amanda Foreman detailed in *Smithsonian Magazine:*

> First, [a girl's] feet were plunged into hot water and her toenails clipped short. Then the feet were massaged and oiled before all the toes, except the big toes, were broken and bound flat against the sole, making a triangle shape. Next, her arch was strained as the foot was bent double. Finally, the feet were bound in place using a silk strip measuring ten feet long and two inches wide. These wrappings were briefly removed every two days to prevent blood and pus from infecting the foot. Sometimes "excess" flesh was cut away or encouraged to rot. The girls were forced to walk long distances in order to hasten the breaking of their arches. Over time the wrap-

> pings became tighter and the shoes smaller as the heel and sole were crushed together. After two years the process was complete, creating a deep cleft that could hold a coin in place. Once a foot had been crushed and bound, the shape could not be reversed without a woman undergoing the same pain all over again.

Noting that "every aspect of women's beauty was intimately bound up with pain," Foreman reported that the practice, over the course of a millennium, variously signified a boundary between the upper and lower classes, determined a daughter's marriageability, and expressed women's allegiance to neo-Confucian values of "chastity, obedience and diligence."

Although the details of this practice are widely known and hideous to recount, it speaks to the ways the culture exerted control over women's bodies by creating a perverse metric for attaining beauty that limits their freedom of movement, stunts their growth, and infantilizes them. Ask yourself: What's beautiful about a woman maintaining the foot size of a child? How can a little girl dance or run or climb or even just enjoy a swift-footed jaunt through a park with her feet bound and crammed into shoes far too small for her feet? How can a girl or young woman even think while managing such extreme discomfort and pain? I could apply the same set of questions to the obsession with thinness in Western culture and the compulsion toward food deprivation that goes with it—or, more comparably, to the corset, which in the nineteenth century was made of steel and whalebone. I once showed you an iteration designed sometime between 1825 and 1835 that was expressly manufactured for a girl as young as you at age nine. You thought it looked benign, like an old-fashioned take on the modern-day bra, but that wasn't quite true.

Originally worn by both genders, for most of its history the corset was designed to mold women and girls' bodies into the beauty ideal of the day—in the nineteenth century, that meant a tiny waist aiming to create or give the illusion of an hourglass figure. One would pull the lace, like string on a pair of sneakers, as tightly as possible around a girl's waist to achieve a coveted waistline. Some mothers believed that if they started shaping their daughters' bodies early, they'd have a perfect figure by the time they reached adulthood. Like bound feet, a bound rib cage could hurt, excruciatingly so, and long-term use beginning in childhood could cause a whole bunch of problems, including difficulty breathing, digestive issues, weakening back muscles, and deformity.

Back in 1990, when I was a freshman in high school, I remember Madonna trying to cast her Jean Paul Gaultier corset as a thing of liberation, wearing it on the outside of her clothes while she danced across the stage for tens of thousands of fans. *Vogue* once called Gaultier's take on the corset "defiant and aggressive," noting that "in place of the soft curves the corset was supposed to shape, the female anatomy became a spiky, phallic weapon, one that Madonna celebrated by exerting her dominance, sexual and otherwise, over the dancers she frolicked with." But I'm not sure how widely accessible or understood that feminist reading was. I know that ideas aren't fixed and we can repurpose language (i.e., the reclamation of the word *queer*, for example, by LGBTQ people), as well as cultural artifacts, but I'm not convinced that the hypersexualization of women and girls in the name of sex positivity as articulated by that decade's "bubblegum feminism," a flimsy, toothless iteration of women's lib, can truly challenge or shake the power structures that subsist on our degradation and disempowerment.

What looks like agency is often submission.

In the 1850s, an American campaign to reform dress codes for women sprang up, spearheaded by newspaper editor and women's rights activist Amelia Bloomer, who advocated and popularized the use of roomier knickers—eventually called bloomers in her honor, to be worn under knee-length skirts, allowing women more freedom of movement. At the time, women wore garments that added about fifteen pounds to their weight with corsets worn beneath six to eight petticoats to enhance their silhouettes. Although pantaloons generated momentary intrigue or bemusement in the 1850s, they did not become a mainstream fashion trend until the end of the century. Ultimately, the corset, draped in petticoats, reasserted its dominion: Women had so internalized the corset's power to feminize and beautify them that they were reluctant to give up the allure and mystique it lent. Some will call that agency—women got to decide, and they decided in favor of restrictive corsets and encumbering petticoats—but was it *their* decision, or was it one they'd been engineered to want and keep wanting, despite its harm, even when they'd been offered freedom? Thinking on the Butlerian notion that gender is something one enacts—or *does*—rather than what one *is*, something universal and innate, I wondered: Had the repetitive use of corsets and multiple tiers of underlayers become so naturalized over time that being without it felt unnatural? How often are we, as women, sympathetic to our captors—human and ideological—like those with Stockholm syndrome? We'll just as soon toss out the keys to the jail cell than risk the new and unknown possibilities that liberty holds.

Another concoction of Western culture that bears mentioning are high heels, which you took a shine to at age six. We bought you a pair of black patent leather ones with a short, square base when you were eight—the pair you still refuse to part with, even though they no longer fit. At shopping malls, I watch you hungrily eye pointy stilettos that to me look like torture devices. "These slay, bruh," you'll say, taking up the language of the older kids on the school bus, as we walk past a particularly unstable and perilous-looking pair of heels. Even though I mock your excess use of "bruh," I still can't stop saying "dude," a California expression I've failed to eject from my vocabulary despite having lived outside the state for twenty-five years. Appropriately enough, in the nineteenth century "dude" mockingly referred to "dandies" or men who were "extremely fastidious in dress and manner," but somehow it morphed into an utterance of emphasis and a very casual greeting. I point it out to show that language and meaning are in constant flux, so our ideas about the world can and do change. We can even work to reshape our world and understanding with new language, like creating nonbinary pronouns—*they* and *them*—to collapse the hierarchies that male/female or man/woman erect. The fact that President Trump had to declare that his administration will recognize only two genders shows how successfully we've begun to reimagine and reorganize our society. As James Baldwin once said: "The world changes according to the way people see it, and if you alter, even by a millimeter, the way a person looks or people look at reality, then you can change it."

In 2007, Christian Louboutin created an instrument of pure pain known as the "Ballerina Ultima" for a collaboration with filmmaker David Lynch. The stiletto's heel extends the length of the sole, requiring the unimaginable wearer to walk through the world en pointe like a danseuse on stage at Lincoln Center. The insane acrobatics and contortions one would have to suffer to slip into them make them more appropriate for a museum shelf than a woman's foot. Louboutin, who expressly designed them as sculptural works of art, not wearable shoes, agrees: He donated a pair to New York's Metropolitan Museum of Art in 2012. With restraint but perceptible censure, the Met calls it an "incapacitating stiletto" that nearly precludes mobility, as well as an "extreme strategy" to "give the illusion of a lengthened leg." In sum, the entry maddeningly understates: "The artifice employed to attain an idealized fashionable beauty is not without its challenges."

While they're a showpiece rather than a practical set of shoes, I find the very idea of them an affront—that they are the brainchild of a man, who isn't equally situated under the rib-and-foot-crushing weight of beauty standards, is almost too much to bear. Like the "Golden Lotus" and corsetry, the high heel, a multibillion dollar industry, restricts women's freedom of movement and cultivates a kind of female fragility, whereby women, in utter discomfort, must teeter—not run, nor climb, nor move too swiftly—or risk toppling over. And yet women will defend these accessories to the death; they will say heels make them feel sexy and powerful, but it's a sexiness and power circumscribed by men.

Just like the word *dude,* high heels have also changed meaning over time, with men being their original clientele, according to Elizabeth Semmelhack's revelatory book *Shoes: The Meaning of Style.* In tenth-century Persia, for example, heels were worn for the practical purpose of helping cavalrymen firmly secure their feet in horse-riding stirrups so they could stably sit on their saddles and more easily fire off their bows and arrows or swing their swords. By the seventeenth century in Europe, heels helped people cut more imposing figures by giving them extra height, which functioned to signal their higher social status, implying exemption from manual labor or extensive travel on foot. As they gained in popularity, the heel went from one inch to as tall as four. When women of the aristocracy began sporting them, the heel became taller and the toes pointier, subtly lifting the feet beneath their skirts to create the illusion of smaller, daintier feet—a beauty ideal that prized delicacy and refinement. By the mid-nineteeth century, heels began to function as they do today—to convey femininity and sexual maturity. Detailing a brief history of the shoe, a commentator on *Origin of Everything* sarcastically, but poignantly, declared: "Everyone knows that super skinny heels that squish all of your toes together into an unnatural point are about as comfortable as walking on hot lava."

Leaving the royal courts of Persia and France, let's fly to ancient Egypt in the northeast corner of Africa, where a different ideal held sway: Artistic representations indicate that ancient Egyptian women in certain epochs may have aspired to a slim body with a high waist, narrow hips, and golden skin. Many sought to set off their eyes with thick black eyeliner—perhaps the modern-day cat eye has roots in Egypt—and the more affluent wore lots of makeup to enhance their looks, but it wasn't just about aesthetics. Cosmetics protected their skin from the blazing sun, and were thought to shield them from evil and impart special powers. In some instances, the palettes they used to grind up the ingredients for makeup, like the ones we might use for mixing oil paints, were shaped like tilapia fish, which they associated with fertility and reproduction.

Finally, to showcase fancy headpieces, upper-class women (and men) sat opulent ornaments or stylish wigs on their heads. Children of the elite are sometimes depicted with shaved heads, aside from a small swatch of hair on one side of their faces. As someone who prizes her long brown hair and is always concocting fruitless strategies to make it grow, I know you'd flinch at the idea of self-inflicted baldness, but hair, with its erotic connotations, was extremely important to Egyptian women as well. As shown in artistic renderings, one way they signaled their sexual maturity was to forgo the sidelock for stylized tresses or ornate wigs.

Traveling on to the Middle East, I want to highlight the beauty ideals of the royal neo-Assyrians (912–612 BCE). Similar to the ancient Greeks, they sought an aesthetic of symmetry and proportionality that even expressed itself in the ways imperial women wore jewelry, where any form of adornment was evenly represented on both sides of the body; they also privileged "a full face with large, cosmetically enhanced dark eyes, thick dark coiffed hair, a voluptuous body and ornate dress" meant to be an "outward expression of intangible ideals, specifically fertility, sexuality, and purity." In fact, their outward appearance held several symbolic significances, according to art historian Amy Gansell of St. John's University, who specializes in the Ancient Near East. Fleshiness suggested good health and fertility, but because the women's bodies were fully clad in lavish gowns and jewelry, they demonstrated their many folds with proud double chins, which also helped demarcate their desirable "soft" bodies against men's "hard" bodies.

"They *wanted* to be fat?" you asked, flummoxed. You've already absorbed the message that a svelte shape is a preferable one. In first grade, I saw you standing in front of the full-length mirror in our bedroom, contemplating your outfit for a long lingering minute. Then, abruptly, you discarded your denim jacket and said, "This makes me look big," which stunned me. While Sabrina felt your comment was about a stylistic preference for a more fitted cut and daintier fashion—not about weight—it still concerned me. "Why, should girls be small?" I asked. "No! It just doesn't look good," you replied in a huff. You were exasperated, as if I was too old to understand contemporary notions of cool. "It's not like the eighties, Ma!" you frequently say when I try to impart a lesson that doesn't resonate, like when I question your texting etiquette.

When a kid says: "Hi, can you call me?" you abruptly write back: "No" if you can't or don't want to. Or, if someone says: "I'm going to go see a movie," you'll respond: "Okay." While it makes me feel that I've raised a Neanderthal, in a culture that expects the plasticity of niceness—not to be confused with kindness, which is substantive, not superficial—from girls and women, I didn't want to hit too hard on how you should, pleasingly, comport yourself. But I also feel that manners are not entirely trivial. They create a mutual warmth and civility between people that seems to be lacking in your generation. Is it all the screens? Is it the self-centered smugness of American culture? My Peruvian friend Liz refers to our country as "a teenager," and she's right. I find our collective arrogance and extreme individualism off-putting because it has resulted in the erosion of our common humanity toward one another. It's a tricky conversation, rife with mixed messages, one I'm sure I've broached with too much contradiction and confusion.

"Can you say that with more finesse?"

"Like what?"

"Like if someone asks if you can talk, you might say something like: 'I'd love to, but I can't right now. Can I call you later?'"

"Ma, if I said that, they'd think I was weird. We don't talk like that."

"Well, if someone says they're going to a movie, you can say: 'Cool! What movie are you seeing?'"

"No, we don't talk like that. You don't understand."

Reflecting on my attempts to mold you into a well-mannered little girl, I'm struck by the parallel ways in which society seeks to mold you into a rail-thin slip of a human, through self-denial and deprivation, making you adverse to fleshiness even at the shockingly young age of six. While Sabrina and I never speak of our weight or dieting, nor do we count calories, the destructive notion that your body should look any way other than the way it does came to you through culture or kids on the playground. You've always been lean, so it seemed like you were mimicking something you'd seen on TV or read in a graphic novel better suited to teenagers when you made your "big" comment. I didn't want to reify the idea or give it too much meaning, so I didn't keep probing, but when you were in third grade, Sabrina overheard fragments of a FaceTime conversation between you and a crew of girls from one of the many summer camps you've attended through the years. Someone asked if you and your posse of girlfriends thought she was "fat." Then she confessed, in a shattering string of words that conjured images of future anorexia, that no matter how much aesthetic praise she receives, she never believes it. Before we're even teens—not even two digits in age—we're bred to feel inadequate. We didn't want that idea to lodge itself into your brain, so we addressed it with you. You admitted that those ideas have sometimes floated through your consciousness, too, after reading *Blubber* and *Smaller Sister*.

Months before, a close friend suggested we read Judy Blume's classic *Blubber,* a book I'd never read, because you like stories about teen drama—"real-life stuff," you say, not fantasy. But the book was too dated and harsh, even for me, despite our shared passion for Blume and her fiction. From *Iggie's House* to *Are You There God? It's Me, Margaret.* to *Double Fudge* and *Tales of a Fourth Grade Nothing,* you love her for the same reason I do: She doesn't condescend to children or hide the pain (pimples, periods, bullies, racism) and pleasures (masturbation, first kisses in closets, and best girlfriends) of adolescence. When we got to the bullying scene in the bathroom in *Blubber,* you were visibly shaken. "Ma, I can't say those things out loud. Kids don't talk like that or do that stuff at my school." You also wondered why everyone was siding with the bully, but it was too hard to explain the cultural reasons why the kid who gets bullied loses social capital and the kid who bullies gains it. It's quintessentially American, a strand in the double helix that is our DNA. We are built on bullying—from our subjugation and exploitation of Native Americans to our enslavement of Africans all the way up to our economic system, which relies on the haves subsisting on the exploited labor of the have-nots. All I could muster was: "They probably want to stay on the bully's good side so they're not bullied." Despite all the social media platforms offering new avenues for bullying kids, I realized that we *had* made significant strides since 1974, when *Blubber* was originally published, especially in recent years with campaigns dedicated to raising awareness and literacy around bullying and body positivity.

But the mutual hurt inflicted on girls by girls is cultural: Our existence is trivialized in frivolity, and we are primped against each other to disperse opportunities to consolidate our power and have a more substantive impact on the world.

We ditched the book, but the idea that being "a woman of size," as writer Roxane Gay puts it in *Hunger,* was undesirable had already taken root and was only reinforced when you read *Smaller Sister,* a graphic novel about a kid named Lucy whose older sister's dissatisfaction with her appearance compels her to start refusing food. As Lucy watches her sister struggle, she begins to wrestle with her own issues around self-esteem, family dynamics, and healing. (I'd never have let you read that book had I known, but weirdly—or appropriately, given the ways we do and don't value girls—it's geared toward readers *eight* and up, according to its publisher, Roaring Brook Press.)

I didn't want to say something idiotically trite and facile, like "inner beauty is more important than outer beauty" or "all the sizes, shapes, and shades girls come in are beautiful," because the culture is telling you otherwise, and honestly, how effective would those limp attempts to reprogram your brain actually be?

Instead, I said: "Let's think about what your body can do rather than what it looks like in those moments. What do you love about what your body can do?"

"I love that I can swim and make rubber bracelets with my loom."

"What about dancing?"

"Yes! And singing."

"Climbing trees in Sunset Park?"

"Yes, and playing tag at the bus stop."

"What about playing *Super Mario Bros.* on your Nintendo Switch? Or games on games on Roblox?"

"Yes!"

In the days that followed, Sabrina enrolled you in a weekend swim and parkour class at a massive gymnasium with physically challenging obstacle courses. We wanted to help you feel the strength and power of your own body, to remind you that you are an active subject, not a passive object for other people's visual pleasure. It didn't wash away the ugly cultural messaging, but you did start to grow in strength and agility and got steadier on your feet, so much so that, two years into the program, you can now easily climb tall trees in Sunset Park or scale the tallest metal poles on the playground with jaw-dropping ease. Your longtime friend Beatrice even shouted out once, "Don't blame me when you come crashing down on your head from way up there," because you'd reached the top of the pole.

Teasing apart your friend's "fat" comment, I thought about how the neo-Assyrians preferred heaviness over thinness. They didn't think in terms of "fat" the way we do. A fuller figure represented health and wealth—suggesting access to food, unlike the poorer and wider population—and that's why it was favored. The point is: Back then, in that part of the world, a skinny woman was the opposite of attractive and desirable, so there is nothing truly good and beautiful about being thin—or about being fat, for that matter. Its meaning shape-shifts through time and across cultures, never fixed, always transforming.

The outward representation of fertility was especially important to the neo-Assyrians because it was believed that the empire would flourish for eternity and thus required women to populate it with as many offspring as possible, ensuring its strength in numbers. To reflect their inner and outer radiance, women wore shiny garments sewn with sequins and gold jewelry because they believed luminosity was a "divine quality," and as royals they were thought to be "touched by the divine, existing as conduits between Heaven and earth." Sometimes, they even wore big "Dolly Parton–like" headdresses, like the Egyptians, to further demonstrate their "larger-than-life" godliness. "We don't have enough information about common people, but ruling is power, and power is placing oneself above another through various devices. So I think this perfected beauty is part of the expression of power, which absolutely would be differentiating the elite from the masses," historian Amy Gansell explained to me.

Looking at your favorite doll, "Maria," an Ecuadorian girl decked out in traditional multicolored Indigenous garb, which we purchased at a shop in Woodstock that exclusively sells various handmade garments and trinkets from the country, I wondered what metrics your ancestors—Ecuadorian on your donor's side—used to measure beauty.

If we went the nearly eight thousand miles from ancient Assyria to Quito, which existed under Incan rule before the Spaniards conquered the region in the 1500s, we'd find women in fabrics made from alpaca or vicuña wool and adorned with intricate geometric designs and vivid, eye-catching hues. Like we've seen elsewhere in history, these rich threads communicated one's elite status and beauty.

Women from various Indigenous Andean ethnic groups in the region enjoyed face painting, which brought to mind your congenital inability to pass up the opportunity to get the odd cat, witch, or zombie stenciled onto your face at the various festivals and fairs we've visited through the years. As far as jewelry went, Incan women were partial to gold and silver, with men, in particular, prizing ornamentation made from shells imported from the coast of northern Ecuador.

Some men and women residing in the Andes from present-day Ecuador to Peru, Bolivia, and Chile also practiced ear gauging, stretching the earlobe out to the size of a baseball in order to fit big golden discs in them, which was associated with aesthetic appeal and stature. In a more extreme practice like footbinding and corsetry—at least to my mind, although scholars may disagree—some thought elongated heads were more beautiful, so they used textile binding around infant skulls to maintain a conical shape. It wasn't just aesthetically pleasing to them; it demarcated one's group identity and social rank and helped the ruling Incans mark their "subjects" as distinct from themselves. What may seem disturbing or harsh through a contemporary Western lens might, in reverse, provoke a similar reaction were they to observe our society today.

I hope a pattern, however vague or nebulous, is taking shape in your mind—that you're beginning to see the harmful impact of certain beauty rituals, that you're starting to notice the ways that these ideals differ across time and space and serve various social functions, that you're starting to question the ones you adhere to so ardently now.

Chapter 3

The Invention of Beauty—and Ugly

Affirming the ever-fluctuating notion of beauty across time and location, Italian scholar Umberto Eco says that even if we were to say the ancient Greeks viewed that which is proportional as beautiful, which they did, their notions of proportionality changed through different epochs. "In the course of time many different ideals of proportion have been produced. Proportion as it was understood by the first Greek sculptors was not the same as the proportion of Polyclitus; the musical proportions that Pythagoras wondered about were not the same as those of Medieval times, because the music that Medieval man considered pleasant was different," he writes.

Just as any history of beauty across cultures and time would be one of difference, not sameness, so, too, is any history of Western beauty ideals. As Michel Foucault observed in one of his many seminal texts, *The Archeology of Knowledge,* the conventions that histories traditionally follow give the illusion of a coherent and linear sequence of events that suggest only one possible reading of the past. But there are several narratives of the past rife with a multiplicity of subjectivities, power relations, and contradictions. The past is one of ruptures and discontinuities—not cohesion. There's not only power and liberation in knowing that there is nothing essentially true and universally enduring—consistent—when it comes down to who and what registers as beautiful or ugly through the ages. Seeing the places and spaces in between one age and the next, where new ideas break off from the old and where alternative significations emerge, allows us to see how aesthetic ideals continually change and to figure out how they serve a hierarchal norm in any given moment. Whom does it benefit to privilege white skin over dark skin in a beauty ideal? Or eye shapes common to Caucasians over Asians? Or noses that are aquiline as opposed to hooked, bulbous, or wide? Or lips that are small and thin versus large and voluptuous?

These aren't superficial, subjective valuations; they're carefully orchestrated ideals socially fabricated to secure one group's value and superiority over another's.

Keeping that in mind, I'll still venture to argue, cautiously, that certain aesthetic ideals developed by the ancient Greeks, in tandem with other countries and cultures, continue to speak to our notions of beauty to this day, however differently they resonate and signify: Proportionality, symmetry, and harmony are the core facets of beauty as articulated in the literature and art of antiquity.

This set of criteria, in part, comes from Greek philosopher and mathematician Pythagoras and his followers in the sixth century BC, who demonstrated that proportional intervals between musical notes correspond to the beauty we hear in a melody or composition. Likely informed by ancient Egypt with its otherworldly pyramids, Pythagoreans also observed that the architecture of Greek temples relied on similar spatio-geometrical intervals between the structure's various parts. To underscore the ways that beauty follows mathematical laws, Pythagoras took up the equilateral triangle as his next point of study. Pythagoras's disciples "swore their oath," in fact, to the Tetraktys, a triangle and sacred symbol in philosophy and mysticism. They believed it represented the perfect harmony and balance of the universe—to that point it's sometimes called the "cosmic triangle"—because it consists of ten points arranged in four rows (1, the monad; +2, the dyad; +3, the triad; +4, the tetrad; altogether = 10). The first row or point on top of the triangle signifies the Source or oneness of all things; the second represents dualities or opposites (i.e., light vs. dark); the third connotes the three points of a triangle, indicating symmetry and proportionality or cosmic order; and the final and fourth row speaks to the physical world (earth, water, air, fire) and the measurable dimensions of it (length, breadth, height, and time). Following the Pythagorean meditation on the equilateral triangle, Roman architect Vitruvius found that our outstretched arms, with our legs perfectly straight and our trunks perfectly erect, correspond to our height and make a perfect square, inspiring him to call the numeral four "the number of man." (Leonardo da Vinci, inspired by Vitruvius's writings, drew the famous *Vitruvian Man*—a nude figure with outstretched arms and legs inscribed within a circle and a square—illustrating ideal human body proportions as a reflection of geometric principles found in architecture.) Four became "synonymous with strength, justice and solidity," with the triangle composed of "three series of four numbers" indicating "perfect equality." (The inverted pink triangle, interestingly, was the symbol the Nazi's used to mark—shame—homosexual men in concentration camps during World War II and was later reclaimed as an emblem of protest and the struggle for LGBTQ equality in the 1970s.)

While early Pythagoreans believed that opposites—odd versus even, male versus female, straight versus curved, for example—consisted of a beautiful side in line with truth and goodness (odd, male, straight) and an ugly side composed of anomaly, wickedness, and dissonance (even, female, and curved),

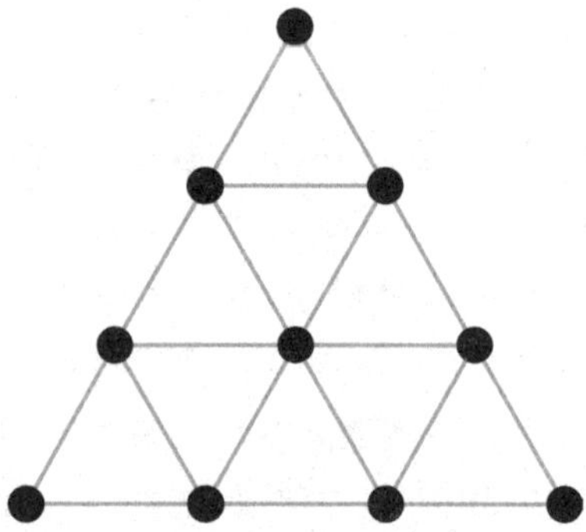

The Pythagorean Tetraktys.

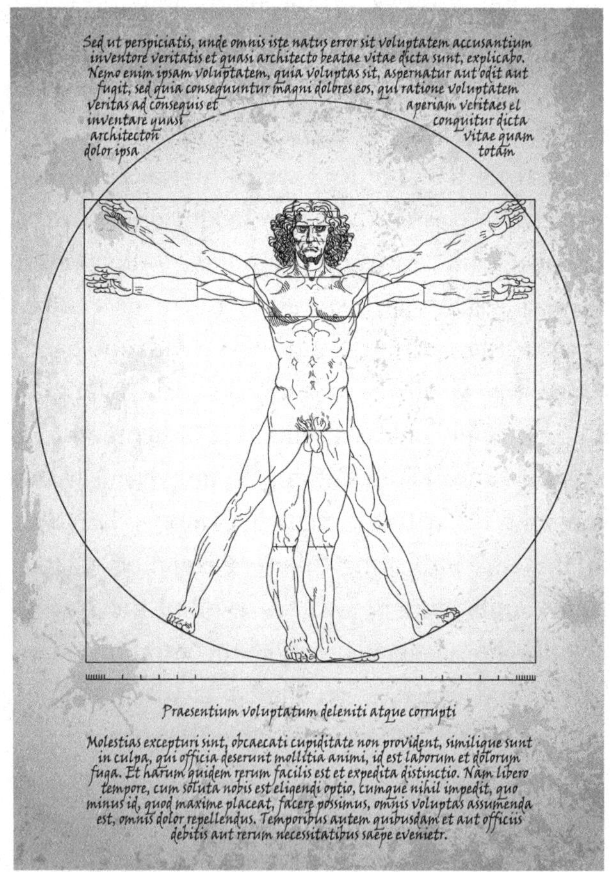

The Vitruvian Man.

Greek philosopher Heraclitus, Pythagoras's contemporary, reasoned that the tug-of-war between incompatible extremes could not be resolved by nullifying one over the other but rather that the tension between two polarities is fundamental to harmony itself: Beauty depends on ugliness for its definitional integrity, as do right and left, dark and light, and so on.

Perhaps the ideas emanating from this formulation hint at why same-sex love is not legible as beautiful. It removes the requisite tension between the male-female binary that gives way to these formative notions of harmony and beauty.

And there *is* something unpleasant, chilling even, about sameness, isn't there? I'm thinking of that Sunday morning when you were playing *Toca Boca,* a digital neighborhood replete with various characters you can design yourself, and the volume was turned up too high, filling your room with a hideous tune that repeated the same riff over and over and over again, bringing us both to the brink as you struggled to mute the sound. Looking at your screen, alive with a rich and diverse array of colors and shapes, it occurred to me that the lack of differentiation—the homogeneity—of the song was what was maddening or unsettling, like tract homes in the suburbs, or spaces where everyone is white, or posses of girls so meticulously sporting the same look that you can't quite tell them apart, or a military march. There's always something a little eerie to me about watching bodies or minds move and articulate in unison. I'm not talking about the frisson you might experience when watching a marathon or a flock of seagulls swoop through the sky, but some forms of expression en masse—even the thunderous clapping or laughing of spectators at a sporting event, like football—blow a cold breeze down my spine. It may be something idiosyncratic about me, but it sounds like collective madness, a stadium of mindlessness operating under the influence of reflexive groupthink, on the cusp of potentially descending into cruelty if the crowd decides it ought. And yet I know that what's allowed us to evolve as a species is social conformity—operating in unity—which itself is a kind of symmetry and proportionality between social bodies in community.

The ideal physical form that would define beauty for centuries was crystallized by Greek sculptor Polykleitos. His statue *Doryphoros* ("Spear-Bearer") was based on a theoretical treatise known as the *Canon,* in which he laid out a system of bodily proportions derived from mathematical ratios. Rather than relying on abstract geometric progressions, Polykleitos used precise, measurable relationships among body parts—A is to B as B is to C—to achieve perfect symmetry and proportion in the human form.

I saw these Greek ideals articulated in reverse while looking at a succession of scary faces you drew in your notebook at our favorite Greek diner. "Which is scarier or uglier?" you asked us after you completed each new composition. "What do you think makes it scary or ugly?" I asked you. "The pointy ears. The sharp teeth. The huge pointy nose. The blood coming out of his ear," you said. "What do *you* think makes it scary?" you asked. "This one is missing a nose, and this one has several eyeballs." Although unschooled in the beauty ideals of antiquity, you've long absorbed the message that that which lacks symmetry, proportion, and harmony is not merely unappealing but unsettling.

After breakfast that day, we went to a local bookstore, where you came across a copy of the DC comic *The Joker/Harley Quinn Uncovered.* Eager to continue our conversation of what features make someone creepy-looking, you called me over and highlighted the characteristics that make the Joker grotesque—his green hair, wrinkles, oversize mouth and teeth, and green makeup. You then pointed out the contrast cut by Harley Quinn, his bisexual paramour, whom you deemed beautiful for her smooth skin, well-appointed makeup, pretty eyes, and cute pigtails. By "pretty" you meant proportional, balanced—and young.

I asked you if an elderly person could be seen as beautiful, and you immediately thought of Grandma Elizabeth, swiftly defending her beauty while also declaring that wrinkles aren't as pretty as smooth skin. Together, we wondered aloud if a man wearing makeup is off-putting just by virtue of transgressing a gender norm. No, you reasoned, but thought the green foundation the Joker applied didn't hit the mark. We also considered the question of whether someone who looked unattractive could be a good person despite their unnerving aesthetic. Promptly you reminded me that Harley Quinn is a villain even though she's attractive. But the idea that our looks correspond with the quality of our character is an idea we've inherited from antiquity, as well. The Greek word *kalokagathía* consists of two adjectives that coalesce physical beauty with inner goodness and a whole host of admirable qualities. Roughly translated, *kalós* means "beautiful, pretty, handsome (outwardly)" and *agathós* means "honest, good, noble." Although the late New York University Classics professor David Konstan told me that this common rendering of the compound expression is inaccurate, noting that *kalos* (fine), *kai* (and), and *agathia* (good) exclusively referred to male citizens of the aristocracy and ultimately meant excellence, he, too, acknowledges that to be excellent and morally fit required that one be in top physical form. Hippocrates and Aristotelians even advanced the pseudoscience of physiognomy, the practice of attempting to discern one's character via his or her facial features. "Mental character is not independent of or unaffected by bodily processes, but is conditioned by the state of the body; and counterwise the body is sympathetically influenced by the affections of the soul," reads a quote taken from *Physiognomonica,* a treatise attributed to Aristotle, though likely written by one of his disciples. Today, we're taught from an early age not to read books by their covers, but the idea that one's bodily condition underpins one's quality of character insidiously informs the way we continue to treat people we find attractive and unattractive, wittingly or unwittingly.

A few years ago, Thomas J. Spiegel, a professor of philosophy and religion at Miyazaki International University in Japan, wrote an academic paper on lookism, a form of "discrimination based on physical attractiveness or the lack thereof," arguing that lookism, similar to fatphobia and cacophobia (fear of ugliness), should be understood as a form of "epistemic injustice" that we can redress only by acknowledging its existence, but we, as a society, resist doing so: It feels too tender to admit that our beauty or lack thereof impacts, even shapes, our lives.

I, too, find it hard to say the words *I am ugly* or *I am seen as ugly*, especially to you, since I'm fairly certain such an insult would be the worst you—and most every girl—could receive. As cultural critic Peggy Orenstein points out in *Cinderella Ate My Daughter,* "The fastest way to take a girl down remains, as ever, to attack her looks or sexual behavior: Ugly. Fat. Slut. Whore. Those are the teen girl equivalent of kryptonite." It feels too taboo to broach, even among women—the fact that our lives, if not defined by, are unfairly contoured by the quality of our looks, which will, in part, determine our well-being and happiness, our opportunities, and our successes. I have never, until now, confessed to anyone that I felt I was ugly. It seemed too shameful to express aloud, but when I have ventured to say more mild things like "My looks aren't my strong suit" or "I'm not telegenic enough for that," people, women usually, have been quick to firmly dismiss my negative self-assessment. Women can't let a thought like that hang in the air without vigorously swatting it away because it's the fate they're chronically trained (and trying) to avoid; it's very nearly the worst thought to think of oneself. But our next-level liberation depends upon our ability to manage the fragile and fraught embarrassment in openly admitting the ways our culturally informed plainness or prettiness impact our lives—and there is ample evidence that it does. And yet, perhaps because it's viewed as a soft and shallow topic, unworthy of serious inquiry, feminism in its many permutations has still failed to adequately address it.

Spiegel compiles research that shows how people perceived as unattractive endure a greater degree of economic, social, and romantic hardship: Individuals viewed as ugly have a harder time securing opportunities in the workforce, are paid less, and receive harsher performance reviews than their prettier counterparts; in their personal lives, they have far fewer affectional prospects; in legal proceedings, they are given harsher sentences; even children judged as ugly receive worse treatment than their fairer playmates. One recent study I found showed that people are more inclined to ascribe immoral behavior to "ugly faces."

You've already seen these injustices play out firsthand at a day camp one summer. One early evening, pre-shower, before the beginning of the school year, you were climbing up the doorframe of our bathroom, explaining to me that one of your peers suffers an assortment of indignities from kids. You attributed it to her size, careful not to use the word *fat,* which is synonymous with *ugly* in our culture and in your mind, too. Rendering it an unsayable epithet, you chose instead to indicate what you meant by size with your hands—"She's like this," you said, extending your arms into a circle in front of your belly.

"I feel like they don't like her *because* of the way she looks," you said, focusing on the bunched-up fists in your lap before taking a sly peek to see how I registered your confession.

I honestly didn't know what to say; I didn't think it was fair to make you feel bad for an ugly thought born of noxious and pervasive societal messaging that carried the weight of a commandment, endowed with moral authority, but I knew I needed to disrupt it.

Then you said, "But *you* think she's gross, too."

"What? I've never seen or met her before," I said, shocked.

"Yeah, but when I said that her entire lunch is just treats, you made a face like she's gross." I reflected on your recent disinclination to eat sweets—"I don't like candy," you'd declared, to our surprise—and forgoing of a popsicle before you'd finished it.

"I am so sorry you thought that. I didn't mean to suggest she's gross. I don't think that at all. In the eighties, my friends and I ate entire meals made up of Ding Dongs, Twinkies, Doritos, and Coca-Cola, and fast food was a staple in our diets. What I was thinking when you told me that is that it's not healthy. Kids are growing, and their bodies need nutrients and healthy foods. Junk food isn't good nourishment. I'm all for a treat alongside a healthy meal." I was trying to normalize eating confections in moderation, not ejecting them from our diets altogether, which seems like a path to disordered eating.

I suggested that you and your peers might feel differently about her if she'd not tauntingly performed a slew of unwelcome antics—she'd stolen a camp mate's toy, she'd broken your eraser, she'd tried to pour pickle juice on your lunch, and she'd refused to participate in group projects because, she said, she's a poet and wants to preserve her energy for her work, a funny assertion from a little kid that made me think she might be a cool one to befriend. (I wondered to myself if she was undertaking to push you and your peers away to preempt the ugliness toward her.)

"Maybe," you replied.

That I managed to refrain from pontificating or judging felt like a small victory, because I had so much more to say. But I knew too much intellectualizing or even the slightest whiff of criticism might make you abstain from future disclosures.

One reason it's challenging to address the disadvantages of less-attractive people stems from the widespread belief that beauty and ugliness are entirely subjective; however, neuroscientific research suggests that certain aspects of what people find attractive—such as facial symmetry, moderate complexity, and proto-typicality—may be rooted in objective brain mechanisms shared across individuals, even if they interplay with sociocultural influences and subjectivity. But would it be that surprising if we did tend to see beauty in the same faces, given the long-standing impact of colonization, globalization, and social media? Collectively, we're scanning faces for similar—largely Western—ideals. Due, in part, to hundreds of years of colonization, for example, the double eyelid as well as light skin and light eyes are coveted characteristics in various parts of Asia. Similarly, a study focusing on print media in Africa found that four influential magazines failed to portray the diversity of physiques, complexions, and hair textures common to African women, instead accentuating and celebrating features common to white women. You'd think social media would help diversify and amplify a wider range of ways to be beautiful, and while it has, it has simultaneously magnified hard-to-attain ideals like excessive thinness. Many images floating through cyberspace have been grossly altered by various filters that reify (rather than challenge) long-held aesthetic standards, making beauty ideals even more out of reach, further chipping away at the self-esteem of women and girls as they compare themselves against unrealizable standards. "There are tons of studies linking social media use and body image issues in girls, but you can't really make a causal claim that it has 'increased disordered eating' based on available evidence," Northwestern University psychology professor and author of *Beauty Sick* Renee Engeln told me via email. "It seems likely to be true to me, but nearly all of the data are correlational, not experimental. . . . There's certainly enough evidence to claim that social media use—particularly, photo/video-focused—is linked with increased body image issues, which includes disordered eating. But the most likely scenario is that girls who are already vulnerable for one reason or another are more likely to be nudged into eating disorder territory by social media content."

Even before you'd expressed interest in social media, I'd begun vigorously beating the drum of its many dangers to ensure you didn't become one of those vulnerable girls. It irked you because it hadn't yet entered your orbit of wants. By age nine, we'd already covered its whole troubling terrain—from strangers trying to court your attention on Roblox to the cruelties and potential legal fallout from saying untrue and unkind things about peers online to the confidence-collapsing perils of measuring one's value against doctored images and the cheap currency of likes. "But I don't even want to go on social media," you said after I'd dramatically rattled off my concerns like you'd been demanding a Snapchat account, but I knew—I know—it's just around the corner.

You happen to be well situated aesthetically—maybe you'd feel affirmed online, or maybe girls who thought you were pretty would dislike you for it—but I knew all too well from experience and research that kids, especially girls, who fall too far below the status quo's beauty ideal are treated unjustly. In more extreme cases, Spiegel argues they ought to be designated a marginalized social class:

> The main problem with not counting ugly or attractive people respectively as a social group threatens to imply that their experiences are merely individual or subjective anomalies rather than recurring patterns of looks-based oppression. . . . If ugly people are told repeatedly that they are not ugly or that their woes are not due to them being ugly, even though they are, then this social taboo of being ugly and telling someone they might be ugly, are what puts those people at a hermeneutic disadvantage of interpreting the social world and their place in it. The taboo upholds a disconnect

> between the way ugly people experience the social world and the way in which they are told the social world actually is.

He goes on to emphasize that people perceived as ugly, in a society that chronically dismisses, challenges, or undermines their ugly self-understanding, are unable to consolidate power as a group to redress the injustices born of their aesthetic disadvantage. Consequently, they aren't able to fully actualize their potential or the worldly possibilities afforded to their prettier peers.

If Spiegel's call to arms on behalf of the disenfranchised ugly seems slightly comical or ridiculous, it's partly because we view aesthetics as the superficial preoccupation of trivial and trivialized women and girls—in other words, nothing to be taken seriously. That's by design: We mock women for their frivolity but then chastise those who don't measure up. Think of aging celebrities who overwork their faces with plastic surgery and Botox or conversely allow themselves to age naturally and are picked apart and criticized either way. (*The Substance,* a feminist satire and horror film about an aging movie star, is a garish illustration of this truth, offering a keen commentary on the overwhelming aesthetic pressures on women and girls and the dangers of submitting to them. The movie's protagonist, Elizabeth Sparkle, aptly named, injects a yellow-green serum into her veins to recapture her youth and desirability, but things go terribly wrong, giving way to a monstrous version of self.) Fear of being perceived as ugly or not pretty enough, in fact, informs every woman's outsized attention to her looks; this is true even for you going back as young as five. You may feel, now, at age ten, that you are freely deciding to put your bright pink headband, just so, over your well-coiffed dark hair after slipping into your prettiest spring dress, the one with vibrant cherry blossoms and Edwardian sleeves, and inserting your sparkliest studs into your ears, but none of it is entirely your choice; you're being puppeteered, in part, by invisible strings that I hope this missive will make manifest so you understand why you—and every other girl—might feel like crying or hiding when your hair or outfit doesn't set exactly as you'd like, so you can stop submitting and start deciding.

Spiegel likens lookism to sexism, racism, and ableism, given that women, people of color, and people with disabilities experience discrimination based on degrading and belittling ideas society ascribes to their fixed characteristics, but those isms also intersect with and define the border between who is and who is not considered attractive, as Princeton historian Nell Irvin Painter shows in her groundbreaking book *The History of White People.* "What we can see depends heavily on what our culture has trained us to look for," she writes. Before unpacking and contesting the beauty ideal, she walks us back to ancient Greece to tease out the complex ways our fairly modern notions of race were strategically constructed during the Enlightenment era to ensure the primacy of white people. Before then, people didn't think in terms of race as we do. The Greeks, for one, didn't ascribe any value to one's pigmentation. Instead they erected their own framework for taxonomizing (and stereotyping) individuals based on the regions of the country in which they were born and raised, a fact Painter highlights simply to show that complexion was not an organizing principal for the ancients. For instance, they attributed qualities of character and temperament to the climate common to the area in which an individual or group of people resided, following ideas put forth by Hippocrates, the fifth-century physician and father of Western medicine. People from the "fertile lowlands," who enjoyed more serene occupations like farming, were thought to be " 'fleshy, ill-articulated, moist, lazy, and generally cowardly in character,' " whereas those in harsher regions, where weather patterns shifted constantly and abruptly and the soil is ungiving, were thought to be hardy, self-sufficient, and headstrong.

Painter goes on to show that our modern concept of race—understood as a biological fact—did not fully take shape until the Enlightenment, when scholars in the sciences (anatomists, naturalists, botanists, anthropologists)—all white, all male—helped usher in a new system of classification in which organisms, including the human variety, were organized within rigid categories, leading, inevitably, to social hierarchies. Since the classifiers were white, they gave Caucasians first place in the pecking order, endowing them with superior intelligence, morality, and, yes, even looks. "They not only wanted the people they called 'their women' to be the most beautiful, and 'their men' to be the most virile. They wanted 'their countries' to have the best politics. So they wanted to have *everything* better. And that included beauty," Painter told NPR.

I knew it was worthwhile, no matter how limited your ability to grasp the finer points, to keep demonstrating over and over again the ways in which words and ideas, inventions of the mind, often work against us and our collective well-being. You understood my mini history lesson with greater fluency than I'd have imagined and even found utility in the way the ancients organized people, although arranging people by groups is always a tricky business. You argued that life in the city and in the countryside places different demands on people and, as a result, may foster different character traits, but arranging people based on their skin tone seemed, to you, intentionally cruel, senseless. "And we're still living with the consequences of those ideas of race," I said, reminding you of all the injustices still endured by people of color, especially African Americans. In various books on the civil rights movement, you learned about slavery, the "separate but equal" doctrine in the Jim Crow South, the murders of Emmett Till, Dr. Martin Luther King Jr., and Malcolm X. In appropriate and plain language that you could understand, we talked about the enduring repercussions of racism, including the way it teaches people to hate their own reflections. In Toni Morrison's first novel, *The Bluest Eye,* she beautifully addresses the ugliness of the racism underlying the Eurocentric beauty standards imposed on Black girls in the character at the center of her story, Pecola Breedlove. Pecola, who has had to bear witness to the horrors wrought by racism—impoverishment, addiction, and violence—has fully absorbed the message that she's ugly and consequently longs for blue eyes, a metonymy for whiteness. As Morrison's narrator explains: "Adults, older girls, shops, magazines, newspapers, window signs—all the world had agreed that a blue-eyed, yellow-haired, pink-skinned doll was what every girl child treasured." This tactically limited and alienating representation of beauty instills in Pecola a longing for light eyes for the better life she believes they'll bestow upon her: "It had occurred to Pecola some time ago that if her eyes, those eyes that held the pictures, and knew the sights—if those eyes of hers were different, that is to say, beautiful, she herself would be different." And she would—she'd be different in a world that recognized her as beautiful because the world treats beautiful people and things with love and tenderness and admiration. To experience herself in the warm glow of that reception *would* be transforming.

I told you about the formation of Pecola's inadequate sense of self in 1940s Lorain, Ohio, due to the beauty ideals that have long excluded people of color. It prompted you to say that you prefer dolls with whom you share skin color, shuffling over to your brown American Girl dolls and your bin full of darker-skinned O.M.G. figures, styled with exaggerated makeup, club-worthy outfits, and accessories. "I don't think dolls of different races were as widely available as white dolls when Pecola was growing up," I said. "If they had been, she might have felt differently about herself."

According to Nell Irvin Painter, "the term 'Caucasian' as a designation for white people originates in concepts of beauty related to the white slave trade from eastern Europe, and whiteness remains embedded in visions of beauty found in art history and popular culture." As the "science of race" continued to take shape, she argues, white ethnographers in the eighteenth century conflated two groups of enslaved people, Africans and Tartars, whom they "associated with brute labor" and ugliness, setting them apart from those of the white slave trade—Circassians, Georgians, and Caucasians of the Black Sea region, largely women used for sex—who would come to exemplify and embody "human beauty."

Guided by a worldview that affirmed the value and aesthetic superiority of lighter-skinned people, late seventeenth- and eighteenth-century thinkers continued to forge the emerging notion of race. One of the first known works to classify humans into discrete categories was published in 1684, laying the groundwork for racialized and aestheticized readings of human beings. The author of the text, French physician François Bernier, gives "pride of place" to the first "species" of humans: groups of people who hail from Europe, as well as regions far from the continent, including North Africa, Asia, and the Americas, which included American Indians. He puts sub-Saharan Africans alone in the second classification but then places Muscovites (Russians) and Tartars (a Turkic ethnic group) with Asians. Finally, he determines that "Lapps" (the Sámi, Indigenous people from Scandinavia) constitute the fourth group of humans, though today they're generally—though not always—considered white. I highlight this befuddled history to expose the absurdity of categorizing people based on some trumped-up concoction like race. Think about it: The white "race" originally included Indigenous peoples; and Russians, whom we now consider "white," were paired with Asians. The new groupings we've fabricated today do not have more integrity or claim on truth. The point is that language and the ideas it contains are always slippery and shifting, often manipulated to justify various agendas and hierarchies.

Bernier's racial pyramid shows the biases informing the categories he created and how they reinforce social, including aesthetic, rankings. In his assessment, sub-Saharan Africans are grouped together due to characteristics he finds distinguishing, like "their thick lips," "snub noses," "blackness," "oily" skin, "wool" hair, which he likens to that of a dog, teeth like "the finest ivory," and mouths "red as Coral." The third race are Asians, all of whom he calls "truly white, but they have broad shoulders, a flat face, a small squab nose, little pig's-eyes long and deep set, and three hairs of a beard." Those on the last rung of his ladder are "Lapps" (now the Sámi), whom he disparagingly describes as "little stunted creatures with thick legs, large shoulders, short neck, and a face elongated immensely; very ugly and partaking much of the bear."

Although Bernier expresses flattering comments about the beauty of nude Black slave girls sold off the coast of East Africa—"I have never seen anything more beautiful"—he endows the white slave girls with superior good looks: "'The handsomest women of the world are to be found . . . [among the] immense quantity of slaves who come . . . from Mingrelia, Georgia, and Circassia.'"

Bernier's arbitrary and often disparaging classification system would be expanded and more widely circulated in the works of French Huguenot Jean-Baptiste Chardin, a jeweler and world traveler. At first, Chardin wrote harshly about peoples from the Caucasus mountains (Circassians, Mingrelians, and Georgians). In his rendering, Circassians are thieves who eat with their hands and go to the bathroom next to their meals—and the Mingrelians are "complete savages," inhumane and cruel, who cultivate overly cosmeticized—and "'erotically adept'"—women. Nonetheless, he lavishes excess praise on them for their good looks, particularly those from Georgia:

> The blood of *Georgia* is the most beautiful in the Orient, & I would have to say in the world, for I've never noticed an ugly face of either sex in this country, and some are downright Angelic. Nature has endowed most of the women with graces not to be seen in any other place. I have to say it is impossible to look at them without falling in love with them. No more charming faces and no more lovely figures than those of the *Georgians* could serve to inspire painters. They are tall, graceful, slender, and poised, and even though they don't wear many clothes, you never see bulges. The only thing that spoils them is that they wear makeup, and the prettier they are, the more makeup they wear, for they think of makeup as a kind of ornament.

Painter wryly points out that his scathing assessment of the women of the Caucacus mountains' foul habits and behaviors would eventually vanish from race theory, leaving us with an idealized image of female beauty—white, passive, young, sexually violable—shaped by the slave trade.

Not long after Chardin's ode to enslaved white women, Circassians, Georgians, and Caucasians became interchangeable terms for the figure of the odalisque (an enslaved woman or a concubine in a harem) with each carrying with it "the aura of physical attractiveness, submission, and sexual availability—in a word, femininity. She cannot be free, for her captive status and harem location lie at the core of her identity."

That beauty ideals were born and developed out of the slave trade is no small irony. Don't women and girls continue to have to forsake certain freedoms for beauty—teetering slowly, delicately, deliberately on high heels, wearing tight bust-defining bras or skirts that restrict motion, starving themselves to achieve thinness, going under the knife to recapture their youthful good looks or improve upon a face deemed less appealing, styling one's hair or cosmeticizing one's face in such a way that makes an enemy of the easy comfort and pleasant messiness of just being? Beautification often requires both physical and psychological suffering, acts of self-denial and constraint, all imbued with the dark legacy of white slavery.

How strange to know that when you paint your nails or put on makeup or cultivate a come-hither look or play into a kind of powerlessness to arouse male attention and interest, you're harkening back to this ugly history of sexual subjugation—rape.

In intersecting and sometimes perplexing ways, throughout the eighteenth, nineteenth, and twentieth centuries eminent thinkers with outsized influence helped reinforce these formative notions of race and beauty, which have given them the illusion of timeless truths that we're still trying to untether ourselves from today: Philosopher Immanuel Kant espoused a universal notion of beauty when he referenced, "The sort of beauty we have called the *pretty figure* is judged by all men very much alike." Tossing Turks, Arabs, and Persians to the ugly sidelines, he declared that "Circassian and Georgian maidens have always been considered extremely pretty by all Europeans who travel through their lands." Following Kant, German historian and archaeologist Johann Joachim Winckelmann praised the Greek profile and believed that white skin enhances one's beauty, but calls Chinese eyes "an offense against beauty" and declared the flat noses of Mongolian Kalmucks " 'an irregularity' equal to deformity."

Contemplating Winckelmann's crude assessment of Asian eyes, I couldn't stop thinking how those ideas have ensured a lifetime of hurt and self-aversion for generations of Asian people, including my friend Grace, who is Korean American. She once told me that as a kid she hated herself and wanted to be white, kind of like Pecola in *The Bluest Eye.* As Cathy Park Hong put it in *Minor Feelings: An Asian American Reckoning:*

> Racial self-hatred is seeing yourself the way the whites see you, which turns you into your own worst enemy. . . . You don't like how you look, how you sound. You think your Asian features are undefined, like God started pinching out your features and then abandoned you. You hate that there are so many Asians in the room. *Who let in all the Asians?* you rant in your head. Instead of solidarity, you feel that you are *less than* around other Asians, the boundaries of yourself no longer distinct but congealed into a horde.

Raised in a predominantly white suburb of Ann Arbor, Michigan, Grace didn't benefit from the diversity you've grown up with in one of the most multiracial and -cultural cities in America. Here in Sunset Park, we live just one avenue away from Brooklyn's Chinatown, where you maintain several friendships, and just last year you had a Chinese American "boyfriend" whom you affectionately called "king of the boys" and fancied the dreamiest guy in the fourth grade. That may not be a symptom of progress so much as the lived reality of dwelling among a multiplicity of identities in a metropolis.

When you were six, we took you to the Metropolitan Museum of Art to see an exhibit called *Chroma: Ancient Sculptures in Color,* which functioned as a kind of corrective to the erroneous idea passed down by Winckelmann and his ilk that the ancient Greeks prized whiteness to such an extent their statuary was devoid of color. As you zigzagged through the bright and arresting figures, we listened intently as a friend, well versed in art history, explained that the pigment had simply oxidized.

The terrible fallout from Winckelmann's misapprehension was that he "elevated Rome's white marble copies of Greek statuary into emblems of beauty and created a new white aesthetic," Painter writes—and worse: "It would apply not only to works from antiquity, not only to Greek art, but to all of art and all of humanity."

Even people who hold an especially dear place in the American pantheon of letters and philosophy succumbed to the biases of their time—and we will, too, as much as we'd like to think we're different. American transcendental philosopher Ralph Waldo Emerson, who championed important causes like abolition and women's suffrage and promoted a more spiritual, as opposed to religious, take on matters of faith, believed that the beautiful were unilaterally English of Saxon descent—and male: "The 'English face,'" he once wrote, "combines 'decision and nerve' with 'the fair complexion, blue eyes, and open and florid aspect. Hence the love of truth, hence the sensibility, the fine perception, and poetic construction. The fair Saxon man, with open front, and honest meaning . . . is not the wood out of which cannibal, or inquisitor, or assassin is made, but he is moulded for law, lawful trade, civility, marriage, the nurture of children, for colleges, churches, charities, and colonies.'"

Emerson, sounding like a proponent of the pseudoscience physiognomy, a theory popularized and advanced by Swiss poet Johann Kaspar Lavater in the late eighteenth century, espoused the view that our looks convey our moral character. German anthropologist and noted skull collector Johann Friedrich Blumenbach, a contemporary of Lavater, though more empirically minded, believed that humans could be classified by cranial differences. He famously idealized the skull of a Georgian woman, arguing that its symmetry and proportion represented the most beautiful and "perfect" human form—a view that helped establish whiteness, specifically Caucasianness, as the aesthetic and scientific norm in early racial theory. Blumenbach's compatriot Christoph Meiners believed that the people *he* deemed ugly, such as Mongolians—Asians whom he lumped together with Jews, Armenians, Arabs, and Persians—*deserved* to be enslaved and controlled because they were "weak in body and spirit, bad, and lacking in virtue," a view he believed naturally extended from their inferior appearances—or ugliness, Painter argues. Ideas like Emerson's celebration of Anglo-Saxons and Meiners's racial pseudoscience reverberate through American culture today. Such notions inform President Trump's remark in a 2024 interview that the violence in or from migrant communities—disproportionately made up of people from Mexico—is due to "bad genes." He draws on this line of thinking to stoke fear and justify the apprehension of immigrants, including, in some cases, their American-born children through U.S. Immigration and Customs Enforcement (ICE). ICE has been known to apprehend migrants in public spaces like streets, hospitals, and schools, as well as from their own homes. ICE has even deported individuals—many of whom were brought to the United States as children—to countries they do not know or remember.

I catalog this formative history of racialized thinking not only to help you pinpoint where contemporary stereotypes and prejudices originate but to show you that the entire epistemology is made up. The proof is in the fact that none of these racial architects could completely agree on who belonged in what category.

Their race-based ideologies eventually gave rise to the pseudoscientific movement known as eugenics, which would go on to influence Nazi Germany's racial policies, culminating in the systematic extermination of Jews, beginning in 1941. Francis Galton, an English polymath who contributed significantly to the field of statistics, drew on the emerging science of craniometry, as well as the core assumptions informing now-discredited sciences like phrenology and physiognomy, to formulate and promote the idea that selective breeding would improve the human race. This notion laid the groundwork for later eugenics programs that targeted people of color, the disabled, queer people, and others deemed "undesirable."

Galton didn't arrive at his premise in a vacuum. Several fallacious beliefs, starting with the invention of race, coalesced in Galton's heinous ideology. Let's take a closer look at craniometry, which American physician and anthropologist Samuel Morton helped popularize in the 1800s. Craniometrists study the size, shape, and proportion of human skulls, particularly in the field of anthropology, but Morton, in the mindset of his time, perceived social distinctions, as well as intellectual capacities, in the cranial differences he observed. He ranked people along "suspiciously stereotypical . . . racial lines" according to Painter, with Pelasgic skulls (the pre-Hellenic peoples of Greece) taking the top spot in his aesthetic hierarchy, followed by Semites (Jews) and then Egyptians (Black people). He writes with absurd adulation—because, remember, we're talking about a *skull* here—of Pelasgic craniums: "The . . . lineaments are familiar to us in the beautiful models of Grecian art, which are remarkable for the volume of the head in comparison with that of the face, the large facial angle, and the symmetry and delicacy of the whole osteological structure," an assessment reflecting the beauty ideals of symmetry, proportion, and harmony passed down from antiquity. Following his adoring take on Pelasgic skulls, he goes on to roughly describe Semitic ones: "[They have a] receding forehead, long, arched, and very prominent nose, a marked distance between the eyes, a low heavy broad, strong and often harsh development of the whole facial structure," inscribing—contriving—their aesthetic inferiority. Next in line are "all smaller skulls [that] belonged to slaves, dumber, darker-skinned examples of the Egyptian type," Painter writes.

Although Morton's anthropological focus was more concentrated on skulls, his reference to the "very prominent" Jewish nose as an identifying feature speaks to a long history of antisemitism going back far with stops in Medieval Europe (see the painting *Jesus Before Caiaphas, Salvin Hours* from 1275), in the

Renaissance (see *Christ Among the Doctors* by Albrecht Dürer from 1506), in the Victorian era's age of phrenology and physiognomy, before culminating in the modern nose job, pioneered by plastic surgeon Jacques Joseph. A German Jew in prewar Berlin, Joseph helped his Jewish clientele pass for Gentiles by altering their noses in the same way that Jews have often changed their names to obscure their identities. To share a little of this history with you, I once told you that Winona Ryder, who stars in one of our favorite Halloween movies, *Beetlejuice,* was born Winona Horowitz, and Bob Dylan, whose raspy, off-key voice grates on you, is actually Robert Allen Zimmerman. I'm not sure if antisemitism motivated their decisions to adopt stage names, but it wouldn't have been unusual, given that Jewish-sounding names were often seen as a liability in show business and could limit one's marketability or opportunities. "I would never change my name," you protested, but I countered that you might if it meant survival—if keeping it meant hunger, persecution, or worse, as it has been for Jews throughout history. Robert Knox, an anthropologist and contemporary of Samuel Morton's, used these cutting phrases to describe semitic proboscises in 1850: "[They are] large, massive, club-shaped, hooked . . . three or four times larger than suits the face. . . . Thus it is that the Jewish face never can [be], and never is, perfectly beautiful." Even today, some Jewish people continue to undergo rhinoplasty, often at great expense, in response to beauty standards shaped by antisemitism and white supremacy.

As of this writing, you don't know that Sabrina had a nose job at the early age of sixteen. She wanted to smooth the bump in the bridge of her nose, the same one your grandfather had. "At least twenty-five percent of the Jewish girls at my school got nose jobs," she told me. Her nose, which she wrote about in a beautiful essay for *ELLE* magazine, became the focal point of everything she felt was wrong about her—the Jewishness of her nose, her secret lesbianism, her social unease. But it didn't, in the end, change how she felt about herself, and as her dad lay dying two decades later, she longed to see him in her face again and regretted that the visible memory of him—and his family, of their shared history as Jews—was no longer there.

Women, too, became subjects of these degrading classifications, as skull size and shape were used to justify gendered hierarchies. They believed that a smaller skull indicated less intellectual aptitude. A statistician named Alice Lee challenged this faulty contention in 1898. She walked into an all-male academic conference at Trinity College in Dublin and began appraising all the men's heads, dramatically pointing out that some of the men with the smallest skulls were, in fact, the smartest among them.

Craniometry, along with physiognomy and phrenology (the pseudoscientific practice of determining an individual's personality traits and intellectual capacities based on the contour, bumps and all, of one's skull) laid the troubling foundation for eugenics that would come to dominate thinking in the late-nineteenth and early twentieth centuries and provide the doctrinal framework for Nazi Germany's justification for murdering more than six million Jews and other "undesirables," such as gay men, political dissidents, religious minorities, and people with mental or physical disabilities.

In the same way that racialized narratives of bodies written over the last three hundred and fifty years functionally placed people of color outside white paradigms of beauty, disabled people have been cast as ugly in historical renderings going back to antiquity, when "Aristotle proposed a law to prevent parents from rearing deformed children, and in Sparta, [where] parents were legally obligated to abandon deformed infants" (although this practice may have been more myth than reality). Even kids with cleft palates might have been killed by the Romans and Spartans because they believed such children were harboring "evil spirits" due to the abiding belief that any "deformities" reflected one's inner crookedness.

When I talked about this harrowing history with you and Sabrina one night, you said that you'd create a wooden prosthetic for your baby if they were born without a leg, recalling the artificial limb Paddler, the beaver in the film *The Wild Robot,* made for Roz, the robot, when she lost hers. We'd just seen this movie of queer kinship in which love and friendship and collectivism are the foundation of community and the essence of family—not blood, not even flesh. The simple act of caring for another is enough to give the word *family* its full weight. I loved that this was the detail you pointed out because everyone thought Paddler was crazy, sinking his incisors into the thickest tree, but he kept at it, trusting the process, knowing it would lead to something good, and it did. You then added that if your baby had a cleft palate in ancient times, you'd put a veil over her face so she could safely go outside, but more often than not you'd ensure her protection by keeping her hidden at home. That made me think of the ways all of us, but especially women and girls, learn to conceal ourselves to get by in this world.

While it's a contradictory and disordered history, as histories always are, and not universally applicable, a recurring belief traceable to the converse of the Greek ideal of *kalokagathía* ("beautiful" and "good") associated the sickly, beggars (*ptochos* in Greek), and the physically disabled and/or deformed with a lack of goodness or morality. "The term *aischos,* also *aischros,* sometimes referred to people with physical handicaps as well as 'ugliness' and 'disgrace.' *Kakos* connoted both 'ugly' and 'evil,'" historian Gretchen E. Henderson explains in *Ugliness: A Cultural History.* Umberto Eco's *On Ugliness* similarly states: "Greek culture produced a vast literature on the relationship between physical ugliness and moral ugliness."

Similar ideas underlie the discrimination and criminalization of people living with disabilities at the founding of the eugenics movement in the late-nineteenth century, when so-called "ugly laws" or "unsightly beggar ordinances" sought to remove destitute and disabled people from public view, which included "diseased, maimed and deformed persons," as well as sexual and gender outlaws. Particularly relevant to me: Uncleanliness and the collective fear of the "diseased" poor—often immigrants and war veterans—played into the hysteria.

Because my physical hygiene was the only thing I could control about my subpar looks when I was a kid, I had—and still have—an outsized preoccupation with cleanliness. When my father was diagnosed with a brain tumor in 1986, my mother, a homemaker without a formal education or career, began clutching her hair in worry and bellowing into the phone to her sister and mother, "We're going to be in the streets! What am I going to do? We have no money!" The specter of poverty seemed to appear, like ugly wallpaper, on every surface, reminding us, everywhere we looked, how tenuous our comfortable state was—the house, the cars, the clothes, the food. I learned early that these things could be taken away in an instant. The loss of my father felt too unfathomably large for my kid brain to process. Instead I was consumed with scary visions of homelessness and hunger—and with the thought that I would no longer be able to bathe regularly, just as I entered puberty. Being well scrubbed—my armor—protected me from the kind of ugliness I could control: bodily filth. Would my hair go greasy? Would dirt and grime collect under my nail beds for the world to see? Would my breath become stenchy in a mouth crowded with unbrushed and crooked teeth? Would kids see me coming and run the other way? Something about sitting in my own stink was an unbearable future to behold. Reflecting on Berkeley scholar Susan Schweik's history of ugly laws, I was able to put my hygienical angst into historical and cultural context.

Many individuals with disabilities excluded from formal employment turned to street-based means of survival, such as performing, begging, or selling small items like poetry, pencils, and shoestrings, which made them vulnerable to ugly laws. Those without regular means preferred living unhoused (aka free) or in rooming houses as opposed to residing in overcrowded and highly regulated group homes. In either scenario, access to regular baths or showers was at a minimum. In contrast, wealthier people with disabilities, who didn't need to rely on alms or street vending and could maintain a kempt appearance, were protected from the indignities of the ugly laws: "Unsightliness was a status offense, illegal only for people without means."

Femininity and beauty have always been intertwined with good hygiene. As Italian Renaissance writer Baldassare Castiglione once put it, "Does she not seem most beautiful and womanly to you then, spic and span in her close-fitting velvet slippers and clean stockings?" Throughout the ages, bodily filth has suggested disease—several of which were real threats before modern medicine, such as cholera, smallpox, dysentery, malaria, leprosy, tuberculosis, typhoid, and measles—and in some ways warranted all the anxiety it produced.

In Naomi Baker's *Plain Ugly,* she breaks down some of the earliest depictions of the "literary ugly woman" in early modern literature. She notes, for example, that Beroe, a figure in Greek mythology, is described as "filthy to look at and repulsive to touch," "a lake brimming with filth," and is "characterized by foul and excessive bodily excretions" and "disease, decomposition and death." In contrast, Helen of Troy is immaculately rendered with "golden hair, milky forehead, snowy neck, starry eyes, rose cheeks and lips, white teeth, dainty breasts and narrow waist," the embodiment of perfect hygiene and beauty. Both Baker's and Schweik's books highlight the relationship between filth and sexual immorality. Mapping out the etymology of the word *slut,* for example, Baker writes that it referred to "a woman of lower social status who is considered 'dirty, slovenly' or 'untidy' in appearance and to a woman 'of loose character.'" That stuck several centuries later in the time of ugly laws:

> In the later-nineteenth-century United States, combining pressures of individualism and consumerism created what Philip Ferguson calls a "broad cultural aesthetic" obsessed with problems of "appearing" and appearance. "[U]gliness became as important a judgment as beauty," writes Ferguson. "Applied to people with physical and mental disabilities, heightened attention to appearance made words such as 'repulsive,' 'grotesque,' 'dirty' and 'slovenly' into accusations of moral and mental failure as well as the more obvious aesthetic transgressions."

Schweik goes on to flesh out the historical connection between prostitutes and mendicants, as well as disability, disease, and queerness, following Rebekah Edwards's scholarship, which may have been seen as a kind of social deformity, visible on bodies that transgress conventional gender expectations and engage in homosexual sex. Quoting a sociological text from 1909 entitled *The Wretches of Povertyville* by I.L. Nascher, Schweik writes:

> This class is composed of those whose propensities, viler than animal since they have no counterparts in the animal kingdom, place them outside of any human category. They call themselves 'faeries.' Such a wretch, born of human parents, in the semblance of man gives himself a female appellative, imitates woman's voice and ways, and as far as he dares wears woman's attire. . . . This effeminate creature is in love with an equally despicable wretch of his own sex. There are women of the same class, masculine women who imitate the opposite sex as much as possible. . . . They assume a gruff

> voice, and in time lose their natural tone of voice, associate with the 'faeries' and in their social intercourse with the latter take the part of a man in his relations to a woman.

I wonder if the ways in which queers and people with disabilities fall short of Grecian ideals of symmetry, proportion, and harmony extend, in part, from our inability to fulfill the proper function of our forms, an idea articulated by thirteenth-century Italian friar, priest, and theologian Thomas Aquinas. Aquinas helped establish the beauty principle that "things must be suited to the purpose for which they are intended."

Bodies that defy expectations, whether because our limbs move differently or not at all, or because our genders don't align with our sex, or because we engage in homosexuality when our "natural" purpose is to couple in matrimony—and produce progeny—with members of the opposite sex, aren't legible as beautiful because they—we—are seen as ugly aberrations, three eyes or two noses on a single face.

I asked you once if you could envision a world where that which was asymmetrical and not proportional—cyclops or visages with uneven and multiple eyes, or a right hand with more than five fingers alongside a left hand with fewer—could be viewed as beautiful for being unique, a delightful deviation from the ordinary, predictable mobs of uniform bodies, but you couldn't see it. The conversation came up because you'd just gotten into Greek mythology, and your book was opened to a page with a big illustration of Polyphemus, the son of Poseidon and Thoosa, who had a large eye embedded into the center of his forehead. When you objected that he isn't attractive, I tried to open a space for seeing things differently by wondering aloud if the rarity of his singular eye could have made him seem unique and beautiful in the same way recessive genes like blond hair and blue eyes are widely viewed as beautiful. Then I told you about the "marvelous monsters," from antiquity through the medieval period, who were valued *because* they looked unusual, *because* they were different.

To the denizens of those days, "ugly things are part of the harmony of the world, thanks to proportion and contrast," Eco writes. "Thus even monsters have a reason and a dignity in the concept of Creation; likewise, evil within the order becomes good and beautiful because evil springs from good, and alongside it, good shines out all the better."

For proof, we looked no further than Pliny the Elder's *Natural History,* an encyclopedic catalog of "monstrous men and animals" that showed up in Hellenic and medieval bestiaries. Pliny the Elder's masterwork cobbles together a large body of knowledge from the ancients that spans topics as wide-ranging as astronomy, art, geography, zoology—and even "monsters," who Christian theologian St. Augustine argued in *The City of God* are "divine creatures" who "belong to the providential order of nature," according to Eco.

We looked at all of them: Fauns, whose eyes resided on their shoulders with a nose and mouth on their chests; Androgynes with male and female genitalia; Astomori, who lacked mouths; Cynocephali, dog-headed beings with human bodies—"Like Dog Man!" you shouted, only these creatures ate raw flesh; Pygmies, who are as small as the length of a forearm and dwell in caves and ravines; and Sciapods, who have only one leg accompanied by a massive foot on which they can run fast and shelter from the sun when lying down.

Thinkers in antiquity were not the only ones to find beauty in things thought unusual and sometimes frightening—or ugly. A movement in the late eighteenth century called Romanticism took shape alongside and in reaction against the neoclassical era's stodgy push to reclaim—and often misinterpret—the aesthetic ideals of the ancient Greeks. The Romantics, as they would come to be called, were less concerned with traditional metrics for creating and measuring beauty and more focused on the impressions produced in the beholder. This tilt toward the perceiver of art and how it impacts them gave way to an emphasis on the sublime, or "a bias toward formlessness, suffering and dread," that inspired artists like Caspar David Friedrich, who painted shipwrecks and loners on mountain cliffs shrouded in fog; bards like Percy Bysshe Shelley, who waxed poetic about the moon—"a dying lady, lean and pale"—and the perverse pleasures of walking among tombstones in search of figments and phantoms—"While yet a boy I sought for ghosts, and sped through many a listening chamber, cave, and ruin"; or novelists like Mary Shelley, whose monster in *Frankenstein,* assembled from cadaver parts, declares, "Beware; for I am fearless, and therefore powerful!" or whose Arctic traveler Robert Walton confesses his desire to explore the unknown: "There is something at work in my soul, which I do not understand." Not understanding, being in a state of mystification or awe and wonder, a frame of mind that "goes far beyond our sensibilities" so that we are "induced to imagine more than we see," encouraged greater subjectivity and new ways of taking in art and the world around us—and for seeing beauty where others, historically, saw ugliness. Romantics were known to seek out and tread among ghostly ruins, which were "appreciated precisely for their incompleteness, for the marks that inexorable time had left upon them, for the wild vegetation that covered them, for the cracks and the moss," and they even saw beauty in death itself. "Yes, my Léa, you are beautiful, you are the most beautiful of creatures, I would not give you up; you, your defeated eyes, your pallor, your sick body, I would not give them up for the beauty of the angels in the heavens!" wrote Jules-Amédée Barbey d'Aurevilly in his short story *Léa.* Some, like Bysshe Shelley, who used to haunt the cemetery where his friend and fellow poet John Keats lay buried, took up themes of Satanism and vampirism, recognizing beauty even in horror. This fragmentation or break from the integrity of measurable beauty ideals, which would reach its zenith in the postmodern era of the 1960s and 1970s, opened up new ways of thinking, seeing, and being in the world. As Eco put it, the movement sought "not to exclude contradictions or to resolve antitheses (finite/infinite, whole/fragment, life/death, mind/heart), but to bring them all together," whereby "the most disturbing aspects of life: sickness, transgression, death, darkness, the demoniac and the horrible" were valued in equal—or greater—measure to their opposites. In this new sensibility, "Ugliness was no longer the negation of Beauty, but its other face."

Romanticism's fracturing of neoclassical notions of beauty, which would be fully disassembled—decimated—in the postmodern era, inform our ability to see beauty where people from ages past might not. You, for one, wondered why a man you thought moderately handsome was portrayed as unattractive on the cover of a book called *Plain Ugly*. The man in question was painted by Italian Renaissance artist Domenico Ghirlandaio in a work called *Old Man with Young Boy*. I explained that his big bumpy nose may have indicated rhinophyma (a nasal deformity). It looked like a kind of illness, which registered as ugly at a time when various sicknesses were often death sentences. But other ideas converged upon his face, likely rendering him homely: classical metrics of beauty, as well as old age.

During the Italian Renaissance, for inspiration, people looked back to ancient Greeks, who defined beauty as proportion and symmetry, and a large knobby nose like his would have seemed out of harmony with the rest of his face.

Even today—and certainly in the past—elderly individuals, particularly older women, are often considered unattractive simply because they have gray hair, wrinkles, and aging bodies. (Common markers of elderly people's skin, moles and blemishes, were "evidence" of witchery by the judges of the Salem Witch Trials.)

Hysteria around witchery started in the Middle Ages but reached its zenith in the sixteenth and seventeenth centuries, when women of advanced years, especially if they looked unwell and emaciated with visible signs of poverty, were "accused of witchcraft *because they were ugly.*" The link between poverty and ugliness, and conversely wealth and beauty, has been well articulated through the ages.

"Attributions of beauty or ugliness are often not due to aesthetic but to socio-political criteria," Eco writes in *On Ugliness.* Citing economist Karl Marx, Eco writes: " 'I am ugly, but I can buy myself the most beautiful women. Hence I am not ugly, since the effect of ugliness, its discouraging power, is annulled by money.' " People of aristocratic or royal standing depicted in portraits in centuries past might read as ugly to us—and even to their contemporaries—but, as Eco notes, their affluence and social positioning "lent them such charisma and glamour that their subjects saw them through adoring eyes." I'm doubtful women deemed unattractive could change public perception of their appeal due to ample wealth in the same way men could, but undoubtedly those who suffered penurious disadvantages were also targets of false allegations of witchery. In 1692, for example, the child of Reverend Samuel Parris—the first ordained minister in Salem Village in the Massachusetts Bay Colony—Elizabeth, age nine, and his niece, Abigail Williams, age eleven, started exhibiting strange behavior: writhing on the floor and speaking unintelligibly. Under pressure to assign blame, the girls accused three vulnerable women who embodied the culture's harsh attitudes toward women who transgress gender expectations and live under socioeconomic duress—Black women in bondage, women living in poverty, and aging: "Tituba, a Caribbean woman enslaved by the Parris family; Sarah Good, a homeless beggar; and Sarah Osborne, an elderly impoverished woman." Tituba and Osborne were jailed—Osborne would eventually die in jail—and Good was hanged.

At nine, when I told you about this chilling history, you reminded me that you once thought of yourself as a witch capable of communicating with cats and casting spells. "And I'm not ugly," you declared, tenuously. "*Would* I be considered ugly?" I promised you that you'd be considered beautiful in every corner of the world at every time in history but pointed out that Jews and people of color were historically excluded from conventional notions of beauty.

"But Ruth Bader Ginsburg was pretty," you reasoned, not understanding that there was no real justification or defensible logic to excluding a whole group of people from the beauty ideal. Your comment came out of a memory of overhearing Sabrina and I gripe about the idiotic chatter that ensued about the former justice's youthful good looks when a documentary about her life and work came out several years earlier. Granted, few of us had seen her in her younger years—we knew only the very thin, small, slightly hunched elderly woman who packed a powerful punch on the highest bench—so it *was* a surprising discovery. But still: Here's a woman of breathtaking accomplishment—tied for graduating first in her class at Columbia Law School, who became the second female law professor in the history of Rutgers University and the second woman to sit on the Supreme Court, a woman who had an incalculable impact on society, helping advance our reproductive freedoms, equal pay, and equal access to state-funded schools, among many other legal triumphs for all of us—and yet people couldn't stop chirping about how beautiful she was in her youth.

These days, representations of beauty are far more diverse than the white, blond-haired, light-eyed standard that defined your grandmothers' generation.

Facts about my mother's early life impressed you, especially her popularity in high school. Walking up 39th Street to catch the bus for a swim at the Y, you told me you intended to write a graphic novel. In it, the protagonist concocts a foolproof plan for advancing her social status at her new school. You'd just read a wide assortment of graphic novels about kids who fail or succeed at popularity, which inspired the "cool girl" strategy you contrived for your main character:

"First she's going to dye the tips of her hair purple. Then she's going to get lots of ear piercings, maybe even a nose ring, and she's also going to wear really cool clothes . . ."

"You know how to make lots of friends and get popular," I replied, having never been popular even among the unpopular kids. "She should ask people lots of questions about themselves because *everyone* loves to talk about themselves."

"No," you said, quick and matter-of-fact. "That's not how."

"Maybe if she's kind to everyone—"

"Ma, that's not how," you persisted.

"Just have her be herself," I pressed on.

"Definitely not!" you said, wide-eyed, as if I'd said something truly ridiculous or offensive.

A city kid far wiser than me in the ways of playground politics, you've already figured out that femininity is a performance, a show, to attract as many eyes as possible; it's surface over substance, like an Andy Warhol print.

You sometimes seem to feel the gaze of others on you even in the privacy of your own home—like the prisoners subject to constant, invisible surveillance in the panopticon Foucault describes in *Discipline and Punish:* Often, the very first thing you do after setting down your book bag is take a quick glance in the mirrored credenza in our living room to assure yourself of . . . of *what*? That your hair looks good? That your face isn't besmirched by food? That your clothes still look nice? Even in a space free from the eyes of others, you want to look presentable. The internalized gaze is always there, whether or not anyone's watching.

I, too, have felt the ever-present sense that I'm being observed and picked apart by legions of eyes. Frequently, in my early youth, they'd follow me, in my mind, with such contempt I felt paralyzed, as if I were an actor on stage in front of a crowd so tough and cruel, I'd forget my lines and ability to move. It happens less now, at my older, less egoic stage of life, but when I was in my twenties and thirties, walking down the streets of NYC, peopled with impossibly beautiful women in ensembles straight out of *Vogue* and leering (or sneering) men, I'd feel so self-conscious, I'd forget how to walk; I'd overthink the movements of my own body and just freeze. In my paralysis, I'd pretend I needed to find something in my bag or needed to stop and text someone. Or I'd call someone. Somehow talking to another person made me feel validated in the eyes of others and would help me unfreeze and carry on with where I needed to go. I thought I was alone in this experience until I read psychologist Renee Engeln's insightful book *Beauty Sick,* which breaks down the harmful effects of our culture's outsized attention on the appearance of girls and women. As a young therapist, Engeln, now a psychology professor at Northwestern University and director of the school's Body and Media Lab, had a patient who expressed a debilitating anxiety about walking across campus to attend her therapy sessions because she felt her peers were "looking at her." When Engeln discussed it with a male colleague, he tossed it up to paranoia, but Engeln's research complicated that pat assessment: "There are many women who suffer as a result of feeling chronically gazed at. You can't just brush off that feeling; it matters. It's the core of beauty sickness," she writes, defining it as a condition in which "women's emotional energy gets so bound up with what they see in the mirror that it becomes harder for them to see other aspects of their lives," so much so that they may feel they're being studied—judged, measured, dissected—under a giant microscope at all times. And aren't we?

Chapter 4

"Lez Alert!"

I was assessing my face against my mother's from my earliest memories, or rather the world around me was, and it was consistently communicating—in a quizzical glance or a compliment withheld or a hostile blank face—that I was falling short, way short. In fact, I remember the exact moment my ugly sense of self went from a hazy half thought to a bright hue of certainty.

On a sunny day in 1986 on Cord Street in Downey, California, where I grew up amid a caricature of '80s paraphernalia and cultural touchstones—Cabbage Patch Kids, Garbage Pail Kids, Little League, crappy fast food (McDonald's, Burger King, Swanson TV dinners), CCD (bible study), talk shows (Jerry Springer, Oprah, and Donahue), sitcoms (*Family Ties, The Facts of Life, Growing Pains*), and regular trips to Blockbuster for movies we watched on repeat (John Hughes films, *The Karate Kid, The Goonies,* too many to name)—I was lost in a reverie of fun. Ten years old, standing in the middle of the street in a swirl of chlorine-soaked kids running through the sprinklers on my parents' front lawn after a dip in our pool, I was showing my first-series Garbage Pail Kids trading cards to Jimmy when a gray minivan disrupted the dreamy flow of fun, taking full residence in the middle of the road. The window on the driver's side rolled down so the mother of a kid we were playing with could talk to Jimmy's mom, Sharon, the sweet den mother to us all. The woman, with a messy bun and wisps of hair framing her narrow face, looked straight at me and contemptuously said: "*That's* Chrysí's daughter?" Her mouth jutted open longwise, like an exclamation point.

It landed as she intended it to—with blunt force. Standing next to my thirteen-year-old brother, Andreas, who *did* inherit our mother's good looks, only seemed to amplify my ugliness. Tall and blond with a chiseled face and green eyes, he gained the affections of nearly all my childhood girlfriends—and even had a secret affair with my best friend in high school.

But it wasn't just my face that made me unattractive to her—it was also the legibility of my queerness.

Girls like me who clung to their prepubescent gender ambiguity, even as our bodies morphed into young women, lost their "tomboy" appeal as soon as their breasts formed. You couldn't inhabit a woman's figure and dress in the same thoughtless array of printed T-shirts and surf shorts, showcasing your scabby knees from bike and skateboard spills, with mounds of flesh taking shape under your shirt—and *not* receive looks of suspicion and disdain from the conservative churchgoing denizens of Downey: the people who voted for Reagan, who watched talk shows to feel morally superior, who believed that HIV was a judgment on homosexuality from God, as did I when I was a child trying to stop the drip, drip, drip of my homosexual urges, a leaky faucet I couldn't wrench shut.

Doubling my confusion and inner unrest was the feeling that my internal and external genders were misaligned—just like

Enrique, your classmate, whom you ardently defend against anyone who misgenders her, even though you sometimes mix up her pronouns yourself. "The boys at school keep calling Enrique 'he,' especially one boy, who won't call *him,*" you slipped, " 'she' even when the teacher said he has to." (I suggested that some might *accidentally* misgender her, telling you about two incidents at work when I did the same, inflicting harm where I didn't intend to, but you believed it was done with intentional meanness.)

Your classmate's refusal to accept Enrique extended from his same refusal to accept our family. Your school's principal called Sabrina and me one morning, concerned about an incident that took place in your first-grade classroom that even now you pretend didn't happen:

"What's something that makes you feel special?" a substitute teacher asked each kid in class.

"I have two moms," you offered proudly, not realizing how that might land in a school largely composed of religious and socially conservative families.

"You can't have two moms. You have to have a dad," your classmate said over and over again, refusing to concede the point.

The principal said the substitute pulled you outside the classroom right after the incident, so you must have been upset. She let you know that all families are welcome at the school, but that was only theoretically true; you were a minority, awash in cultural and religious condemnation meant for us—your queer parents—not you. A social worker from the school called to affirm our welcome at the school. "The student who made the comment said that your family goes against his religious beliefs," she said apologetically, "but we let him know that there is no legitimate basis for discrimination and bigotry in our school"—an ethos that may begin to radically shift with arguments handed down from Trump's Supreme Court allowing people to appeal to religious justifications for their prejudices toward LGBTQ people.

When I picked you up that day, you charged at me with your usual puppylike affections and didn't mention it, so neither did I. When I tried to tease it out of you in play, and when your beloved teacher, who also grew up with two moms, tried to address it with you, you kept it locked up. Did it embarrass you? Were you trying to protect our feelings? Was it a nonissue, or did such things happen so frequently that it failed to register as anything out of the ordinary? Either way, Sabrina and I started thinking about transferring you to a different—more queer literate—school near Park Slope, which was once known as "Dyke Slope" because so many lesbians lived there at one time.

—

Unlike Enrique, who is growing up in a world with greater gender fluidity, trans literacy, and acceptance, I didn't have the language to make sense of my inner conflict and confusion. I still don't, really. I just know that I didn't feel like a girl in my early youth. I felt like a boy in female flesh. Womanhood came to me later. Maybe I was compelled into gender submission as I grew up, maybe my sense of self shifted, or maybe my desire to be a boy extended from my reluctant lesbianism or the fact that my brother received the larger share of love and affection in the world, but looking in the mirror at that time was a jarring and withering experience. My exterior gender and interior one were out of alignment, and every attempt to sync them—with corresponding clothes, a rich fantasy life, and standing up over the toilet bowl to pee, messily—ultimately failed.

—

Were I seen as the boy I was in my mind, I might have been perceived as cute in an off-centered sort of way—the way that all boys, just by virtue of being boys, are—with their mismatched dirty clothes, bad haircuts, and smears of pizza grease lining the sides of their goofy smiles. Being the kind of girl I was, even "cute" was unattainable, especially in contrast to my mother.

My face juxtaposed beside *Yia Yia*'s elicited cruel double takes so frequently in my childhood that I dreaded being introduced as her daughter; I could always hear the silent disbelief. "How could *that* woman have made *that* child?"

The many iterations of ugly in which I was cloaked—my genetic constitution, my burgeoning sexuality, my more masculine affect—were visible to the mom in the minivan. She didn't just see a face cut up, unpretty—she saw disordered sexuality and gender, the specter of moral depravity and social dissolution.

As it's often been fabricated in various Western historical contexts, one could say that I was the definition of ugly.

According to research collected by Gretchen E. Henderson in a book called *Ugliness: A Cultural History,* while the "classification of 'ugly' proves unruly," continually shifting and morphing over time in various historical settings, the common thread running through the ages is that those deemed ugly conjure unease and angst, even terror, in the eyes of their beholder. Tracing the etymology of the word, she notes that *ugly*'s Middle English roots meant that which was "'frightful' or 'repulsive'" and derived from the Old Norse word *uggligr,* meaning "'to be feared or dreaded.'" By the eighteenth century, it more commonly connoted deformity and moral depravity. (Does this etymological history help explain why genderqueer lesbians—morally "crooked" girls—aren't legible as attractive?) Through the Enlightenment era, when "practices of investigation, classification and display" proliferated, Henderson writes, "bodies who refused to fit categories seemed to demand attention."

I was a body like that. I existed, on multiple fronts, as "matter out of place," a phrase Henderson takes from social anthropologist Mary Douglas's 1966 book *Purity and Danger.* Douglas was referring to the cultural relativism that determines that which we see as dirty or impure, as a violation of "a set order of relations." On my body one could see the collapsing social structure, binaries colliding and shattering, a mess, confusion. I was a girl who was a boy who desired girls. Like Julia Pastrana, the Mexican-born singer and performer in the nineteenth century who traveled across America and Europe in exhibitions that billed her as "The Ugliest Woman in the World," my ugliness sat in the middle of the organizing dichotomies on which society rests—normal and pathological, male and female, feminine and masculine, homosexuality and heterosexuality—threatening its collapse.

Even my elementary school peers perceived my incongruities: "Lez alert! Lez alert!" my friend Sharon yelled as she and our fifth-grade crew ran crazily in all directions away from me on the playground at recess one day. I'm not sure who originated the game, but it was a form of tag in which the tagger (aka the Lez) could pass her lesbianism on to another girl with one touch until that girl could pass it on to another.

Being called a lesbian was a uniquely harsh insult.

Culturally, the word is synonymous with ugly, not just for the ways lesbians defy traditional gender roles in the popular imagination but for their disinclination toward and unavailability to men. By patriarchal design, there is nothing less desirable and less attractive than a woman who refuses to be the vessel of men's pleasure, literally and metaphorically—lesbianism is the ultimate rejection of the role prescribed to us as women. I believe, controversially perhaps, it's part of the reason some women opt for the word *queer* as opposed to the word *lesbian,* even if they are exclusively attracted to women. By foreclosing our accessibility to men, we lose social and cultural currency. *Queer* keeps that possibility—and our desirability—intact.

To tease out the knotted history that melds lesbianism with ugliness, consider the discourses around the earliest iterations of feminism in the nineteenth century. Back then, women who loved women could (kind of) fly under the radar in what was once termed, in the eastern United States, "Boston Marriages," in which middle- and upper-class, college-educated, largely white women from prestigious all-girls schools like Vassar and Mount Holyoke cohabitated in long-term unions. Renowned lesbian historian Lillian Faderman suggests that the reason some formed such unions was because they couldn't find men secure enough to couple with educated women, women with minds—and rooms—of their own. Others, after experiencing the joys of being in intellectual communion and on equal footing with like-minded women, decided they could do without the opposite sex. When considering the mind-numbing drudgery of maintaining a home back then (without modern conveniences like washing machines and dishwashers and electricity), raising children, and catering to the wants and needs of a husband, it's understandable why some felt "same-sex relationships were far more preferable and even practical for many women than any form of heterosexuality would have been." As one woman demurred to an interested suitor in a 1897 novel called *Diana Victrix:*

> I am not domestic the way some women are. I shouldn't like to keep house and sew . . . It would bore me. I should hate it! Sylvia and I share the responsibility here, and the maid works faithfully. There are only a few rooms. We have time for our real work but a wife wouldn't have. . . . Please go away! I have chosen my life and I love it!

By the end of the century, middle-class women with same-sex desires could more securely reject marital unions because they had access to higher education and could pursue careers that earned them their own money.

But "educated spinsters" weren't immune to social disapprobation and stigma. Some conservative thinkers thought them "manly" or "masculine" or "unfit for . . . traditional roles," and believed their existence would lead to the collapse of society because the highest-quality women among them—which meant affluent women of Anglo-Saxon descent—would eschew marriage after college and "the lower orders of society" would breed deficient offspring who would destroy America. (This is the age of eugenics, after all.)

I told you about this early history to underscore why a newly out lesbian in the queer teen television drama *Heartstopper,* Tara, was told she was "too pretty to be a lesbian," which struck you as odd because you've been exposed to a diverse range of lesbian representations in your pop cultural—and actual—life.

As we sat in the living room waiting for Sabrina to join us to watch *Enola Holmes,* a character I love for her independence, bravery, and cleverness, I explained that women, especially straight women, don't want to be seen as ugly or manly because they desire men—and want to be desired in return. Male supremacy's maneuver was to sabotage the efforts of these early feminists by casting such women as unpleasant and unappealing. It was an extremely effective strategy—still employed today. Women, not wanting to seem loathsome to potential suitors, absorb the message that to be a feminist is to be ugly, compelling them to reject rallying for their own rights, which ensures their continued subordination.

Back then, women couldn't vote, own property, or keep their own wages from work. They *themselves* were seen as the *property* of their husbands. Already boy crazy with a long string of crushes, you avowed that you would never have married a woman back then but would have found a way to even the playing field with your future husband, even if it required John Waters–esque theatrics of distaste and perversity. The plan you concocted sounded benign enough at first—you'd work without him knowing and secretly save mountains of cash—but it quickly devolved into committable offenses, which included killing a string of handsome husbands over and over to keep amassing more wealth. You didn't understand, of course, that your new husbands would be the recipients of your deceased husbands' fortunes, not you. But you were having too much fun, cackling like a wicked witch, so we let you believe you'd discovered a winning scheme. And there *was* a knowing underlying your murderous plot—that the only real escape from the injustices endured by women back then was a radical takedown or savvy manipulation of the social structure upholding the patriarchy, which the gathering at the Seneca Falls Convention of 1848 attempted to do.

But some men, of course, found the convention vexing—and threatening—to witness three hundred attendees advocate for a woman's right to be "as free as man is free," as one of the assembly's organizers and Susan B. Anthony's longtime friend, Elizabeth Cady Stanton, put it. We'd once visited Anthony's house in the Berkshires with cousins Roberta and Peter when you were eight. There we learned that after meeting at an antislavery gathering, Anthony and Stanton became close confidantes who, together, fought for our right to vote and even founded a radical newspaper called *The Revolution.* I asked you afterward what societal issue you and your best girlfriends would want to tackle. Without pause, you said "climate change," after having just had a nightmare about an environmental catastrophe that put the inequalities between the sexes, then and now, into perspective, because without a planet viable for human life, social issues don't matter a whole lot.

In your dream, a massive tidal wave gathered up all the water in the Brooklyn Harbor at the base of Industry City in Sunset Park and was coming for you and Sabrina as you ran. You found a police officer—"he was part bear," you said—and he allowed you and Mom to hide in an underground jail, where he and Sabrina coupled and had six bear babies, all of whom you hated. You said

I was teaching a class and that you missed me. It was hard not to interpret your longing for—and ambivalence toward—a more conventional family in this horrifying vision. Ominously, you said that if the ocean ever comes for us, you'd end your life before allowing yourself to be submerged in water, or you'd board a jet plane and live above the clouds and bad weather forever. (Your midnight fears were a sobering reminder that the existential crises of your generation might one day render the rights won by first-wave feminists—and the concerns of this letter—terrifyingly irrelevant.)

Nonetheless, early feminists like Anthony and Stanton wanted to establish a female bill of rights, inspiring ridicule and wrath. Naomi Wolf, author of the widely influential *The Beauty Myth,* highlights some of the uglier thoughts critics expressed about those first-wave feminists who gathered at the iconic symposium. One called them "'unsexed women,'" "'too repulsive to find a husband,'" and "'entirely devoid of personal attractions.'" The same detractor, quoting an antifeminist contemporary, described the congregates as a "'hybrid species, half man and half woman, belonging to neither sex.'" In response to a senator's positive assessment of the attendees as being "'beautiful, intelligent and accomplished,'" another retorted that they were "'not beautiful or accomplished,'" that they were "'*passé*'" with "'hook-billed noses'" and "'crow's feet under their sunken eyes.'" Speaking of feminists in general, a male doctor at the time argued that you could spot "'degenerate women'" by their "'low voices, hirsute bodies, and small breasts.'" In these denigrating comments, you can start to see the ways in which feminism eventually gets conflated with lesbianism (or inversion), as Lillian Faderman demonstrated in her groundbreaking history *Surpassing the Love of Men*—and both are synonymous with ugly.

Although there was a brief moment in the Roaring Twenties

when experimenting with lesbianism or bisexuality was a subversive kind of "chic" (in certain privileged milieus), it wasn't until World War II, when men left home and women entered the workforce en masse, that a full-fledged community of queer women began to emerge.

An iconic image from the time depicts a robust and determined woman in blue denim with a red-and-white polka dot headscarf flexing a bicep over a tagline that read WE CAN DO IT! She would come to symbolize the broader mobilization of women—wives, mothers, daughters—who took on industrial jobs vacated by men fighting in Europe and the Pacific. For many, it was a self-esteem-enhancing enterprise because, for the very first time, they got to make their own money, use their minds outside domesticity, and rub shoulders with an eclectic mix of women they'd ordinarily never have met. You learned about this iconic image after reading a book entitled *Rosie Revere, Engineer,* a story about a little girl who hides her inventions underneath her bed and keeps her ideas to herself in fear of embarrassment, ridicule, and failure. When she's given encouragement from her great-great-aunt Rose—who helped build the planes she never got a chance to fly—she ultimately learns the success in store for those who dare to actualize their dreams, for those who speak up, for those willing to fail. You're long past picture books, but we still remind you of the lessons the story imparted when we notice the mouselike cadence of your voice while presenting projects at school events or hear that you've been scaling back participation in class even though your teacher said you've got such interesting things to say. She wants to hear from you more often—and more loudly. Only by getting practiced in being uncomfortable and trying new things can you find your confidence and strength—and *yourself.* It's kind of like when we've given you new freedoms, like going to the corner store on your own or walking to get an ice cream by yourself in the park. You felt a little uneasy at first but slowly built the self-trust you need to manage yourself and the world on your own.

That's what happened when men headed for the frontlines. Free and independent of men, women discovered themselves anew—new aptitudes, new ambitions, and in some cases, new desires, including homosexual ones, along with a fledgling lesbian community ready to embrace them.

Faderman calls the sexologists (i.e., Havelock Ellis, Richard von Krafft-Ebing, etc.) the "midwives" of lesbian subculture because they gave us a self-concept (before *lesbian* was in popular parlance), the "female sexual invert" to build a community around. But the phrase *female invert* implies abnormality and recalls the masculinizing language used by antifeminists in the nineteenth century. To call us inverted is to identify us as women turned "inside out or upside down"; thus, we were seen by sexologists from Karl Westphal to Sigmund Freud as psychological males, which helped conflate sexuality and gender for generations to come, a flawed assumption that the influential work of scholars like Gayle Rubin and Judith Butler has helped dismantle.

Without any other social templates to draw from other than heterosexuality and traditional expressions of femininity and masculinity, many lesbians absorbed the sexological message that they were "men trapped in women's bodies"—some, indeed, might be considered transgender today—and articulated their lesbianism in rigid butch-femme relationships. Although sex researchers like Karl Heinrich Ulrichs and Havelock Ellis believed homosexuality was congenital and argued that it shouldn't be seen as a moral failing punishable by law, in the age of eugenics that was cold comfort: While a biological basis for our "condition" may have generated societal sympathies in some quarters, it also encouraged others to see homosexuals as freakish malformations.

The notion that homosexuality was a psychological, rather than a biological, manifestation was no shelter from the haters, either. The widespread misinterpretation and misapplication of Freud's theory—that we are all born with a freewheeling sex drive that gets tethered to a specific object-choice through our psychosexual development—amplified society's already condemning attitudes toward lesbians and gays. Although Freud's theory made heterosexuality as psychologically contingent as homosexuality, the dominant culture—and Freud himself—took the view that homosexuality was a deviation from normal heterosexual development and thus saw lesbianism as "sick," "'antisocial,'" "a symptom of illness," a "character disorder," and "'borderline or outright psychotic.'"

And it got worse after the war, in the conformist '50s. When men came home from combat, women were expected to return to unpaid domestic labor and forsake their wage-earning jobs and independence. A pervasive desire for normalcy returned—"a time when authority became king and nonconformity became close to criminality," Faderman writes—and with that an impulse to mark, stigmatize, and punish transgressors.

Joseph McCarthy, the disgraced Wisconsin senator who led high-profile anti-communist hearings, exemplified the era's intolerance for dissent and nonconformity. Along with his aide, Roy Cohn, who was rumored to be gay, McCarthy helped fuel the persecution of gay men and lesbians in the government in what became known as the Lavender Scare.

In a shaky bit of logic, the government linked communism with homosexuality, believing that because homosexuals "'lack emotional stability'" and "'moral fiber'" gay civil servants were as threatening to national security as communists.

As Glenn Close narrated in the documentary *The Lavender Scare:* "The United States was gripped in the panic of the Cold War. There were fears that Soviet spies had infiltrated the government and that gay men and lesbians could be blackmailed into betraying national secrets." A report put out by the State Department in 1950 argued that even one "sex pervert" could damage the collective body of the agency because the homosexual "tends to have a corrosive influence upon his fellow employees. These perverts will frequently attempt to entice normal individuals to engage in perverted practices. This is particularly true in the case of young and impressionable people who might come under the influence of a pervert. . . . One homosexual can pollute a government office."

By 1953, President Eisenhower had issued an executive order to identify and remove suspected or known homosexuals from government posts. One victim, Frank Kameny, who'd been arrested by two plainclothes police officers at a cruising site in San Francisco in 1956, would lose his job in the Army Map Service in 1957. Although Kameny held a PhD in astronomy from Harvard University, he once told Eric Marcus, the author of *Making Gay History*, about his life after being terminated from the government: "I had no source of income. And the next two or three years were extremely difficult. In fact, by the time I got into 1959, I was living for about eight months on twenty cents worth of food a day, which even by 1959 prices was not terribly much. It was a great day when I could afford five cents more and put a pat of butter on my mashed potato." His bold appeals to the government, including a lawsuit filed with the Supreme Court that the justices refused to hear, ultimately failed. It's estimated that between five thousand and tens of thousands of gay people, mostly men, lost their government posts—some died by suicide, others remained unemployable, and many were ruined financially.

Lesbians were vulnerable, too—especially those working in public sector roles as military personnel, social workers, and schoolteachers, three of the few professional posts widely available to women at the time. Madeleine Tress, a Brooklyn-born lesbian who earned a degree from Georgetown University, was working as an economist at the U.S. Department of Commerce when two federal agents called her into an office to question her, crudely, about her sexuality. "They say they have evidence that I'm a lesbian. And then they say, 'How do you like having sex with women? You never had it so good until you get it from a man.' It was the most demeaning thing," she said. Her informant described her as "not at all feminine. Looks and acts very mannish. Uses very little lipstick. Wears severely tailored suits," indicating that those who violate gender norms were prime targets for persecution, which might explain why the first LGBTQ organization, the Mattachine Society, compelled members to try and assimilate into mainstream society via a strict dress code. The group, according to one attendee, demanded "presentability":

> 'To be invited to Mattachine . . . you had to be wearing a Brooks Brothers three-piece suit. Those who were unusual dressers or had unusual hairstyles were not invited. If you made the mistake of bringing someone who was too flamboyant, you could be asked to leave.'

People who displayed their sexuality and gender nonconformity "loudly and proudly" were unwelcome. Men had to wear suits and ties, and Kameny, who co-founded the Mattachine Society of Washington, D.C., encouraged men to sport a clean-shaven look (no beards), women to wear dresses, and both to wear nice shoes.

Reflecting on this bit of LGBTQ history and the masculinized feminists from the nineteenth century, the urgent and insistent desire to demarcate one's manufactured femininity no matter the cost to oneself makes sense. The fallout and punishment for not doing so can be detrimental, even dangerous, especially in the case of gender-defying lesbians and gay men. I told you about the dress code of Mattachine and the police raids on queer bars, where, according to urban legend, women had to have at least three articles of feminine clothing on or risk arrest. You didn't think that was a big ask until I proposed forcing you to wear a suit and tie to school every day—"As long as I can wear accessories," you joked. Together, we considered how Val and Ruben's mom, Eli, a handsome soft butch, might feel being forced into girly attire, but you teasingly replied that she could easily find feminine clothes in the closet of her beautiful wife, Liz, whom you love. (Once, after a weekend getaway with the family during which Liz painted your nails better than a professional manicurist could, you confessed that you wished Sabrina and I enjoyed such girlish rituals.) You deliberated over the questions I put to you a little longer and decided that if wearing gender-appropriate clothing protected LGBTQ people from social disapprobation or harassment, then it was a small price to pay. I wanted to explain that for me—and, I imagine, Eli—to be compelled into frilly outfits would feel like a self-transgression, but you'd hit on a larger truth that I couldn't argue with: that all of us learn early on, men and boys, too, but especially women and girls, that we must subvert our inner truths for the comfort and ease of social acceptance, like when you echoed your friend's aversion to avocados while you love them, or when Sabrina pretended she was more Jewish than she is, faking her way through Hebrew songs at sleepaway camp, or when I made an amped theater of my ardent "heterosexuality" so no one would find out I was a lesbian.

The problem with constantly reaching for the utility of normality and the protective shield it provides is that eventually you start to forget or lose who you actually are—or could be.

While the original Mattachine Society, conceived and spearheaded by Harry Hay, espoused a more radical and liberationist politic, as the '50s progressed, it adopted a more assimilationist one. A desire to seamlessly blend in, to go unnoticed, makes tactical sense, considering, as you pointed out, that so many of those who were visibly queer were targeted and ruined by the government. But bolder acts of resistance began to subvert the status quo and stifle the urge toward homogeneity. The propulsion toward social change was gaining momentum: *Brown v. Board of Education* ruled that segregation was unconstitutional in 1954. In 1955, Rosa Parks helped ignite the Civil Rights Movement by refusing to surrender her bus seat to a white man in Montgomery, Alabama. That same year, local activists launched the Montgomery Bus Boycott, which lasted 381 days and cost both the bus system and the city nearly one million dollars combined in lost fares. Together we read about these painful—and inspiring—historical events in a book called *What Is the Civil Rights Movement?* by Sherri L. Smith, a slim and accessible history written for tweens. You enthusiastically pulled it off the shelf at a local bookstore, feeling a pull toward and commonality with marginalized people. Hearing your gentle kid voice narrating the atrocities and injustices inflicted on African Americans, along with their collective efforts to right the wrongs they suffered, created a perverse—but deeply affecting—juxtaposition.

> A Black group called the Montgomery Improvement Association bought station wagons to use as taxicabs to help boycotters travel to their jobs. Women raised money to pay for the cars, gas, and insurance by selling food. The bus company was losing money daily. Without buses to bring Black customers downtown, white-owned stores began to lose business.

Montgomery bus activist Aurelia Browder, who once said, "If you live and you haven't stood for anything, you didn't live for anything, either," filed a successful lawsuit against the mayor of Montgomery with three other plaintiffs. "On December 20,

1956, the US Supreme Court declared Montgomery's segregation laws unconstitutional," you read with a voice full of triumph. "Browder had won!"

We marveled at how much people can accomplish when they come together for a common cause, as we've seen with protests across the United States since Trump's second term. In defiant opposition to the cruel, unlawful, and unjust executive orders he's signed targeting trans people, immigrants, and people of color, millions of individuals have turned their anger and pain into collective action. In reaching for histories of marginalized people, I felt you were seeking something in their stories—healing, strength, inspiration, identity. You wanted to forge a connection between the African American experience and that of your Latinx, Indigenous, and Jewish ancestors. "Did you know there were 'No Jews' and 'No Hispanics' signs in America, just like there were 'No Negroes' signs? My teacher told us that," you said. It was too hard to explain the differences in the history and forms of discrimination endured by these different groups of people, but the basic truth, which is perhaps the more fundamental one, was that people were being excluded and treated unfairly—hideously so—and maybe you felt that way, too, navigating the world as the child of two moms amid Trump's hateful rhetoric and policies toward marginalized communities and in settings where the queerness of our family is sometimes unwelcome. Even in a progressive bubble like Brooklyn, you've felt the pinch of not fitting in.

Taking cues from the burgeoning Civil Rights Movement, especially the now-famous antisegregation sit-ins organized by four Black college students at the F. W. Woolworth lunch counter in Greensboro, North Carolina, in 1960, some LGBTQ activists wanted to take a more affirming and aggressive approach to queer politics, including Kameny, who told Eric Marcus's *Making Gay History* podcast that he and his fellow LGBTQ activists were done with the message that "we were sick. We were sinners. We were perverts," calling the more "unassertive, apologetic, defensive" organizing "drivel." By the 1960s, the formative days of many of our modern leftist movements were well underway: the Civil Rights Movement, including its more radical contingent, the Black Panther Party; the Women's Rights Movement with its "lesbian separatists" and "Radicalesbians"; as well as the post-Stonewall militant group the Gay Liberation Front.

On June 28, 1969, in New York City's Greenwich Village, cops arrived at one of the most popular gay clubs in the city, the Stonewall Inn. Under the pretext of investigating illegal alcohol sales—as a club, members could bring their own alcoholic beverages, but the owners could not sell alcohol—officers stormed in taunting, harassing, and intimidating the establishment's clientele, largely comprised of working-class gay men and trans people of color. Because homosexual acts were criminal offenses—and would remain so in New York City until 1980—getting questioned and identified by the cops was serious business. Officers could arrest people for homosexual solicitation and wearing gender-inappropriate clothes (i.e., men in drag and women in butch attire) and would threaten to "out" patrons to their families and employers. Although there had been uprisings at other queer establishments throughout American cities—Pepper Hill Club Raid in Baltimore, Maryland, in 1955, where 162 were arrested; Hazel's (Hazel's Inn) in Sharp Park, California, in 1956; and Black Nite Brawl in Milwaukee, Wisconsin, in 1961, to name a few—the Stonewall Rebellion's timing was central to its impact and success. It was "an idea whose time had come," Faderman writes, noting that it could not have transpired and galvanized the modern-day LGBTQ Movement without the traction gained by other militant factions like the Black Panther Party, founded in 1966; the Students for a Democratic Society, established in 1959; and the Youth International Party (aka Yippies), started in

1967. Fronted by heroic trans African Americans like Marsha P. Johnson and Miss Major Griffin-Gracy and Latinx New Yorkers like Sylvia Rivera and Raymond Castro, Faderman writes that the success of the uprising—the "shot heard around the world"—could not have happened twenty or even ten years earlier:

> Although violent protest had been unimaginable to the largely conservative middle-class men and women who made up the homosexual movement during the two preceding decades, a handful of activists, made militant by the general militance of the '60s, had the foresight and imagination immediately to seize upon the riots, which had been started by more flamboyant and working-class homosexuals, and present them as an event that heralded a new gay militant movement of justified fury. They understood the importance of drawing parallels between the sufferings of other minorities and those of homosexuals.

I shared the CliffsNotes on LGBT history with you and even checked out a children's graphic novel about the Stonewall Riots when you were in third grade. The trajectory of the movement provided a rich and inspiring set of lessons for a girl, any girl, trying to mold herself into what society expects (early Mattachine) and then deciding to break free from societal imperatives, choosing instead to celebrate the ways she stands out, even at the risk of social censure and stigma (Gay Liberation Front). Things really got going for all these social movements when people decided they'd risk it all to be themselves, to stop toeing the line to fit in. As soon as they decided to step out, fists up, and demand their right to be exactly as they were, things really started to change for the better, and in the process, they created new ways of existing in the world—new ideas, values, and points of view. Creativity is born against, not in conformity with, the norm. I reminded you of all the ways you, too, have helped challenge norms and expectations in our little corner of the world: calling out a friend's racism, sporting an outfit that made you look like a goth girl, going high fashion among classmates who dressed down, dancing off script in pre-K, and boldly declaring, at braver junctures in your history, your queer family—two moms, donor siblings—no matter how icy the reception. I wanted you to know that each time you honor yourself in these ways—the parts that fall outside the lines of expectation—you're helping expand the ways for all of us to freely exist in the world, which is, in a way, what the second-wave feminists sought to do as they grew more aggressive and norm-defying in their politics, taking particular aim at traditional beauty standards.

In an historical rendering that's partly—maybe even largely—mythological, they burned their bras, let the hair on their legs and underarms grow wild, slipped into blue denim bell-bottoms and T-shirts rather than frilly dresses and constricting skirts, kicked off high heels for sneakers, and defiantly refrained from wearing makeup. They wanted to free themselves of the "vestiges of the 'female slave mentality,'" opting for a natural form of beauty rather than a manufactured one—a dignified kind of ugly over a self-abnegating kind of pretty. More emphatically, they eschewed any form of "polish," preferring, as they did at the first National Women's Music Festival in Illinois in 1974, singers who reflected their own "declassed, unslick image on the stage. Making a mistake, being 'human,'" Faderman writes, "was better than being perfect." A scrappy, smudged aesthetic showed one's allegiance to egalitarianism and rejection of hierarchy: A professional appearance "represented artificial and destructive categories, barriers set up by the patriarchy that limited the possibilities of women 'creating a vision together.'"

Second wavers who identified as "lesbian-feminists" are the class of feminists responsible for solidifying the link between feminism and lesbian that's still with us today—and makes some loathe to label themselves feminists. They argued that "the lesbian was the same as any woman and that any women could 'existentially' convert from heterosexuality to homosexuality in the name of women's liberation." Some, in fact, used the qualifier "political lesbian" to indicate feminist choice, not sexual orientation. To some, Faderman points out, " 'lesbian' has always been a kind of code word for female resistance." Although they may or may not have been genuinely attracted to women, they nonetheless sought to create with other women their own utopian communities, even aspiring toward establishing a Lesbian Nation. Radically separate from and anathema to heterosexuality and patriarchy, they would produce their own culture (music, books, zines, folk art), values (nonmonogamy, spirituality, pro-woman, pro-child, "nonracist, nonageist, nonclassist, and nonexploitative"), and institutions (women's health clinics, financial institutions, childcare facilities, food and living cooperatives). They wished to "return society to the maternal principle in which life is nurtured" as opposed to being destroyed by the patriarchy's insatiable thirst for power, sexual and economic exploitation, and war.

But those ideals looked like a form of hysteria—pragmatically impossible and naive—by the time the conformist 1980s rolled around. During the Decade of Greed, against the backdrop of Reagan's neoliberal economic policies and loud appeals to traditional family values, more lesbians—and women in general—had obtained college degrees and entered the workforce, seeking professional ascendence and monogamous coupledom during a "minor baby boom," marked by the rise of sperm banks. A drive toward domestication and "clean and sober" living replaced the wilder and loftier ambitions of the movement's previous two decades—and *feminism* became a dirty word. As one scholar put it: "In the 1980s, feminism was out of fashion with most young women. Like flappers in the 1920s, these women looked on feminists of the previous decade as old hat, stodgy, and unpleasantly angry." By then, feminism was firmly linked with "man-hating dykes" and the more rigid butch-femme dyad.

I heard and felt the daggers of all this disparaging history when the word *lesbian* was first ascribed to me on the playground in 1986. After the bell rang and we began shuffling back to class, I overheard Sharon, with her cool-girl shrug and effortless good looks, say, "Stephanie probably *is* a lesbian," to which someone replied, "Yeah, totally."

To shake *lesbian* off me—and the ugliness it conjured—I started feigning interest in boys I liked only as friends to hide what was already apparent to many.

At age eight, you are having the exact opposite experience I had growing up, in which people frequently point out how beautiful you are—your skin, your face, your style—and although we are on opposite sides, we exist on the same coin. Whether you're given or denied the compliment, it's the same thing: Our value rises and falls with our ability to deliver on the imperative to be cute, which trivializes our existence and pits us against ourselves—and each other. The compliment is also the insult.

A woman nurtured and regrown in every wave of feminism might reject this harmful value system, but it will continue to stalk her consciousness and undermine her self-worth.

That's why you frequently assess your reflection, trying to spot the flaws, trying to fix them, admiring where you succeed. The psychological violence done to you in those moments is the same violence that's compelled me to pretend I am straight, to avoid mirrors, to hide my disfigured feet, to opt out of photos.

—

"Mama, let's take selfies," you said one Saturday morning. We were preparing to go to Industry City to meet your friend Maximus.

"I hate being photographed," I said. Immediately I wanted to suck those words right back into my mouth.

"Why?" you asked. You were genuinely confused, not only because you are a child of the Selfie Generation but because you delight in seeing photographs of yourself—of memories we've made, of stories you like to hear over and over again about your younger years.

"I just don't like how my hair looks today," I said dumbly, reinforcing all the values Sabrina and I are trying to overthrow.

"I can fix your hair," you offered. But then you changed your mind and collapsed on my feet to tickle them.

I shrieked and pushed you away a little too hard. You fell off the bed but came back for me as I ran through the house, screeching, trying to escape your clutches. "Okay, now, enough of that," I huffed and puffed from the bathroom, where I'd locked myself in. I started to feel upset—not with you but with the condition of my feet and the shame I feel for them, still, at forty-nine.

As a kid, my family always joked about the tragic condition of my feet with toes that look like alien fingers amid a giant bun pushing my big toe sideways. "You didn't get those from me!" my mom would joke. Even my paternal grandfather, an elegant Argentine who drank wine with every meal and loved opera and classical music, would tower over me from his height of six feet at a swimming pool in Palm Desert, where he and my grandmother Fébé had a time-share, and say, "You could be a great swimmer with those, Estefanía!"

The idea of you seeing them in close proximity, or worse, handling them—dry, calloused, and malformed—felt too vulnerable, like it would make me less lovable to you. Ugly.

Chapter 5

Daddy

Even my brother's sweet eyes could feel like daggers. One memory stands out with particular poignancy: I'm in our parents' small bathroom, which is painted a depressing baby blue—a hue so weak it feels sorrowful, half alive. The walls, the toilet, the tiles, the sink, the shower—blue, blue, blue. I'm ten. A spray of sunlight comes in through a small window over the toilet. Outside, I hear a swirl of children's voices, the soundtrack of my youth. With my brother biking a few blocks away and my mom "hitting balls" at a local golf course and my dad, a man who never stopped working even when he wasn't working, hunched over a keyboard or a book, I am safe to explore a secret desire.

I open my parents' medicine cabinet and quickly grab my father's shaving cream and slather it all over my face and neck like icing on a cupcake, imitating his hand strokes. Then I turn my Princess Leia toothbrush upside down and proceed to carefully faux shave, casting the thick layers of foamy gel on my brush under the running water as I'd seen my dad do hundreds of times.

"What are you doing?" my brother asks, appearing in the doorway out of nowhere like an apparition.

"Just messing around," I reply dumbly.

"Dude, you're *weird,*" he sneers, disdain spreading across his pretty visage like poison ivy, his eyes showing me to myself in such a way that I can only see ugly.

I struggle to wipe away his contempt—it feels like dirt on my face—as I close the door and swiftly splash off the rest of the cream.

I knew I could never let him—the golden boy who traversed the world with an ease I'd never know—be your donor.

I would have felt left out of the dyad formed between him and Sabrina and the affections you'd inevitably feel for him. It would be to relive my youth on the lesser end of all things—in beauty, likability, and love—and it would be more crushing the second time around for all the ways it might create tension and distance between us and further confuse a very literal—unimaginative—world that was already going to struggle to make sense of our queer family: "Wait, so you're her mom *and* her aunt?"

At the height of Sabrina's and my romance, five years in, when I was still yearning to close all the gaps between us and become one—is that early stage of love a longing to return to the oneness we knew in utero? Before we were jettisoned out of our mother's wombs and into the overwhelmingness of space and time, as Austrian psychoanalyst Otto Rank proposed? Against my better reason, I wanted to forge a biological link with her, to root our love in a new life—your life—one we would love above all others. It felt primal, an impulse outside of logic. And yet, ironically, it was a desire as queer as Lee Edelman's call for the end of futurity (the child) because ultimately it was an utterly hopeless urge—a baby that can never be, a stillborn idea. That's what sobered me up—the realization that you would not, in the end, be *my* child—you would be *his.*

Fortunately, I never had to share my growing ambivalence or misgivings with my brother or talk my way out of our ask: His then girlfriend, now wife, wisely persuaded him against it, highlighting all the potential problems that Sabrina and I were too rash or romantic to initially see. I returned to my former position—one that refused pride of place to biology and the narrow view of family it holds. I had to, because we would not share blood, and I needed to believe that it wouldn't matter. But it did, it does.

A lesbian couple we knew here in New York City found their donor at the Sperm Bank of California (SBC). They'd done extensive research and concluded that it was best to use a donor from across the country—to ensure their kids didn't unwittingly fall in love with local half-siblings—and informed us that SBC was one of the oldest and most ethically run banks in the country. That's how we ended up on their website, scrolling through innumerable intakes that mapped out anonymous men's biographies and genetic histories. For me, it was disheartening, an exercise in eugenics. Even though it wasn't my body that would grow you into a life—for reasons I'll explain—the idea of a stranger's seed merging with Sabrina's egg iced the blood in my veins. Was it jealousy—or just an all-pervasive feeling of *ick* around the idea that the fluids of a man unknown to us would be placed in Sabrina's uterus via intrauterine insemination (IUI)? We considered a known donor, but we couldn't agree on whom to ask. We knew that a friend-donor could, potentially, put us in a more complicated and precarious legal position should he want more rights to you than we'd agreed on beforehand. One thing I intuitively knew then and know for certain now: You can't possibly know how you are going to feel when you hold your baby in your arms, and you'll feel far more than you ever thought possible.

A few years ago, Sabrina and I watched a three-part series on HBO called *Nuclear Family,* directed by Ry Russo-Young, that reaffirmed our decision to use a sperm bank. As a child, Ry, the daughter of two moms, was at the heart of a famous court case that captured national headlines in the 1980s when her known donor—a gay civil rights attorney, no less—sought visitation rights by leveraging the law's built-in prejudice toward same-sex couples. I watched that series in pain for Sandy Russo, the non-bio mom, whose rights were being undermined by the donor's paternity claims. As much as I wanted you to have some semblance of a father in your life, it wasn't worth risking the integrity and stability of our family.

Browsing through pages and pages of online donor profiles, Sabrina, patiently enduring what I could not, whittled it down to twelve possibilities. She printed them out for us to read and discuss on a getaway to Kerhonkson, New York, a picturesque hamlet in Upstate New York's Ulster County, sometime in the fall of 2013.

It was a bright day, windy and crisp—the kind of day that feels like a happy memory, a place you want to keep returning to in your mind. We packed up our brown leather weekender and piled into our tiny Impreza. Cruising north on Interstate 87, I read the first four aloud, feeling nothing for any of them but a subtle contempt. It was similar to the desperate feeling I've experienced dating online after reading far too many uninspiring—or off-putting—profiles. You keep scrolling with a sick compulsion in the faint hope that maybe the next one or the next one or the next one will stir you.

When I landed on your donor's profile, it was like that—we knew immediately that he was the one. It wasn't any factoid about him, nor his picture, which we didn't have at the time, that moved us; it was his beautifully chosen words—compassionate, contemplative, and insightful. I felt his depth in the reflections and stories he shared about his life, which he narrated in a straightforward and simple prose style. His intellectuality and quest for knowledge reminded us of our own very cerebral fathers, your grandfathers, for whom you are named. He felt familiar, like an old friend or a favorite family member you look forward to seeing at Thanksgiving. He graduated from college with a double major in economics and music and wide-ranging intellectual appetites. He descends from Ecuador, loves science, and has a knack for learning languages, which reminds me of you when you pretend that you speak Spanish fluently because you want to so badly. "Because I'm Ecuadorian, Mom, it comes to me easily," you say. Sometimes you feign a Spanish accent for the sheer joy of enunciating in a new, almost musical way. You even make up your *own* languages at times—"What did you say?" I'll ask. "Ma," you reply, "it's okay. It's my own language, and only I can understand it." Like my dad when I was growing up, he subscribes to journals on science and world events and even weighed whether or not to pursue a career in engineering, another similarity he shared with my engineer father. He also thought about becoming an attorney—Sabrina's dad's profession. A voracious reader with a passion for the arts, music, poetry, and philosophy, he admitted to a youthful rebelliousness that has since evolved into a mature thoughtfulness. I catch wisps of you—a faint silhouette—in his phrases, in the gentle strength that comes through his words, in his kindness. I felt the joy and aliveness of him on the page, his sweet essence—like yours—tenderly carving out a life for himself.

It's strange to feel so much for a person you've never met, to hold psychic space for and curiosity about a nameless, faceless man. I try to picture his life now from the bits of biography he composed in his profile. Since we used a sperm bank in Berkeley, California, where I went to college, I imagine he went there, too. It's uncanny, knowing our feet, his and mine, may have walked across the same city, perhaps even the same campus, down into the same stacks, through the same classrooms and around the same neighborhood, separated by a span of only fifteen years.

I've envisioned his life there—sipping coffee and talking animatedly with a friend about a piece of music he's composed or about a great book he read in one of the several cafés lining Shattuck Avenue; or living in a small apartment complex in Poet's Corner, where the streets are named for famous writers—Chaucer, Poe, Byron. Maybe he's a writer, too. Or a lawyer. The canvas can be covered in all sorts of colors and shapes. He's a shape-shifter in my mind—he can be anything, he can be anyone, at any time. I sometimes look for him—or think I catch a glimpse of you—in the faces of strangers. I've created stories about him—maybe you have to—with the thin threads of information I have.

While I was cleaning out my metal filing cabinet one day, you caught a glimpse of your donor's profile on my desk and asked what it was. When I told you, I pointed out his sloppy scrawl (like mine) and that you two share the same birthday month. You asked if you could keep it and greedily stowed it away, like a secret treasure or a map that no one could touch but you. You resumed your search for fun in your toy-filled room and landed on your looming kit. Looming, a popular pastime among your peers, is the practice of stitching together colorful rubber bands to create bracelets, necklaces, and figurines, which I call your "rubber sculptures." You like to create families—large families with fifteen to twenty people—that you name and rank according to age and familial connection. You'd moved on so quickly that I didn't think seeing his profile affected you, but it did.

The next morning you woke up late for school: 7:00 a.m. When Sabrina nudged you to wakefulness, you told her that you'd had "the best dream of your life" about your donor. The two of you were playing soccer. "He had a jersey on, and I knew it was him, and I was so happy. I didn't want to wake up," you said. After telling Sabrina about your vivid dream, you zoned out, your eyes glassy and still. Sabrina had trouble bringing you back to the present, to this life, to this small apartment in this big city where you have two moms and no father. "My stomach hurts," you complained, clutching your tummy, when she urged you to get dressed for school. Like many kids, you hold all your difficult feelings in your stomach. When I walked you out to the bus stop, you weren't yourself. Usually you dash out the door like a puppy unleashed to play tag with your friends. But that morning you moved slowly, pensively, and stayed by my side. Everything about you was muted, a sun hidden behind clouds.

When you were younger, you sometimes tried to insert yourself into the proper order of things by telling people you did, in fact, have a father. During a weekend playdate in second grade, your friend outed a story you'd concocted for your schoolmates. You'd both insisted on McDonald's—specifically, a Six Piece Chicken McNuggets Happy Meal with french fries, apple slices, and chocolate milk. Although you'd sworn off the fast-food joint after a friend told you "the food is cooked in sweat and is not real," you confessed that you were over it, thereby concluding a six-month hiatus, which surely extended your lifespan. Eating on a wooden bench at our mini farm table, you locked into the *Baby-Sitters Club* television series while your friend turned to me and asked:

"Does she have a dad?"

"No, she has two moms," I replied.

"Then why does she keep telling people she does?" she asked.

I glanced over at you. You pretended you didn't hear any of this and kept your eyes firmly fastened to the screen.

"I'm not sure. I'll have to ask her," I said.

"I don't know," you piped in, aggravated by the disclosure.

"She tells everyone at school that she does have a dad, but he doesn't love her, so he won't let her live with him. Is that true?" she persisted.

"No, that is not true, but I'll have to ask her about that later," I said, anxious to steer the conversation in another direction.

That evening when Sabrina came home from work, she wondered if, perhaps, that wasn't a fabrication but an honest misinterpretation of your history. In the end, she couldn't figure out if it was that or just an expedient explanation for kids who don't understand our type of family, but she assured you that you were not unloved, but known, by him. He was never meant to be a part of our family.

You similarly sought to shroud yourself in normality when you befriended a new girl at your school who said she couldn't be friends with gay people, so you emphatically assured her of your heterosexuality. "I will marry an Ecuadorian man and have twenty kids!" you proudly declared.

Submerged in a Lush bath bomb in our claw-foot tub that same night, you triumphantly said: "Since I'm not gay, my new friend said we can be friends!" Then you asked: "Can you exchange numbers with her mom so we can have a playdate?" You didn't understand that her parents wouldn't let their daughter visit our queer home.

She wasn't the only kid who had parents, especially religious ones, uncomfortable with our "lifestyle." As frequently as I tried to organize playdates with certain friends from school, their mothers and fathers would refuse every time, often ignoring my overtures outright or devising elaborate reasons for why their kids couldn't make it, even if I threw a date out several weeks in advance. Sometimes I'd even suggest that the parents join me during the playdate for pizza so they could be assured that I wasn't defiling their children with our queerness. They shared a common story: immigrants, largely religious, navigating a new country, language, and way of life, each carrying the weight of uncertainty and hope in equal measure. I was sympathetic toward their unknowing suspicions and their desire to protect their children from things they themselves didn't understand. They weren't being intentionally hurtful; they were trying to ensure their kids' safety. And while I could hold their fraught feelings and beliefs about me, I resented the position they put me in vis-à-vis you: I had to repeatedly share their fake reasons for not allowing their kids to visit, as you continued to ask over and over again, until you figured it out and stopped trying.

A few months after transferring to your new school, which was more diverse (with several same-sex families), better resourced, and more established than your former one, you enthusiastically told me that you didn't have to explain what a donor was to your classmates because "everybody already knows." It was a school holiday, so we spent the day together. After we had lunch, we were walking up Fifth Avenue to buy some arts and crafts for home when you spotted your friend.

"Ma, let's walk faster."

"Why?"

"I see my friend whose parents don't like gay people. She's right behind us."

"You don't want to say hi?"

"No. I mean, I would say hi, but then you'd be forced to talk to her mom."

"Oh, I don't mind."

"No, I don't want to. Let's move faster," you said, slyly looking over your shoulder to be sure we kept a lead on them.

When you were as young as three, a friend at daycare insisted that you had to have a father while she made a Father's Day gift and you made a present for Uncle Heinrich.

"I don't want a daddy," you roared, and scampered off to a corner of the room to cry—because you did.

Toward the end of first grade, you told me you'd begun asking friends at school what it's like to have a dad but got upset when kids, some unwittingly and others intentionally, trumped up how great it is and how much you're missing out.

Weeks after that conversation, you spotted a movie on

Disney+ that none of us had ever seen called *The Parent Trap*. We piled onto our tattered gray pleather couch, regularly assaulted by the mighty claws of our two cats, with blankets and pillows and popcorn. Starring Lindsay Lohan, Dennis Quaid, and Natasha Richardson, it's the story of two long-lost identical twins, Hallie and Annie (both played by Lohan), who met by chance at a summer sleepaway camp. After their parents divorce, each parent retains custody of one of the twins: Hallie lives with their father, Nick (Quaid), on a sprawling vineyard in Napa, California, while Annie resides with their mother, Liz (Richardson), a famous fashion designer, in London. The duo sneakily switches places to fulfill their childhood dream of meeting the parent they had never known.

After camp, on the car ride from the airport to Nick's home, Hallie (masquerading as Annie) urges her father to "just imagine someone's life without a father," telling him that he's an "irreplaceable person in a girl's life" and ending every sentence with "Dad," an endearment Hallie has never gotten to say—just as you haven't. It killed me a little each time Hallie said it, but then she brought it to a devastating crescendo when she explained, point by point, the many losses a girl suffers without a father: never getting to say "Dad," or purchase a Father's Day card, or sit on his lap, or say "Dada," which, she says, is often a baby's first word.

The happy feeling in the living room vanished. I saw something in your face—something rising, too big to hold back. I didn't have the right words—maybe there weren't any—so I moved close and wrapped my arms around you.

Later that night when I asked you about that scene, you said it made you feel a little sad and left out, like you're missing something you know you'll never be able to find.

"When I was little, I thought *you* were my dad," you remembered. We laughed, and I reminded you that I said you could call me "Daddy," thinking it would satisfy some primal longing. The irony is that I was misidentified as "male" on your initial birth certificate before I had it changed. I wondered if the office clerk, who, perhaps, didn't agree with our "lifestyle" wanted to make a point. As early as eighteen months, you started asking, "Who's my daddy? Where's my daddy?" You saw your friends, cousins, and kids on the playground with dads, and you wanted one, too.

And sometimes, I wonder if you resented me for it because I was the one standing where a father normally would.

—

The afternoon after you'd had your first sleepover at Grandma Elizabeth's house, we went to lunch at a Japanese restaurant across the street from her apartment building in Manhattan. You pulled out a pen we'd just purchased from the Museum of Modern Art's gift shop and a pink notebook and drew an unflattering picture of me. When you were done, you turned the page.

"Now, I'm going to draw Mama Sabby," you said with a love and adoration in your voice reserved for her alone, the "cookies-and-milk" mom whose calm, welcoming face matches her sweet demeanor. You kept grabbing her face with your tiny hands and pulling it close to yours.

"Look how cute you are, Mama Sabby," you said just before queering her with a long shaggy beard. When we expressed our surprise that you didn't call us to pick you up in the middle of the night and, in fact, slept long and well, you said: "I felt comfortable because I was with Grandma and she looks like you, Mama Sabby, and one day I will look like both of you."

In that moment, I felt an outsized sense of hurt at the biological triad those words formed, of which I can never be a part. It seemed to delegitimize the connection between us—unsteadily linguistic rather than unshakably genetic, and tenuous, even illegitimate, to twenty-nine percent of Americans, according to a YouGov poll in 2018. You may want to anchor and stabilize yourself in blood relations because you may feel unmoored and incomplete walking through the world, an ancestral tree cut in half, with me on the side that's missing, trying to hold you up unevenly, stumbling.

I try to comfort myself with the flimsy notion that you can't really miss something you've never had, but that's not necessarily true, is it? Maybe you do miss the father you never had, the mysterious man whose body helped make yours. Maybe you miss him when you see Uncle Jamie toss your cousins into the air above the pool, far higher than I ever could; or when you watch *Bluey,* the Australian cartoon whose dad *outdads* us all; or when you see movies and read graphic novels in which girls interact with—and joke about—dads; or on Father's Day, when all your girlfriends are discussing weekend plans and gift ideas. I find myself missing him on your behalf.

Or maybe it's my father I'm longing for. He died unexpectedly from a brain stem stroke in the winter of 2004, when I was twenty-seven. But then again, longing is an intrinsic part of the human experience, isn't it? Aren't we all built with the impossible yearning to reunite with the body that severed our wholeness, our mother's, and the wish to sustain our lives indefinitely alongside the ever-present knowledge that we *can't*—that we will, one day, be lost to this world forever? We're all longing for something, and it's larger than whatever it is we happen to fasten our yearning on to at any given moment.

Some years ago, when I heard Australian musician Nick Cave discuss the topic with *On Being* host Krista Tippett, I realized how human it is: "I think that most people have that feeling and a kind of lostness. . . . An incompleteness and the need for something beyond ourselves to make sense of things. . . . And that yearning feels to me a kind of universal condition, based on a universal feeling of loss."

The ancient Greeks knew this feeling well, as captured in

Plato's *Symposium.* In Aristophanes's myth, there were originally three kinds of humans: Each had one head with two faces, four arms, and four legs in male-male, female-female, and male-female pairings, but they grew too powerful and prideful and attempted to overpower the gods and goddesses towering over them on high from Mount Olympus. To punish them and diminish their strength, Zeus split them in two, leaving them—leaving us—to forevermore long for our other half. For you, that longing has sometimes attached to your paternal absence, to a desire for a *daddy,* a word you've said at various stages of your young development with such pathos and pleasure, it would show up in your play often—the missing genetic link, the opening in the circle, which you may want to close in predictable ways because you don't yet understand that there's power in maintaining the gap, a place to form new kinds of being and beauty and family. Our kind.

Chapter 6

Perceptions

—

"Ma, did you and Mama Sabby fight over who got to have me in their belly?" you asked me one day after declaring your wish to have as many children as possible and as soon as possible.

"Not at all. I didn't want to carry you. I just wanted to love you," I said.

"But why didn't you want to carry me?" you asked, surprised by my admission.

"Well, if I *did* carry you, you wouldn't be you—and I don't even want to consider that because you're the love of our lives."

"But why didn't you want to carry me?" you persisted.

"It sounds strange, but for me it would have sort of felt like wearing a dress. Moving through the world as a pregnant woman doesn't match up with how I see myself," I said, reflecting on my gender-dissonant youth, when I hated the vulnerabilities inherent in being a girl—my bony legs, my growing breasts, my soft body: my fragility.

"But I'd be half you if you had me."

"Yes, but you wouldn't be you. You'd be a different child, and the child I love and want is you, exactly as you are."

I couldn't fully unpack how the idea of walking through the world pregnant felt too shatteringly vulnerable to me as a person who continually experiences varying degrees—far lesser today than in my elementary school days—of gender dysphoria, the sense that my body doesn't accurately speak to my self-concept, and dysmorphia, the ever-present feeling that I'm aesthetically inadequate. I couldn't tell you that I didn't *want* to reproduce myself—that I couldn't imagine seeing my face in my child, that I actually didn't believe I could love such a child or that the world would love such a child. It was a consideration too heavy to hold because I could not absorb that burden on my child's behalf; I'd just have to bear witness to his or her suffering, which I knew would be far worse than experiencing it for myself.

"Beauty prompts a copy of itself," it prompts "begetting," Elaine Scarry, the Walter M. Cabot Professor of Aesthetics and the General Theory of Value at Harvard, writes in *On Beauty and Being Just.* "It is impossible to conceive of a beautiful thing that does not have this attribute." Conversely, it then follows that that which is ugly—unless it's so ugly it, like beauty, seems "incomparable, unprecedented" and "conveys a sense of the 'newness' or 'newbornness' of the entire world," decentering and enrapturing onlookers, as Scarry says of beauty's effects—eschews self-replication. Scarry's logic resonates with my own resistance to self-generation and my desire to see Sabrina's beauty in my child. It also explains a friend's rationale for why Sabrina should carry you, not me.

At a theater to see the movie *Lincoln,* Sabrina confessed to our mutual friend—not realizing I was in earshot—that her friend had said, "You have to have the baby because you're prettier." Even though this truth was not unknown to me, I felt as I had on Cord Street when I heard, for the first time, someone express externally what I vaguely knew internally. It struck like a sudden fist to the gut. Was that the way Sabrina saw me, too? I don't remember a single thing about the film, only the irony of sitting there, the ugly one, watching a movie about a man who was considered a human eyesore in his day, too.

In one popular story about Lincoln—albeit likely apocryphal—a political rival slams the sixteenth president for being "two-faced," to which he's said to have replied: "If I had another face, do you think I'd be wearing this one?" Among his contemporaries, Lincoln was thought to be homely; poet Walt Whitman said Lincoln's face was "so awful ugly it becomes beautiful," and a pundit wrote these ego-crushing lines: "Lincoln is the leanest, lankest, most ungainly mass of legs, arms and hatchet-face ever strung upon a single frame. He has most unwarrantably abused the privilege which all politicians have of being ugly." At one point, Lincoln wondered if he should grow a beard to hide his "horrible lantern jaws," stating: "It is allowed to be ugly in this world, but not as ugly as I am." One evening in the woods, when Lincoln stopped to let a woman rider pass, she commented: "Well, for land sake, you are the homeliest man I ever saw." To this he replied: "Yes, madam, but I cannot help it." She quipped: "No I suppose not, but you might stay home."

When discussions of abolition and Lincoln's part in ending slavery came up at school, you were surprised to learn from me that he was considered unattractive in his day, because you thought him handsome.

The summer you turned eight, you offered a similarly generous assessment of me and my face.

I picked you up from swim camp on a cool, sunny day. We were walking up Sixth Avenue, a tranquil street, toward the playground when you suddenly had to pee, urgently. We stopped at a local bar. You ordered lemonade—"Ew, too sour," you'd said—

and I ordered a beer. We sat outside to enjoy the unusually non-humid day and talked.

"I'm a green cap now," you proudly declared, having tested out of the red cap, which formerly confined you to floaties in the shallow end.

"I'm so proud of you," I said.

"Now I'm ready for the ocean in the Outer Banks," you said, excited about our upcoming trip to North Carolina with your cousins Mari and Emmy and Uncle Jamie and Aunt Joanne.

I was wearing a baseball cap over my shaggy uncombed hair when you spontaneously grabbed the sides of my face and said, "You're pretty, Mama."

"What?" I said, unsure if I'd heard you right.

"You're pretty," you repeated.

A series of dissonant thoughts and feelings converged on me in an instant. My first thought was that you were saying it because it wasn't true and you were trying to be kind. My second thought was that you were saying it because it wasn't true and you wanted to make it so by declaring it. My third thought was *I'm so happy you see me that way.*

If I'd felt differently about my aesthetics—if I saw myself as, perhaps, you saw me—would I have felt differently about carrying you? I can't say for sure, but I was struck when a friend gushed with delight after I told her that she and her son looked so much alike: "Oh, thank you for saying that! At least one of my kids looks like me. Because my daughter and I look nothing alike," she said with disappointment. I can't imagine what it would feel like to *want* my child to look like me or to be disappointed if he or she didn't. And I can't imagine outwardly admitting my pleasure at seeing my own face in my child's, which is tantamount to expressing satisfaction with one's own looks. I say that with envy, not judgment; we should all take pleasure in our reflections. I've even seen Sabrina light up when someone points out how much you look like her. Maybe seeing yourself in your child—whom you love and value above all others—helps you realize your own beauty. If we shared a face, how could you be beautiful and I still be ugly? Would my love for a child born from me have changed my self-perception? I'll never know, but none of it matters now: Sabrina brought you to life, and I wouldn't have it any other way.

But you didn't come to us easily . . .

We did several rounds of IUI, each time spending one thousand dollars, at a fancy clinic in Brooklyn Heights—"You'd move here if you had a lot of money, right, Ma?" you always say, quoting me to myself, when we go to Monty Q's on Montague Street for lunch and visit the neighborhood's spectacular library on Cadman Plaza West—and still, Sabrina wasn't pregnant. Because Grandma Elizabeth effortlessly got pregnant with Sabrina and Aunt Joanne in her late thirties and early forties, we naively thought a pregnancy would take the first time. When it wasn't happening and I saw our slim savings growing slimmer, I asked Sabrina: "What if we just got a dog instead?" But I, too, now longed for this baby we were struggling to make. *Yia Yia* generously sent us a three-thousand-dollar check to help us weather the next several rounds of IUI, which brought us relief.

At the time, we'd been watching TLC's *Long Island Medium,* mostly because we loved spiritualist Theresa Caputo's idiosyncrasies—the big bleached bouffant, the long colorful nails, the funny way she frequently says, "You understand me?" in her thick regional accent—but it gave me comfort, too. Even if I didn't fully buy her psychic powers, I felt comforted by the idea that the energy of our loved ones—like that of compost, as Ron Finley, the Gangsta Gardener, once told me—never dies; it takes different shape, becomes part of the formless eternal, and is an energy we can tap into and commune with at any time.

When I met Sabrina and fell in love at age thirty-two, I missed my loved ones who'd passed away more than I ever had. I missed my father, who had died five years before, and his parents, my grandparents, who'd lavished me and my brother with enough love and affection and fun to nurture an entire village of children. Falling in love opened the floodgates—I mourned them as if they had just died. In Sabrina's love, I could be vulnerable to the pain of their absence in ways I couldn't formally access. I thought of them constantly, like an old vinyl record stuck on the same scratchy riff. To this day, Sabrina says some cosmic tug, my father, led her to me, and it was uncanny how we met.

It was a little before midnight, and the movie she'd just seen with two of her friends had finished. They were walking down Smith Street when a volt of energy compelled her to promptly abandon her friends and head over to Cattyshack, the lesbian bar, where I was enjoying a second date with a girl named Kathy. It was the first and only time Sabrina went to a bar alone, stone sober. "I felt like I was floating through the streets with no will of my own. I remember going through the doors, up the stairs to the dance room, ordering a drink and heading straight out to the roof deck, spotting you immediately and walking right over to you to stand by your side." I felt her hovering. When I looked up and into her disarming brown eyes, she said, "I like your glasses," then introduced herself to me and Kathy, making us laugh with her wit and old-man humor. As the night wore on and we proceeded to get more drunk, we had a "kiss orgy," where each of us took turns kissing each other to see where the sparks might catch. The kiss I shared with Sabrina persisted past a reasonable stretch of time, compelling Kathy to huff, "Okay, okay, we get it," and then head to the bathroom long enough for us to exchange numbers. The extra irony of all this is that I'd actually invited my friend Susan to the "date," thinking that perhaps Kathy and Susan might like each other because my attraction to Kathy felt like the slow-burning kind that I was too impatient to wait for. But Susan forgot her ID, and the bouncer wouldn't let her in—despite the fact that she was forty. If she'd been there, Sabrina may have been too intimidated to come up to three lesbians sitting on a bench—that sounds like the start of a joke—but everything aligned just right for us to meet and fall in love. And without our queer love, as strange as it may seem, you would not be here.

To call that August night one of the best of my life is an understatement—it was the beginning of everything good in my life, a spot at the top of the highest peak with breathtaking views.

I wanted my departed loved ones to meet Sabrina, the love of my life, and this baby—you—we were struggling to make.

I'd picture my father talking to Sabrina, who's like him in so many ways—deeply kind, compassionate, intelligent, silly—about some dorky tech thing he'd read about in *Wired.* I'd see him listening attentively, slightly shaking his head in agreement with pursed lips, to my father-in-law, Samuel, a successful attorney, about his philosophical take on the fragility of democracy or universal healthcare. I'd see my grandmother, who always made me feel seen and loved, holding our cooing baby in her arms. I know she'd have made you feel as special as she made me feel in the '80s when our maroon Thunderbird would pull into the driveway of her house in North Hollywood—a modest three-bedroom, two-bathroom home that was pleasantly dark, like the contemplative insides of a monastic library with warm lamps and lots of books in dusty stacks and a haunting organ. She'd stand at the top of the steps outside the entrance to her door, jumping up and down like a cheerleader with invisible pom-poms, welcoming us.

She took all my childhood fears and anxieties seriously but dispelled them by turning them into things of beauty—magic—like when we'd visit their time-share in Palm Desert for the weekend, where the winds swept through with a persistence and velocity that scared me, shaking the windows of the bedroom in which we slept side by side. My grandmother would kick the sheets up in our bed and holler in her thick Argentine accent for the rest of the units to hear, like a harmless maniac, "I love the wind! I love the wind! I love the wind!" Assuring me that the windows would not break, she'd list out the reasons why it delighted her so, turning it from a threat to a comfort: Like God, the wind is invisible, but yet ever present—a force that stirs with strength and a hint of something divine, sharpening the air with an electrifying crispness, whispering through the trees, rustling our hair, and brushing gently across our faces. From then on, I could no longer see the wind as anything but beautiful, no matter how loudly it rattled the odd window.

Playful and silly, she'd march through the house for no apparent reason, loudly singing, "Nobody likes me! Everybody hates me! I'm going to eat some worms!" and would stop by me and my brother, asking if we'd join her "friend of the friendless" conga line, and we'd all parade through the house, asking anyone we passed, including inanimate objects, to be in our tiny procession. I wanted to see her again, even if only in a dream.

One night, I kept trying to visualize my father and grandmother, hoping I'd catch a glimpse of them in a dream. When I finally went to sleep, instead I dreamt of some kind of celestial being—an angelic, feminine presence, beautiful beyond comprehension—floating on a pool raft attached to a Volkswagen Beetle on an endless stretch of highway that cut through infinite flatlands on either side. She breathlessly drove up to my green station wagon, the one from my earliest youth with wooden side panels, and said, "A girl. December." She'd begun to speed away when I called out, amid a face covered in tears, "Is she healthy?" "Yes!" she yelled back as she flew away imperceptibly fast, like an alien spacecraft, defying the laws of physics. It's one of the most vivid dreams I've ever had; I woke up and knew you were coming with a certainty as sure as my own heartbeat—and you were: You were conceived, on the fourth try, that December.

When you arrived at a hospital in Brooklyn in the summer, the euphoric love I felt despite the destabilizing challenges of having a newborn—nature's mad medicine for propagating the human race—quickly made my past a shadowy memory, a grainy half-life I barely remembered nor wanted to. I was no longer drifting in some theoretical world or trying to escape, to be somewhere, anywhere, other than where I was, as I did in my early youth and adulthood. I wanted to be here, in the flesh, holding this baby, this woman, this life, in my hands.

You love to hear about that prescient dream—and about the very moment you left the womb after twenty-two hours of labor, as we held our breath, waiting, in uneasy anticipation, to hear you cry—the first sign of a healthy infant, her ability to assert her voice—and how we burst into happy tears like none we'd experienced before or since.

That moment, in that hospital, felt preverbal, pre-cultural—holy. In that room, there was no question that I, too, was your mother and you were my child. But the world beyond that hospital room, even just outside our door, didn't always see it that way. It was a telling start to our life as a queer family that the administrator who filled out your birth certificate listed me, despite my feminine name, as male. (Although it may have been an honest administrative oversight, I kept the original birth certificate as a time capsule or funny keepsake to joke about when you're older.) I was standing where a father normally would, and the world treated me accordingly. The full force of the congratulations was largely directed at Sabrina when you were first born; she did the hard work of carrying and delivering you, so that seemed warranted. But I never actively wanted to be a woman, ever, until I had you: I wanted to be the primary parent—the *mother*—not the secondary one—the *father*.

The biologization of motherhood—the idea that this child that came from your body is quintessentially *yours,* not *his,* and, consequently, you are the ultimate authority on all things baby—feeds into the system that ranks dads beneath moms, which thwarts the goals of feminism by burdening women with the lion's share of parental responsibilities. Occupying the position I do in our family, I'd begun to see why some fathers may feel a lesser investment in parenthood. It's not just the feminizing nature of nurturing that conflicts with their gendered self-understanding but that they're relegated to the margins of parenthood like a footnote in a book. Women don't seem to want to relinquish their superior status vis-à-vis their children, as Stephanie Coontz has pointed out, but at a big cost: It keeps the familial imbalance of power intact and plays into the inequalities women suffer in the larger world.

I didn't want to be your father; I wanted to be your mother. I had my sex on your birth certificate changed, but the form's designation, "Mother/Parent" and "Father/Parent," still classified Sabrina as your mother and consigned me to the more neutral, watered-down label of "parent," proving that I am, as my friend and fellow non-bio mom Eli says, "supporting cast" to Sabrina's leading role as mother. The designation of "parent," of course, is progress, but if it were applied equally to us both, it would be transformative. Changing the language we use changes the way we experience the world. So many inequities—quietly corrosive—stem from the asymmetrical ways we position mothers and fathers as well as biological and nonbiological parents, in both language and law.

Culturally, it's so embedded in our mindsets and how we've organized society that it's challenging to think outside or against biology and binaries. Whether we were sitting on a park bench or walking through the playground area in Sunset Park or standing in a grocery line, strangers would sometimes ask unintentionally insensitive questions when they found out we are a two-mom family: "Who carried her? Where did you find a donor? How did you decide on your donor?" rendering me—not the mother, nor the father—invisible on the spot.

My queer positioning in our family exacerbated my feelings of ugliness, if ugliness is understood as that which upsets the conventional order of things or, using anthropologist Mary Douglas's useful phrase, as "matter out of place," making me hypervisible in some situations—unpleasantly so—and totally erased in others.

Those first few months, we were bleary-eyed and exhausted, waking up every three hours to feed you, taking turns lulling you back to sleep, placing your body between ours as we watched a show with divided attention, too consumed with you, too tired to successfully focus on anything else.

During your colicky fits, I'd walk you up and down the hall in our apartment, whispering to you in my best ASMR voice about the abstract paintings hanging on our walls that your grandfather Samuel composed in the 1970s, before Sabrina was even born. One piece is called *Sabrina: A Conception.* It's a blue-and-yellow line—Grandpa Samuel and Grandma Elizabeth—merging to form a green one: Sabrina. Even the art on our walls spoke of the fusion of two becoming one. But I still found a place for myself in that painting. Green, my favorite color, is Sabrina—the life that I'd one day love, the body that would make yours. It's also the color of nature—trees, grass, everything vibrant and alive. Yellow is the sun, the force that sustains all of it. When I walked by each painting, naming the shapes and colors, trying to soothe you back to sleep, you seemed to listen—eerily still, as if you knew exactly what I was saying.

Neither of us made enough money to keep you home full-time for longer than four months. We had to entrust your care, too soon, to strangers at a newly established daycare center in our neighborhood. I went back to work after a month; Sabrina stayed with you for another three. Placing you in the care of others felt freeing on the one hand—like we could return to some semblance of normalcy, moving through the world unencumbered by the needs and wants of a tiny human fastened to our bodies—but after being inseparable for sixteen weeks, Sabrina felt like a vital part of her body was being severed each time she put you in another's arms. Life's like that sometimes, or maybe that's what life is fundamentally—a series of ruptures, separations, and endings and a longing for wholeness.

The nursery caretakers were wonderful—warm, kind, and loving. The staff started to feel like an extended family, but the owner's husband, a kind and well-meaning man, sometimes said thoughtless things, unintentionally causing harm, confusing you and making me feel like a nonentity.

When you were about ten months old, he'd scoop you into his arms at drop-off and say, "Come to Daddy! Come to Papa!" Lifting you into the air amid your smiles and baby babbles, he'd say: "Who's your daddy? Who's your daddy?" You mutually adored one another, so for a long time, I didn't say anything. I didn't want to create any tension or negative feelings toward us as a family, especially given how much we depended on them to care for you. One could only hope they'd love you as if you were their own, and didn't the phrase *come to Daddy* suggest he did? I also didn't want to seem threatened, although I was, or like a man-hating lesbian chiding him for overzealously expressing his affection for you. I still carry the baggage of that term with me and never know how others are filtering what I do or don't do, what I say or don't say, how I look or don't look, through that historically dingy—ugly—lens. What compelled me to finally say something was the worry that it might start to confuse you. As you began to acquire language and comprehension, you might have actually started to think that he was indeed your father. And it might create ambivalence toward—mystification about—me. "If he's my daddy and she's my mommy, who are you?" you might have wondered.

When you were no longer an infant, I finally told him that as you started to make sense of things, it was imperative that he stop referring to himself as "Daddy" or risk confusing you. I also said that I understood that he didn't mean it literally or with intentional insensitivity. He apologized and never referred to himself that way again.

But when you turned two and transferred to the daycare's sister site down the street, the lead teacher, whom you still say is your favorite teacher of all time, struggled to manage your growing awareness of—and complex feelings about—your fatherlessness. She'd call us worried about how to manage Father's Day art projects when you didn't have a father or when your peers expressed confused agitation about our two-mom family. A simple line, like the one that concludes Todd Parr's wonderful picture book, *The Family Book*—"There are lots of different ways to be a family. Your family is special no matter what kind it is"—or the line uttered by the kind teacher in Lesléa Newman's classic *Heather Has Two Mommies*—"Each family is special. The most important thing about a family is that all the people in it love each other"—would have helped introduce a more expansive definition of family. Sabrina and I considered donating both books to the daycare, as well as Suzanne and Max Lang's children's book *Families, Families, Families!*, not just for the children but to give the carers language they could use to explain our familial configuration, but we decided it might come off as heavy-handed and off-putting.

Other years, you'd come home with a Mother's Day gift for *us* on Father's Day. The daycare did the best they could, as did we. We created inconsistent family traditions around Father's Day, where we'd tell stories about your grandfathers, pointing out similarities you share with them. "You have the best qualities of them both," we'd say. "Your big heart and daydreaming remind me of Grandpa Armand," I'd say. "Your knack for art—drawing and painting—and your fondness for perusing piles of books on the toilet and your silly sense of humor are *all* Grandpa Samuel," Sabrina would add. Then we'd share stories about them—how Grandpa Samuel fell asleep, snoring loudly, during a talk at Harvard on a campus tour Sabrina took her junior year of high school and the speaker said, "Harvard isn't for *everyone,*" while looking directly at Grandpa Samuel as onlookers snickered. Or how small crowds would gather around him during frequent trips to the Met, the Guggenheim, and MoMA because he spoke with a loud, authoritative voice (in a fake British accent) and had an encyclopedic knowledge of Western art. And I'd tell you about Grandpa Armand—how he dreamed of coming to America from Argentina his entire childhood, how he learned to speak English (with only a slight accent) by listening to shortwave radio and watching American movies, and how he got his visa on his own when he was nineteen and boldly declared to his parents that they could come with him to the United States or stay in Argentina, which was faltering under a military coup, but he was moving to the country he'd come to love.

Other years we ignored Father's Day entirely, not feeling the need to adapt ourselves to a holiday that didn't speak to the reality of our lives.

But it wasn't always other people who didn't know how to manage the queerness of our family; sometimes it was us. We unintentionally created shame—maybe it was our shame, or maybe it was our desire to protect you—where you initially felt pride by urging you to forgo telling the kids in your new third-grade class that your Ecuadorian doll represents your donor's ancestry. You'd just experienced the slow devolution of your closest friendship since babyhood and felt on the outs of your mutual friend group. The next year, we left the school for many reasons, but that was the leading one for you. The whole place was sullied in the memory of a love lost. "Do you miss anything about your old school?" we'd ask as we passed it along the avenue, and you'd half yell, "No!" firm and resolute. At that school, you'd sometimes had to absorb prejudices meant for us, not you. That's why we thought you ought to disclose the bit of information about our family *after* you forged friendships with your classmates, once they knew and loved you.

We told you as much when you did a run-through of your presentation for show-and-tell.

"This is Maria. She's a doll from Ecuador. She represents my love of the Spanish language and the country my donor comes from," you said.

"Well, if you say 'donor,' you're going to have to explain what a donor is, and that's hard to explain," Sabrina said.

"No, it's not. I'll just say I have two moms, and they couldn't make a baby on their own, so they used a donor."

"That's a lot to reveal on a first meeting with your classmates," I said.

"Some kids may give you a hard time about it," Sabrina added.

"Why? I'm proud of my family, and I don't have anything to be ashamed of."

"Of course not. We're proud of our family, too. We just want you to get situated in your new friendships before you share that, only because some kids may not be so nice about it," I said.

The next day, when we asked how it went, you said: "I just said it was my favorite doll and it's from Ecuador," which may have been more heartbreaking than had you weathered difficult, or even mean-spirited, questions. We realized we should have had faith that you could handle whatever questions or comments came from your peers rather than try to control their perception of you and in so doing supplant your pride with shame. The myopia and wrongheadedness of our excessive protectiveness was on full display when you came home some days later and emphatically shared that there were several other LGBTQ families at the school and no one needed "donor" explained.

We stumbled through other things, too, like when we told you about your biological "brothers" and "sister."

Sabrina had reached out to the Sperm Bank of California to get on a list to meet your donor siblings. We thought it might be useful to connect with other families for various reasons, including medical ones. We also thought it might be good for you, as an only child, to make connections with your donor siblings. The couple, Rebecca and Joan, that eventually contacted us was a two-mom family living outside San Francisco, preparing to move to New Jersey because Rebecca was pregnant with twins, Tina and Lenny, and they needed the support of their family.

After exchanging a few pleasant emails with videos and pictures that showed an undeniable likeness between you and their son Marlo, we organized a day trip to a play space in New Jersey.

We've always been transparent and clear about your donor-conception, perhaps to a fault, but you were only four when we finally met them, and it was too complicated to explain, so we lied: "They're old friends of ours from San Francisco, and they have a little boy your age you'll get to play with," I'd said.

Seeing sweet Marlo for the first time stirred feelings that were hard to place. It wasn't exactly love but maybe a silhouette of it. Seeing your dark eyes and smile in his face, your physicality in his movements, was affecting. It stirred an ineffable feeling that lives somewhere beyond conceptuality and is more powerful because we've not invented language to articulate—limit and contain—it. It wasn't just the similarities visible in your mannerisms and look—he is of you, and you are of him; there was also something about his essence that felt familiar. Was it the phantom trails of the unknown man who helped make both of you—the shadow man, indistinctly seen but fully felt?

Marlo was delightful. Like you, he's kind with a fiercely independent streak, creative with a built-in aptitude for music, naturally warm and effervescent with eyes brimming with soul and intelligence. We synced well with his parents, too—how lucky were we. They were kind, open-hearted, and easy to talk to. Both work in helping professions—Joan, a schoolteacher, and Rebecca, a social worker serving LGBTQ youth.

On another trip to see them, when you were six, you got to meet two new donor siblings—fraternal twins Tina and Lenny—and enjoy more time with Marlo in their spacious two-story house in New Jersey. You loved being in their roomy digs, as you often do when we go on vacation and rent spaces far larger than our meager 687-square-foot apartment in Brooklyn, and had fun playing in Marlo's toy-filled bedroom when you weren't following Tina around as if she were your very own live doll.

You and Tina resembled each other the most. I wondered if you'd noticed. Once, you caught a glimpse of a picture of her on my phone and thought it was you, but we still hadn't told you that the four of you were related. When we learned that Joan had told Marlo you were his half sister by way of our shared donor—in a simple, nonchalant sort of way—we decided to do the same when we got back to Brooklyn. But unlike Joan, we made it spectacularly complicated.

Our explanation had three parts—all too complex and inappropriate for your age and comprehension—and for mine, too. First we explained the science of how a man and a woman make a baby: "The man's sperm joins with a woman's egg, and a fetus is created that will eventually grow into a baby." Then we said, "A nice man donated his sperm to a place that helps women like us make a family." And finally: "The same nice man who helped us make your life helped Joan and Rebecca make Marlo, Tina, and Lenny, so you're all related through your donor."

We've always thought that being open about your lineage

would foster mutual respect and communication, so you'd feel comfortable asking questions and expressing feelings, happy ones or sad ones, about your origins or paternal absence. We told you about your donor siblings in that same spirit, but my bumbling articulations were too much. It confused and unsettled you. The light in your eyes dimmed after my explanation. You asked: "But why can't they live with me if they're my brothers and sister?"

"They live with their moms, and you live with yours. We have a connection with them through your donor, but we aren't the same family," I said. "But how wonderful to have them in our lives."

"But I want to live with them," you said, brow furrowed, face frowning.

All I could come up with in reply was "I'm really sorry it makes you sad that you can't live with them." You love people—and cradle ongoing, elaborate fantasies about having lots of kids and living with all of your extended family in the same big house—so I knew a part of the sadness was your longing for siblings, for more family. "Love, not blood, makes a family," I explained, trying to carve out a space for myself as your nonbiological family member. Over the ensuing days, you continued to brood over their absence: "But I do love them," you countered, and how could I argue with that?

I wanted to say what I will say now: Love, the glue that coalesces a family, is not the stuff of one-off meetings in a play space or a big house in New Jersey; it's the joys and sorrows and anodyne tasks of everyday togetherness: grocery shopping, setting the table, sharing meals, doing the dishes, brushing teeth, squabbling over silly differences.

It's the good stuff—laughing like hyenas at the pair of sweats that give Sabrina plumber's butt; or running through our tight quarters playing "Mommy Monster" and tickling you until you shriek; or Mother's Day brunch with Grandma Elizabeth, hard of hearing, sending us into stitches as she repeatedly mishears and misinterprets things we've said, hilariously and nonsensically.

It's traveling together to Provincetown: fun on Commercial Street, buggy rides over sand dunes, sunsets at Nauset Beach, full moons over gray-shingled cottages, hot buttered lobster rolls on the boardwalk at Native Cape Cod Seafood, and ice cream at Lewis Brothers.

It's long weekends in the Berkshires—cousins in Monterey, ghosts at the Red Lion Inn, "the way we never were" in the visions of Norman Rockwell, sugar highs at Robin's Candy in Great Barrington, *The Taming of the Shrew* and August Wilson's *The Piano Lesson* at Shakespeare & Company.

It's lighting the menorah each night of Hanukkah while you trip through the prayers in Hebrew—a language you don't actually speak or understand.

And it's the bad stuff, too—the time I forced you to wear a pricey coat we'd just purchased that rankled your ever-evolving style, reducing us to fury and tears; or when the pandemic peaked and you retired your colorful feminine wardrobe for a dark palette of jeans, overalls, and printed T-shirts and sneakers—and your levity faded along with the color; or when your bond with a friend dearer to you than anyone began to wane, and we watched your confidence and joy diminish with it; or when I struggled to hide my own anxiety and depression as my lifelong insomnia reached a near-debilitating extreme as the Covid crisis raged on.

That's what makes a family—memories, love, heartache, and the sweet banality of daily life. Blood has little to do with it, but the world beyond this tiny box we call home often makes it seem otherwise.

Chapter 7

Weird Girls Rule

Is an era without ugliness an era without progress? Or, to ask another way, is ugliness a cultural quest?" Gretchen E. Henderson asks, pointing to the concept's radical potential and, to my mind, its kinship with queer theory—a system of thinking that seeks to destabilize normality and all the ways it rigidly and harmfully contours our psyches and perceptions.

"Ugliness is unpredictable and offers an infinite range of possibility. Beauty is finite. Ugliness is infinite, like God," Italian historian Umberto Eco muses. Taking a swipe at its fairer counterpart, he says: "Beauty is, in some ways, boring. Even if its concept changes through the ages, nevertheless a beautiful object must always follow certain rules."

There is indeed an order to beauty that makes it ordinary against the unruly and unexpected delights of ugliness. Some people, like Isadora's mother in Erica Jong's iconic novel *Fear of Flying,* see ordinariness as a kind of failure—uninspired, bland, lazy. Her most withering insult is to simply call something "ordinary."

That struck me. I've never really idealized or aspired to normalcy, either—maybe because I knew I could never deliver on its demands. But one thing I know for sure: It's in the places where *you* push past the ordinary that you—and the world—get to revel in the rewards of your extraordinariness. When you dance out of sync with the beat, or sing with a voice full of broken glass; when your hair is tangled and leaf-strewn from climbing the tallest branches in Sunset Park, or your dress and face are smudged with delicious drips of ice cream on a hot sunny day. Like the beauty of the natural world that underlies and pokes through cracks in the pavement on the grimiest streets and sidewalks of New York City—the long, lush green weeds of Star of Bethlehem that sprout alongside vibrant clusters of grape hyacinth, the untamable world refusing to be disciplined—I hope you triumph over your false conditioning, the man-made ideologies that overlie your body and throw a paralyzing net across your mind. "Look, Ma, these purple flowers are growing here," you said, pointing to the few that pushed through the base of the rock wall encircling our park. We talked about how beautiful things can grow in the most unlikely places. Even rock and concrete can't hold them back.

I wish your body could absorb these sentiments like rays of light from the sun when someone criticizes the way you dance, the way you sit, the way you stand, the way you sing.

You came home from school upset one day because a friend said she couldn't stand your singing voice and demanded you stop. She also made fun of your outfit. "What are you wearing? You look weird," she'd said.

That day, you'd gone to school wearing what you identified as a "Jewish style," referring to the Hasidim who live in Borough Park, the southwestern part of Brooklyn, a few avenues away from our apartment. There the streets are populated by men in black suits and biber hats or *shtreimels* (rounded fur hats) and women in sheitels (wigs) and dusky garbs that hide everything but their faces and hands. You wore a dark shirt tucked into an ankle-length black skirt and a deep navy blue sweater with black boots. Jewish on Sabrina's father's side, you were eager to explore the religion and culture—to go to Hebrew school and one day have a bat mitzvah.

To me, you looked like Wednesday Addams, very goth and so cool.

But it was too outside the lines for your classmates, and as much as you loved that particular ensemble, you retired it to an IKEA bin stuffed with old Halloween costumes.

I tried to coax you into revisiting it—that part of you that's out of sync with expectation—but you refused.

Other people's eyes—even the idea of them—can be a hard place to sit if you can't find a way to insulate yourself from their judgments. A certain look can grow noxious weeds in our psyches that spread out multidirectionally around our self-confidence.

Hearing an adult publicly declare my ugliness in her surprise at my aesthetic misalignment with my mother—reinforced, a few years later, when my mother's friend said to my teenage face, hit by the adolescent trifecta of zits, braces, and poodle-perm hair: "It must be hard to have a pretty mother"—made me feel like I was a moral failing, an assault on the eyes so absolute that I, like your uncelebrated ensemble, should hide away, and eventually I did. But now I wonder, if I'd grown up today—with more queer visibility and a larger range of ways to express my often confused and always contradictory gendered existence—would I have been as quick as you to relegate a beloved outfit that didn't square with popular opinion to a rarely visited bin of costumes? Maybe we weren't doing enough to expose you to the infinite variety of ways to embody and articulate your femininity and *girlness*—or teaching you the subversive thrill of expressing yourself *against* expectation. But we found a song that provided a portal into a broader realm of possibilities while driving home from cousins Peter and Roberta's house in the Berkshires one evening.

Coasting along the highway, we shared the airwaves as we often do. You pick a song, I pick a song, then Sabrina picks a song. Sabrina usually picks a song you like—"That defeats the whole purpose of this lesson in *sharing,*" I'll say to your gratified snickers from the back seat—but this time she chose one for you and herself, Le Tigre's "Deceptacon." She wanted to expose you to new music, mostly because our psychological health was rapidly deteriorating with the excess doses of Taylor Swift and Olivia Rodrigo you interminably beat into our ears. Although the lyrics are peppered with curse words, we liked that "Deceptacon" is an anthem to the queer disco of yore and a feminist battle cry expressed in the fun flamboyance of a high-energy punky pop song. You loved it, too, and asked us to play it on repeat. Instead we introduced you to another Le Tigre favorite—"Hot Topic"—a track that celebrates women who've resisted and reshaped various productions of knowledge and culture, who've broken through the pavement meant to overlie, bury, their unruliness: queer writers giving voice to the historically voiceless, like Dorothy Allison, who wrote *Bastard Out of Carolina,* which centered on the life of a poor "illegitimate" girl in the rural South who suffers sexual and other forms of abuse at the hands of her stepfather; Leslie Feinberg, the "anti-racist white, working-class, secular Jewish, transgender, lesbian, female, revolutionary communist" who brought awareness to the experience of growing up in 1950s Buffalo, New York, as a working-class trans-inflected masculine dyke in *Stone Butch Blues;* radical thinkers and theorists like Gayatri Spivak, who famously critiqued the structures that prevent the subaltern—those marginalized by colonial, class, and patriarchal power—from speaking but cautioned against speaking on their behalf; revolutionaries like Angela Davis, who called for the abolition of the prison industrial complex that preys upon the bodies of Black and brown people; visual artists like Lorraine O'Grady, whose performance and conceptual art decenters dominant paradigms about race and gender; Carolee Schneemann, who grappled with the struggles of female embodiment, using her own body as a canvas to help us rethink how we see our bodies from a feminist perspective; tennis star Billie Jean King, who confirmed her lesbianism in 1981 and championed the enforcement of Title IX, a law prohibiting sex discrimination in education and athletic programs receiving federal funds; and writer Gertrude Stein, whose literary innovations—including stream of consciousness, repetition, and fragmentary language—have had a lasting impact on poetry and fiction, who defied societal expectations by living openly with her partner, Alice B. Toklas, at a time when same-sex relationships were largely taboo. The track goes on to spotlight other heroic individuals—queer poet and novelist Eileen Myles, nonbinary transgender singer and actor Justin Vivian Bond, trans jazz musician Billy Tipton, and several others—who've had a reverberating impact on our culture.

You picked up the refrain quickly and repeated it endlessly, a clear message to marginalized people: Challenge norms and hierarchies, refuse erasure, take space. Our survival depends on resisting the status quo and amplifying our voices and realities. Like Gertrude Stein, we'll have to shatter the way we think by turning the language we use upside down to see what new ideas and structures of thought might emerge, just as the song does when it rejects—reinvents—what it means to "rhyme" by defiantly declaring in a nonrhyming string of words: "Hot topic is the way that we rhyme."

Listening to Le Tigre's paean to fabulous women and queers, I was reminded of advice I received from the author of *Beauty Sick,* Renee Engeln, who studies the psychological and physical consequences of uncritically submitting to beauty imperatives.

"You don't get to live in this culture and not be shaped by it. So the fact that your daughter is being shaped by the culture she's surrounded with—that it's acting on her—that's just how humans work. All you can do is open other doors, give them other options. Show them other things."

In that spirit, let's walk through a little *herstory* of dissonant women who've refused to squeeze themselves into the existing order of things. Maybe they didn't know how to conform to what was expected of them, or maybe they didn't want to, but either way I hope you'll take a little from each and create something wholly unique to yourself, a patchwork of influences, or find an opening into a whole new dimension of being and self-creation.

I'll start with my entry into the world of fairies and freaks, drag kings and dykes, as a newly out nineteen-year-old in 1995. Before I landed on University Avenue in Hillcrest, an LGBTQ enclave in San Diego, I had only a smattering of queer icons to look up to—and only one self-acknowledged queer classmate. Singer-songwriter Elton John had come out as bisexual in 1976 and gay in 1992; country singer k.d. lang confessed her lesbianism to *The Advocate* in 1992; rock star Melissa Etheridge revealed her homosexuality at a queer event celebrating President Bill Clinton's inauguration in 1993; the year after that, *Friends* aired its first episode with Ross cut up over his wife leaving him for another woman and moving out; then Enrique "Rickie" Vasquez came out on my *My So-Called Life* that same year. But the only direct experience I had with queers in my actual life was based on inference—or gaydar: my now-out friends Ashley, a lesbian, and J.P., a gender-queer artist; the pair of schoolteachers my mom golfed with who cohabited in the same home for decades; a moody gym coach from a summer sports camp; and maybe a few others, but not many. So, I knew that people like me existed, but I wanted to see them in larger numbers—I wanted queer friends, a first kiss (with someone to whom I was actually attracted), a girlfriend—so I came out to my brother over the phone while he was away at college. He said he was proud of the courage I'd mustered to tell him what he already knew and offered to take me to my first gay youth meeting at the San Diego LGBT Community Center in downtown when he came home that summer. His good looks would reel in a bunch of disappointed gay boys who would become my good friends. Soon I had a queer circle of friends and could finally experiment with an assortment of things I'd missed out on in my closeted adolescence: crushes I could confess and talk about, make-out sessions with near strangers, parties, a writing group called Queer Players, meaningful conversations about queer books—*Stone Butch Blues, The Well of Loneliness, Rubyfruit Jungle,* lesbian pulp fiction—and being kicked out of our homes or leaving them too soon because we felt unsafe or knew we'd never be accepted.

Walking down University Avenue at that time, flanked by my new queer posse, I felt desirable—if not attractive—for the first time ever. In queer culture, a woman thought undesirable and unappealing in a heteronormative context is rendered sexy and good-looking in a queer one. What's pretty and ugly is truly contextual. The range of ways a woman might be read as attractive in queer culture—a subtle swagger (Roberta Colindrez), a deep voice (Jodie Foster or Linda Perry), strong arms (Nicola Adams), a flat chest (Katherine Moennig), a distinguished set of wrinkles (Jane Lynch), or a gnarly-footed "tomboy" like me—gives every iteration of odd girl a chance to feel the thrilling heat of another's gaze. Throughout my teen years, I neutered myself in boxy androgynous clothing—polyester slacks, maroon wing tips, and oversize collared button-downs—to hide myself from unwanted male attention, but as soon as I came out, a new version of me emerged in which I wanted my femininity to be visible—and desired. I started wearing amply heeled open-toed shoes, fitted sweaters and tight jeans, a light and natural-looking palette of makeup and long hair. I enjoyed getting attention from women, but the few trysts I had offered only moderate excitement, and I couldn't stop obsessing over my high school crush, Chelsea, who came out to me as straight our senior year, and nor could I stop living in the longing of an ongoing childhood infatuation with an actor, Jodie Foster, who became the focal point of all my teen lusts from seventh grade through the end of high school. I even had a binder of articles about her that went back to the 1970s; my mom would drop me off at the downtown library in San Diego while she played golf, and I'd spend hours poring over old magazines and newspaper articles, dissecting her every phrase and thought. I had spent so many years—from nine to nineteen—in a state of longing that I didn't know how to—nor did I want to—return the feelings of women I could actually have. Intimacy necessitated a level of bodily visibility that made me feel overexposed and uncomfortable. The thrill of subverting norms as an act of resistance, celebrating the uncelebrated, failed to provide me the wherewithal to confront my face, my body, my fragile humanness in naked communion with another woman. Fantasies provided safety—but also prevented me from living life materially.

A few years later, when I entered the University of California, Berkeley, I continued living theoretically, as opposed to actually, but made a few inroads in learning to take pleasure in my "radical ugliness." I was encouraged by queer faculty and texts written by everyone from Judith Butler to Eve Kosofsky Sedgwick to Michel Foucault to delight in being the queer disruption, the odd girl, the ugly girl, the pervert, the freak. I took a class taught by the brilliant nineteenth-century French and British scholar Sharon Marcus called "Odd Women and Queer Men in Victorian Fiction" that feted freaks: I learned about lesbian diarist Anne Lister, an early-nineteenth-century businesswoman, world traveler, and defier of gender and sexual norms who lived openly in romantic relationship with other women, even detailing sexual adventures she undertook with various love interests in her private journals. I read *Salomé* by English dandy Oscar Wilde, who once wrote, "Disobedience, in the eyes of anyone who has read history, is man's original virtue. It is through disobedience that progress has been made, through disobedience and through rebellion." I also learned about his chilling two-year imprisonment for "gross indecency" in a highly publicized 1895 trial, sparked by his intimate relationship with Lord Alfred Douglas. Our professor helped us unearth the queer subtexts in Charlotte Brontë's deliciously subversive *Villette* as we rallied for protagonist Lucy Snowe, who challenged the orthodoxies of her day in nineteenth-century England and continental Europe with her intense self-reliance and gender trespasses, epitomized by her theatrical turn as a male character courting a female love interest in a school play. Described as having "no attractive accomplishments—no beauty," she expresses a disinclination toward marriage, describing her suitor's three-year absence as "the three happiest years of my life." In combination with lessons learned in a course taught by the incomparable medievalist Carolyn Dinshaw, who helped establish the LGBT studies minor at U.C. Berkeley, I was able to apply various theoretical tools to deconstruct the social creation and negative positioning of the dazzling array of oddballs in Marcus's class. I was introduced to a socially constructivist understanding of the world through my rudimentary readings of Judith Butler's take on gender performativity—i.e., what masquerades as natural is just a series of repetitive acts that calcify over time so as to seem inevitable and true—and Foucault's *The History of Sexuality,* which elaborated and illuminated the ways that discourses of power (medical, political, cultural) shape our sexual self-understanding, our mores, even our personal desires and kinks. I learned that all the things I formally took for granted—my gender, my sexuality, my race, or values I'd never fully questioned like monogamy or capitalism, or even beauty—

were socially constructed to support the reigning power structures of any given time and place. If everything was all just made up, I reasoned, then it was foolish to mindlessly try to conform to norms, and I could start to imagine a world reconceived for the betterment of people relegated to the peripheries.

When you're old enough to read this missive, I hope, by sharing a little of this intellectual history with you, I might help free you from the shackling notions of beauty that will inevitably try to assert dominion over your self-worth and life choices.

Social constructionism was formalized in academic discourse by sociologists Peter L. Berger and Thomas Luckmann in *The Social Construction of Reality* (1966), but the essence of its insight—that our beliefs, values, and social institutions are human inventions, rather than eternal truths—existed long before. I encountered the more developed forms of this theory through thinkers like Butler and Foucault at Berkeley, but its groundwork had already been laid—not in the twentieth century, but as far back as the Renaissance. In the late sixteenth century, French philosopher Michel de Montaigne began to unravel certitudes. "There is more ado to interpreting interpretations than to interpret things," he observed, suggesting that what we take for knowledge is a web of subjective readings we mistake for truth. A century later, in *The New Science,* Italian philosopher and historian Giambattista Vico put forth the idea that human knowledge, especially of history, law, and culture, is shaped by the customs, languages, and institutions of particular societies—marking an early recognition that meaning and truth are not timeless givens but are historically constructed through human invention and action. In the nineteenth century, German philosopher Friedrich Nietzsche took it further, famously declaring that there are no facts, "only interpretations." He challenged the very notion of essential truths, writing in *Thus Spoke Zarathustra* that each of us may find our own path—but as for the right path, "it does not exist." Around the same time, Swiss linguist Ferdinand de Saussure argued that "the linguistic sign is arbitrary." In his understanding, the connection between words (signifiers) and the concepts they represent (signified) are not natural or necessary. This foundational insight laid the groundwork for later theoretical movements, especially structuralism and post-structuralism, which questioned the stability of meaning and highlighted how it is shaped by dynamic and shifting linguistic systems. By the twentieth century, French sociologist Émile Durkheim contended that there is nothing inherently criminal or immoral; society makes it so. And finally, we arrive at French philosopher Jacques Derrida, who argued in *Of Grammatology* that meaning is always unstable, contradictory, and contingent on what it excludes.

I highlight these revolutionary ideas from this pantheon of great minds for your future self, when you're old enough to grapple with theory and start the project of disentangling from the cultural imperatives you might experience as universal truths you must heed—that your hair must look just so; that your body must be trim or well sculpted ("Look, Ma, look at my muscles from parkour"); that your outfits must attract the admiration (or envy) of others; that you must be likable and liked at all times. These are the hallmark concerns of the role society has prescribed for you as a girl, and unless I can help you cultivate an inner resistance and defiance, they will be with you through every season of your life, weighing you down, taking your attention off more meaningful and fulfilling endeavors, making you feel small no matter how big you are.

Little by little, when this new queer ethos took root within me, I started to see myself—the disorder of me, the crooked frame around my unusual colors and shapes—within this outsider history. I began to recognize myself as a critical component of the whole, essential to every other part, vital *because* of my unexpected twists and turns, my radical counterpoints to normality and beauty.

In this welcoming space, I began to cultivate all sorts of weird quirks in active defiance of social norms, including wearing flip-flops year-round to intentionally expose my ugly feet and going by a made-up name, Fairyington, which I officially changed in an Alameda County courthouse in 1999.

My self-created name was an attempt at reinvention and a feminist acknowledgment of how our surnames carry the legacy of patriarchal lineage and colonial power. By taking up an epithet usually hurled at gay men—"Fairy!"—and breaking a spelling rule in not dropping the *y* to add *ing,* I intended to show the mutability of language, believing that if language can change, then ideas can change, and if ideas can change, then we, like fairies, can transform the world in the form of fairness. It was also a way to re-signify myself as "pretty" by calling myself "fair." I wanted to insert myself into unreachable echelons—signified by the august ring of 'ington'—to claim space where I was neither wanted nor seen.

As my conservative parents feared, my time at U.C. Berkeley radicalized me. I went in a cohesive subject and came out a dismantled one. But I found strength, even power, in my state of disassembly and in living and thinking against norms. It was like a deep diaphragmatic breath locked in my lungs was finally released. I could be myself, whatever I wanted that to mean on any given day or in any given moment. I could even cultivate "ugly" like some girls cultivate "pretty," or fuse the two in some startling and unexpected way, or transcend both . . .

Like rocker poet Patti Smith, who once said, "I felt alien my whole life" but leaned into it rather than hide or try to disown it, even when some listeners thought her "weird" and were so unsettled by her androgyny, her unusual vocals, and her pointed disregard for feminine theatrics that they attacked her—revealing their misogyny, or rather the misogyny that lives in all of us—with lines that would wither any other woman: "She couldn't sing worth shit, she dressed like a man and she was as ugly as fuck." An American original like none other, she's never let the naysayers confuse or stymie her vision or direct the ways she chose to self-invent. During an interview in Stockholm in 1976, for example, she told a journalist: "I'm not hung up on anybody's idea of how I should be. I'm outside of society. I'm an artist, and rock 'n' roll is my art." Showing that beauty ideals can expand—or subvert conventions—to include people who formally fail to fit, *Vogue,* the fashion bible for a more than a century, would celebrate her "mold-breaking good looks" in 2017, with her long stringy—witchy, some would say—gray hair, slender frame, gender-clear style, and distinct way of being and moving through the world. As she once told *Harper's Bazaar* about the challenges of being a woman musician in a male-dominated and sexist industry: "I was aware that being a female in some ways was a detriment, but for me it wasn't so much that I was a female; it was the fact that I was such a weird one, and I didn't really fit in, even in, sometimes, the female world, and that's why I always used to say that I was beyond gender. . . . But I didn't let anybody intimidate me. I just realized that some things still needed work. We needed to make breakthroughs, and for me, the way to break through is just to follow your vision, and if it costs you a bit of fame and fortune, so be it." Honoring her own creative direction served her well; her first album, *Horses,* a challenging collection of tracks, is considered one of the most important rock albums of all time.

Despite what I sometimes perceive as your worrisome subservience to the status quo around what it means to be a girl, I also see a defiant iteration of self forming at the edges of you, like when you grabbed a pair of thigh-high boots designed for your witchy, gray-and-green-skinned Shadow High dolls, outlandishly done up, and told me that if you had a pair, you'd wear them with a miniskirt so everyone could see the full length of their fabulousness. At first I stayed silent because I wasn't sure what to say, but I couldn't restrain my dated 1970s-era feminism, reminding you that your clothes megaphone a message to the world about who you are, for which you will be judged, so you ought to be thoughtful and intentional about your choices. You tried to trump me by saying, "I don't care what people think. I'd wear them because *I* like them," which is the kind of refrain I often hear from younger generations of feminists, the ones who might be inclined to boast tight half shirts with *SLUT* scrawled across the chest or ass-grazing skirts in the name of sex positivity and personal autonomy. As much as I understand that the meaning we intend is never fixed or certain but full of unpredictability—moving, turning, crashing in ways wholly unexpected—I remain unconvinced that these expressions of self are "decisions" untethered from the desire to please and command the male gaze in ways that compromise one's dignity and self-respect. Still, I liked the proto-defiance in your hubristic display of confidence, the bit about eschewing public opinion in favor of your own. It brought to mind Patti Smith's creative ethos—as well as disgraced, then redeemed, televangelist singer Tammy Faye Messner, former wife of scandalous minister Jim Bakker.

After the duo's TV ministry, the Praise the Lord Club, came crashing down with the revelation that Bakker had paid Jessica Hahn, a church secretary, nearly $279,000 to keep their sexual encounter secret—she later alleged that he sexually assaulted her—and defrauded his followers out of $158 million, Messner became a beloved gay icon for her ability to commune with drag queens one day and rabid conservative Baptists the next—a skill worthy of respect in an age marked by declining civility and mutual understanding between people of differing views—and for her AIDS activism. She wore makeup so loud and garish that she was often the punch line of jokes. On *The Tonight Show* in

1988, Johnny Carson cracked, "Tammy Faye Bakker had taken her makeup off, and people thought it was Ernest Borgnine." Even Messner herself made quips about her lavish look, telling Larry King: "Honey, I am going to my grave with my eyelashes and makeup on." Despite being well aware of the comedy made of her face, she kept her mascara, eyeshadow, rouge, and lipstick on full display because, as she told a caller on King's show, "I like it so much," adding this self-deprecating rejoinder: "If you knew what was under here, you would be so glad I was wearing it." Raised by Pentecostal preachers in the Midwest, makeup was a sin, but she didn't let that stop her once she experienced the magic of mascara's power to amplify her beautiful blue eyes: "God didn't strike me dead, so I didn't believe in that after that," she told Larry King when he asked if she wore makeup in high school. While her love affair with cosmetics wasn't without the dark underbelly of self-loathing—"I think I feel ugly without it. I think that's it. I feel ugly without it. I don't like looking at my own self in the mirror without it," she said during comedian Roseanne Barr's relentless interrogation of her "extreme" makeup—she also affirmed, "I do it for me. I don't do it for you." When Barr said: "People criticize you about your makeup all the time. How mad does that make you?" Messner said, "You know, it's gotten to where I just laugh at 'em. . . . I think everyone deserves to be who they want to be, who they are. I think everyone needs to be able to wear the face they're comfortable with," she gently, but firmly, pushed back.

It may seem odd—or off—to cast Messner as an admirable iteration of womanhood in a missive urging you to see the deleterious effects of blindly following imperatives to fashion yourself—cut yourself—into a paragon of some unachievable cliché of beauty. After all, she ignored a year of colonic bleeding because she was too embarrassed to see a male doctor and eventually died of colon cancer. But she also articulated herself exactly as she wanted to, bucking the conventions of cosmeticization with no regard for the cheap seats' sneers and jeers, offering a soft-landing "fuck you" to the mocking gaze of Barr and legions like her, which *is* admirable. She obviously wasn't just trying to look pretty in the traditional sense; if she were, she'd have conformed to the standards expressed by the chorus of people making fun of her look. She was playing with the form in her own unique way—fabulous in her gaudiness like the drag queens you admire on Commercial Street in Provincetown, Massachusetts, or more like Fauxnique (aka Monique Jenkinson), the first cisgender woman to be crowned Miss Trannyshack in San Francisco, who Michael, your beloved gay uncle, introduced us to after I began expressing concern with what I perceived as your preoccupation with aesthetics. "I understand what you're saying, but on the other hand, not all adornment is a form of self-denigration," he said. And I agree, but it's impossible to parse the tangled threads that compose a woman or a girl's impulse toward beautification: When is it a harmless form of fun and creativity, and when is it self-abnegation or degradation? Maybe it's always a little of both.

While writing this to you, I've encountered several people—some with PhDs and professorships at prestigious colleges—who have subtly indicated to me that the framing of my questions, as well as my concerns, around this topic are somewhat heavy-handed or overthought. "Oh hush, let her be. She'll experiment with lots of things," a distinguished professor at a top-ranking university told me when I shared my fraught history with my own face and my concern that you might be internalizing too many of society's beauty standards. Similarly, a deeply intelligent friend with a PhD and lectureship at a high-ranking college balked when I said I didn't want you wearing crop tops to school, a battle we've had in our household on a few occasions. "Ah, I wore them all the time as a kid," she said. "Well, why doesn't your son wear one?" I asked. She smirked. "Because *he's* meant to be a sexual subject and *she's* meant to be a sexual object," I said before she could answer, feeling the veins in my neck pulsing with fury over the countless men who've leered at—yes, *leered* at—my *eight-year-old* daughter when minimally clothed to defend against the sweltering summer heat in New York City. And *yes:* The problem is not what you—or any other woman or girl at any other place or time—are wearing but how certain men trespass with an inappropriate look, comment, or touch. But the larger question for me has always been: Why don't we question these cultural constructs of what constitutes "sexy" or "cute" as if they reflect women's natural preferences rather than broader social—patriarchal—conditioning? I'm all for sexual empowerment and freedom of choice—to the extent that anything *is* a choice—in all aspects of life, but we don't live in a theoretical world as much as those in the ivory tower would like us to believe; we live in a flesh-and-blood reality that is ugly and cruel with a set of rules that are unfair and weighted in men's favor, and it's my job to protect you from the indignities and vulnerabilities inherent in this unjust equation—or at least to help you work it to your benefit. And while it's puzzling to me that the critical implications of the beauty imperative's impact on women's and girls' well-being has at times been underappreciated—and, in some instances, even trivialized—I know that it's no small thing when I look at these startling statistics: 40 percent of school-age girls, from ages five to nine, want to be thinner; 34 percent of five-year-old girls occasionally and deliberately restrict what they eat; 50 percent of adolescent girls are dissatisfied with their bodies; 15 percent of women in one study "met the criteria for a lifetime eating disorder" by midlife, and a death from the condition occurs every fifty-two minutes, with women accounting for the majority of those deaths.

I'm not sure if it was a soft protest of my strident views on the topic, but a few days later, the crop top advocate showed up for another playdate while donning one herself. But she's not the only one with an ample IQ and feminist bent to swat down my concern over what feels like an early push to prematurely self-sexualize ("Can I buy a training bra?" you'll ask, or "Do you think my period will start soon?") or cosmeticize ("Can I wear a little lipstick, Ma?" "What about a little blush?"). At dinner with a queer feminist friend one evening, I took umbrage with Sabrina and her friend creating a tradition of taking you to get your nails done: "Why are we encouraging her self-objectification so early?" I asked aloud, to which my friend defensively countered: "You don't *hate women*, do you, *Steph*?" as if getting one's nails done were some quintessential expression of *womanness* or *girlness*—like the crop top. Her point was that nail polish is something women and girls care about, so it's misogynistic to disparage it. I didn't want to sound like an unhinged has-been from a feminist commune in the 1970s, so I dropped it, but what I wanted to say was: *The more important question is: Why do women and girls care about nail polish? Why have we, as a society, cultivated that desire in them? And why am I being dismissed and gently chided for questioning the very forces that trivialize—and oversexualize—women and girls?* But I already knew the answer to that . . .

This ongoing—unstoppable—cycle of attempting to morph our bodies and faces into whatever the culture deems beautiful is inextricably linked to maintaining our desirability to men, a form of cachet even many lesbians are loathe to forsake. No one wants to put their appeal—and the possibilities for sexual and romantic partnership that it promises—at risk. Unless men are socialized to desire women very differently—perhaps through widespread, authentic representations of women and femininity—our "beauty sick" culture will continue to damage girls' and women's self-esteem. This fuels troubling phenomena like "Sephora girls" (tweens as young as *eight* seeking expensive skincare products), unwarranted dieting, and disordered eating:

In a 1999 study of 1,932 boys and girls (ages twelve to sixteen), 52 percent of girls and 25 percent of boys considered themselves overweight, contrary to having a normal body mass index. A decade and a half later, more research found that between 2013 and 2016, 37.6 percent of adolescents (ages sixteen to nineteen) were dieting the previous year, with nearly half being girls (45.2 percent) and less than a third being boys (30.1 percent). Some of these young dieters will go on to have an eating disorder at some point in their lives (approximately 20 million women versus 10 million men in the United States); others will undergo costly cosmetic procedures (22.6 million women versus only 1.6 million men) to try to achieve other unrealizable ideals.

The superficial and fluffy iterations of feminism that came out of my teen years and young adulthood in the 1990s reinforced, ironically, these self-destructive impulses but tried to package it all as progress and self-affirmation. "Bubblegum feminism," or "cute feminism," as it's variously been called, commodified and defanged the more radical work of the feminist punk scene and particularly Riot Grrrl bands like Bikini Kill and Bratmobile, with their DIY clothes, anti-corporate zines, and makeup that looked like an aggressive attack on prettiness, a kind of cultivated ugliness. The mainstream quickly co-opted and perverted their more unruly and disruptive politic with forms of enslavement masquerading as empowerment (i.e., Britney Spears, the Spice Girls, etc.), a subservient kiss-off to the patriarchy in bright red lipstick, a tight-fitting miniskirt (in the name of "sex positivity"), a crop top with *Cunt* or *Bitch* scrolled across it and a "girl power" fist pump. Their ineffectual forms of reclamation and "rebellion" overtook the more radical Riot Grrrl template that helped undermine male supremacy and traditional edicts about how women and girls should look and be.

As much as one may like to say that nail polish is *just* nail polish—it doesn't have a gender, as Bad Bunny might say—it *isn't.* No matter how many cool men—Bad Bunny himself, Lil Nas X, Harry Styles, and the hip, artsy Brooklyn boys you come across on the playground—paint their nails in a rainbow of hues, culturally it's still understood as the provenance of women, which is what makes male usage subversive. The intellectual theatrics and disruptions of the academy or whimsical forms of play coming out of Hollywood haven't fully, not even close, changed the reality on the ground in the larger culture, and so, at this moment in time . . .

It's not *just* nail polish.

It's not *just* jewelry.

It's not *just* lipstick or foundation or mascara.

It's not *just* a pair of high heels.

It's not *just* a diet.

It's not *just* Botox.

It's not *just* plastic surgery.

It's *not* trivial.

It's grave: They want to reduce you to an assembly line of cosmeticized parts, to a stack of bones, fragile and small; to limit your food to such an extreme you can't think of anything substantive; to care more about the pretty color and shape of your lips than what you want or have to say; to feel that the sum of you, the weight of you, adds up to how pleasing you are to other people, especially men. And here's what's *really* grave: Your objectification escalates into dehumanization—you're no longer an entity unto yourself, but something made for man, subject to his will, his mercy—and this is inextricably linked to the disrespect, harassment, and violence endured by women across the globe, as argued by feminist research and analyses going back to the '70s.

Even when you perform your proud theater of self-affirmation and sass, like when you, at seven, took to the runway in our living room—our distressed wooden coffee table bench—belting out self-satisfied lines about being "a certified classic" with "diva appeal" from the L.O.L. Surprise! album on wobbly footing, it looks like a form of hubris underpinned by uncertainty.

And what, exactly, is the L.O.L. Surprise! doll crew—plastic *baby* figurines dressed as *high-class escorts*—affirming? Their looks? Their ability to successfully operate as society has programmed them to with their ample makeup, accessories, and styles?

Your performance is so amped up and exaggerated, I wonder if you're mimicking the drag queens in Provincetown. Once, at age four, you unzipped your sparkly jacket as you walked down the street in their direction, letting it fall to the pavement like a scene from *RuPaul's Drag Race,* gliding past so they could admire your sequined dress. "Work it, girl! That's right. Cover girl! Show us what you got!" they sang out, enthusiasm you received in kind, telling them what you loved about each of their jewel-encrusted gowns.

What you don't yet understand is that it's not subversive when you do it; it's submission.

L.O.L. dolls—and the oversexualized and controversial Bratz from the early aughts—were born at billionaire Isaac Larian's behemoth toy company MGA Entertainment, which makes it impossible to see their over-the-top displays as the delightful queer camp you admire in the queens of Ptown.

"The master's tools will never dismantle the master's house," as the radical feminist writer Audre Lorde famously put it. And you can't own—rather than be owned by—the lines someone else has written for you. While women, too, can show the artifice and insubstantiality of the role and gender society has prescribed to them by mocking it with the excess flourishes, silliness, and fun that Susan Sontag lauds in "Notes on 'Camp'"—there is an *imperative* for cisgender women to be aesthetically pleasing, which is where the fun ends.

When you were six, you teared up, for no obvious reason,

and then grew sullen right after watching *Descendants,* a movie about the children of Disney's most iconic villains and heroines. Why? Did you find something in the actresses' faces that you didn't find in your own? You seemed dissatisfied with yourself suddenly. Maybe you were too young at six, too literal in your interpretations, to understand that you—a small girl—are not meant to look like those performers who are stylized to an otherworldly degree. "It's just pretend. No one is expected to look like that," we assured you, but that is a lie, and you knew it. The impossible *is* the beauty standard that every woman is expected to strive toward, a futile effort that keeps us in an eternal state of self-dissatisfaction, upholding entire industries.

In the United States alone, American women—and men—spend hundreds of billions of dollars trying to improve, adjust, hide, obscure, correct, and perfect their aesthetic condition through weight reduction ($90 billion in 2023); beauty, cosmetics, and fragrance ($67.5 billion in 2024); apparel ($304 billion in 2024); cosmetic procedures ($11.8 billion in 2022); and gym, health, fitness clubs ($44.8 billion in 2024).

We're all climbing a mountain that has no peak, no end in sight, no place to sit atop in satisfaction.

"It's really a great tactic of capitalism—to create ideals that are unattainable and then create publications that compel people to strive, never-endingly, for that ideal and blame themselves for not attaining it," Robin M. Mathy, an LGBTQ researcher and activist, said with a sardonic chuckle when I wondered aloud if body dysmorphia isn't a natural by-product of being a woman in our culture.

Defined in the fifth edition of the *Diagnostic and Statistical Manual of Mental Disorders,* or the *DSM-5,* the bible of the mental healthcare profession, body dysmorphia is a "preoccupation with one or more perceived defects or flaws in physical appearance that are not observable or appear slight to others." The irony of defining obsessive bodily dissatisfaction as a mental disorder is that it is so common, so pervasive, so inextricably linked to what it means to be a girl and a woman—a defining quality, in fact—that to call it a psychopathology is to classify womanhood itself as a disorder of the mind. When I consider how the *DSM-5* begins to elaborate its definition of mental illness—"a behavioral or psychological pattern" that causes "significant distress or disability" in an individual—it doesn't seem far-fetched to argue that it is: Aren't the demands of femininity—especially as they pertain to the beauty ideal—a destructive pattern of thought that breeds both harmful behaviors and psychological distress? Like when a girl feels too ugly for love, as in Janis Ian's haunting song "At Seventeen"; or when a teenager refuses to leave the house because she's run out of foundation to even out her blemished skin, convinced that her perceived imperfections will eclipse her beauty, her likability, her value; or when she forgoes attending a party or social event because she thinks she can't find a single flattering outfit given her current physique, which she experiences as a series of dissatisfying parts—thighs that kiss, a belly deemed too big, a butt thought too laden with cellulite. Citing a 2003 University of Sussex study, Engeln explains in *Beauty Sick* that women tend to see themselves in parts that, more often than not, disappoint them, while men "experience their bodies as one unit, not as a series of pull-apart components that need to be altered or fixed." (More tellingly and consequentially, men, in the study, were more focused on what their bodies can *do,* while women were more consumed with how their bodies *appear.*) She also points out that around 90 percent of young women can easily identify a body part that displeases them. Can't one argue, then, that the Western conception of "woman"—as a fragmentary set of parts brooded over with frequent dissatisfaction amid the persistent hope of crafting herself into a desirable whole for men's pleasure—is a kind of illness of the mind? ("Woman" as "part," rather than "whole," has roots that extend back to the Book of Genesis, in which Eve is created from Adam's rib for *his* gratification, rendering her, literally and symbolically, incomplete—an entity insufficient on her own, a mere bone trying to find its missing parts.)

And yet there's no way out of it. Our subjectivity depends on a "discourse we never chose but that, paradoxically, initiates and sustains our agency," Judith Butler writes in *The Psychic Life of Power.* These cultural ideals are the sutures that hold your intelligibility in place, which leaves you with only two options—you can be played *by* these imperatives or you can *play*—mock, resist, have fun with—them . . . like Fauxnique: Her lipstick bleeds boldly past the outline of her lips while her thick black eyeliner and eyelashes flare out impossibly high, surrounded by a saturation of hues on her eyelids, and the bright pink blush on her cheeks spills up into unusual places, like her forehead. By announcing herself as the fake, the imitation, in her rendition of femininity (as reinvented by drag queens), Fauxnique calls into question the whole production of gender, bringing the theater of it all to an operatic climax.

Discussing the wonders of Fauxnique seemed too complex for your eight-year-old brain to grasp, especially since you don't yet wear makeup. When I showed you a picture of her, in fact, you thought she was a drag queen in the traditional sense. Instead, Sabrina and I wanted to find a way to take the focus off the way your body *looks* and help you see all that it can *do,* so we enrolled you in a parkour class with a friend. While you loved—and triumphed in—their obstacle courses, climbing up and sliding down cushy plastic red walls, working your way up ropes or across wooden rings descending from the sky, even bringing your Spidey skills to scaling up and down structures like the doorframes and windowsills in our apartment, you marveled—as you should—at your hard-won calluses and growing muscles. "Look how strong I am," you said, flexing in the shower, asking me to show you my biceps as a point of comparison. "Dang, bro," you yelped like a teen, because I did inherit my mom's ample biceps. It quickly descended into yet another way to self-objectify and compare yourself. Post-shower, while slathering on your Mustela body lotion, you beamed at another comparison: "Ma, a friend told me she wishes she had skin as smooth and hairless as mine." While your beautiful skin may inspire the envy, and sometimes even the disdain, of others, appearances are always in flux. Maybe you'll get a smattering of pimples when you enter puberty; and you'll surely get wrinkles as you age. That's the trouble with constantly weighing yourself against others. If you're on the upswing of the comparison, you feel affirmed and fabulous, but if you're on the downswing, you feel like crap. It puts your self-worth on a seesaw, continually oscillating between highs and lows. I imparted this lesson head-on, maybe a little too indelicately, and it riled you one afternoon when you came home from school upset over a low score on a math test.

"*Everyone* got an A but me. *Everyone* understands it but me," you said. A few wet ones rolled down your plump cheeks while you lay on your bed with your feet kicked up against the wall.

"You're not everyone. You're you—the one and only. Stop comparing yourself to others," I said unhelpfully. "You'll get it in your own time, and I doubt *everyone* got an A."

You insisted that they did. I could only remind you that it's senseless comparing yourself to others because there will always be someone smarter and someone dumber, someone richer and someone poorer, someone cooler or someone dorkier, and someone prettier and someone uglier than you. Despite the seeming futility of my efforts at the time, I tried to encourage you to compete against yourself, not other people, to enjoy your strengths and work on your weaknesses.

Before our culture of comparison became a sick epidemic of

sorts in the Selfie Generation, where girls can bask in the spotlight of their self-designed digital stages, perhaps only celebrities experienced the psychological duress of chronic comparison—and no one more than the world-renowned diva Barbra Streisand.

Streisand reached superstardom in 1968 with her jaw-dropping vocals and theatrical flair in the movie *Funny Girl,* winning her critical acclaim and an Oscar. *Funny Girl* takes inspiration from the real-life story of early-twentieth-century comedian Fanny Brice, whose history uncannily resembles Streisand's own. Like Brice, Streisand is Jewish and grew up in New York City—Streisand in Brooklyn, Brice on the Lower East Side—and dreamed of becoming a performer but was told repeatedly that she wasn't pretty enough, a message that Streisand received early and in the cruelest way: She once recalled that her stepfather told her when she was six or seven that she couldn't have an ice cream because she was "too ugly." As reported on *60 Minutes* by Mike Wallace, her own mother told her she was "odd, skinny and not pretty enough to be a movie star" and that she should, instead, take up typing. But she persisted, telling Wallace that she knew as young as seven that she would be a star—despite the many who didn't believe in her. But throughout her career, Streisand, like Brice, was measured against the more traditional representations of beauty of her time—blond-haired and blue-eyed beauties like Julie Andrews and Joanne Woodward—and criticized for falling short. The running commentary on her looks included directives to "cut your nose off, cut your nails off, cap your teeth . . . change your name, change your face," she confessed to Barbara Walters in 1993, but she resisted: "The truth is that there are things that are right for me. They may not be right for you or anyone else, but I go by my instincts." That goes for her now-iconic nose, too—with its classic mid-ridge bump, not unlike the one Sabrina shaved off, regretfully. "Why would I take off my bump? It makes me look more unique," Streisand told Gayle King in 2023 on *CBS*

News Sunday Morning. And it's true: I've gotten countless Hollywood actresses confused because their beauty is remarkably unremarkable in the ways it predictably follows a similar set of criteria, but who could ever confuse Barbra Streisand for anyone else? When her record label photoshopped the bump off her nose on the cover of her album, thinking it would please her, she demanded they put it back. Her nose, after all, may have been the source of her incomparable vocals: "Who knew what it [rhinoplasty] might do to my voice? Once a doctor told me I had a deviated septum . . . maybe that's why I sound the way I do," she wrote in her memoir. I couldn't stop thinking about how a condition the medical establishment considers problematic may, in fact, have given her the gift of song.

The potential impact of her genetic "error" reminded me of a powerful anecdote I heard in a documentary about the '80s pop duo Wham! Their megahit, "Wake Me Up Before You Go-Go," a high-energy dance song you discovered in third grade through the wide-ranging tastes of your school's dynamic music director, was inspired by a mistake. George Michael, the lead singer of the group, was staying at a friend's place, and the friend scrawled a sloppy message for Michael that was meant to read *Wake me up before you go,* but instead read *Wake me up before you go go,* which Michael heard like music because of that extra *go,* an error.

I want that idea to bloom in your head like weeds of surprising beauty—the idea that deviations from norms can lead you to unexpected opportunities and gains. I wanted you to marvel, as I do, at the ways flaws, mistakes, failures, and misalignments (like deviated septa and erroneously rendered scrawl) can bring such beauty—or alternatively, engrossing ugliness, thrilling originality, or even weird forms of dissonance and confusion, worthy all the same—into the world, an idea powerfully fleshed out in cultural critic Jack Halberstam's *The Queer Art of Failure.*

Offering his own meditation on queer negativity—a reaction

against humanism and its anodyne notions of progress, as well as the domestication and normalization of LGBTQ culture and politics—Halberstam makes an impassioned case for foundering, challenging the positivity of the "try, try again" ethos, and creating space for the darker or more fraught emotions that attend messing up or defeat:

> What kinds of reward can failure offer us? Perhaps most obviously, failure allows us to escape the punishing norms that discipline behavior and manage human development with the goal of delivering us from unruly childhoods to orderly and predictable adulthoods. Failure preserves some of the wondrous anarchy of childhood and disturbs the supposedly clean boundaries between adults and children, winners and losers. And while failure certainly comes accompanied by a host of negative affects such as disappointment, disillusionment, and despair, it also provides the opportunity to use these negative affects to poke holes in the toxic positivity of contemporary life.

Freedom from positivity seems like an especially important form of liberation for women and girls: We are groomed to be in a suspended state of artificial cheer to please and comfort others and are even heckled by random strangers (men, *always* men) when we let our false agreeability relax into a more appropriate scowl (appropriate given the psychological pressures and indignities bred by our gendered existence)—"Smile, sweetheart, it can't be that bad," I've been commanded by men on the street. There's a perfectionism built into the construction of "woman" and "girl" that is dying to shed her gendered embellishments, both aesthetic and behavioral, to fully let herself go.

How light and buoyant might you feel if you allowed yourself to fail and wallow in the deliciousness of total surrender—to keep those knots in your hair, those stinky beat-up sneakers on your feet, those oily whiteheads on your chin, those bitten and blunted fingernails on your unwashed hands, to stare down gendered constraints with your best Billy Idol sneer.

Go punk and make a delightful mess of things, like Poly Styrene (aka Marianne Joan Elliott-Said) of X-Ray Spex.

"Some people think little girls should be seen and not heard, but I think, 'Oh bondage, up yours!'" Poly yells in her raw, intentionally unpolished vocals at the beginning of her iconic track from 1977. Formally trained as an opera singer at Wigmore Hall in London, according to music critic Lucy O'Brien, Poly strategically "subverted her voice and used it as a weapon almost" to rail against the ways that society enslaves people of color—Poly was biracial with a Scottish-Irish mother and a Somali-born father—women, and consumers. She pointedly mocks our collective submission to the status quo. Despite its harm, we uphold and submit to it.

Eschewing traditional beauty standards, she even stood apart from the punk clichés of dress (bondage pants with straps, zippers, or chains; shredded band T-shirts held together with safety pins; black leather jackets decorated with band logos, statement patches, and studs; Dr. Martens or tattered old Chuck Taylors), telling the United Kingdom's *Penny Black Music:* "I wanted to be different. I didn't want to copy them." Despite the DIY nature of the punk aesthetic, its adherents, like normal-aspiring girls and boys across our country and the globe, could just as passionately and unthinkingly ape one another to fit into the *unorthodox* order of things, but not Poly. She went for whimsy and fun, even optimism and joy, a decided departure from the angry nihilism reflected in their dark, anarchic rotation of garbs. She wore chunky metal braces, puffy fluorescent DayGlo sweaters and shirts, berets and Brodie military helmets and smiled brightly through intermittent scowls with affirming lyrics that grappled with the societal issues of her time—and ours—environmentalism, excess consumerism, sexism, racism, all while believing in the possibility of our collective liberation through higher consciousness. She rejected the pretty iterations of female punks with their miniskirts and fishnet stockings in favor of eschewing sexiness, telling *The Quietus* that she'd shave her head—which she eventually did—if anyone ever tried to turn her into a sex symbol. "I did cover myself up a lot with my clothes. I had a very quirky style, but I wanted to be respected for my music, my lyrics specifically," she said, taking umbrage with the fact that men's looks are always secondary to their music and questioning, in a *Flux* interview, the hypersexualization of women as a form of feminist liberation: "There are a lot more girls in bikinis looking sexy in videos. I don't think that's gender equality myself."

While "Oh Bondage Up Yours!" is seen as a feminist anthem, she explained in the documentary *Poly Styrene: I Am a Cliché*, which was codirected by her daughter, Celeste Bell, that it is more broadly about all forms of bondage, especially consumerism. She got the idea for the song while looking at a pair of Vivienne Westwood bondage pants—and landed on the idea that we are purchasing our oppression. On "Germfree Adolescents," she takes further aim at the ways our individuality—the traces of our human touch and stink, the smudges left by our bodily existence—are wiped out by capitalism and materialism, by taking a swipe at "deodorant," mouthwash, "disinfectant," and other forms of "antiseptics" that "scrub away" and sterilize our humanness and individuality.

I played the song for you, but your ears were too attuned to the overly produced, smooth vocals of Taylor Swift, Olivia Rodrigo, Harry Styles, and your latest obsession, Marc Anthony—"Alexa, play 'Vivir Mi Vida' by Marc Anthony, please!"—to withstand the cultivated harshness (purposive "bad" singing) to endure its full three minutes and sixteen seconds. I introduced you to the track to expose you to a female artist completely indifferent to creating conventionally pretty sounds, but it didn't have the impact I'd hoped. "This is *horrible!*" you railed. "Mama Sabby, do *you* like this song?" you asked in disbelief, desperate for confirmation that this was a terrible assault on the ears.

"She is *intentionally* singing in an off-centered way. It's a rejection of norms," I said.

"And it's *horrible,*" you said, asking if we could switch to the *Mamma Mia!* soundtrack.

"It's an acquired taste," I said.

"It's a *bad* taste," you replied.

Even if I thought you'd be receptive to the ways the song confronts and rejects our materialistic impulses, I knew your religious devotion to all things *mall* would hinder your ability to appreciate Styrene's subversions. The night before, Sabrina's longtime friend, a talented poet who started a nonprofit dedicated to preserving Coney Island's rich literary history, and another of your beloved aunties, asked for a one-line bio about you for a poem you'd written. She planned to showcase your words on a banner advertising a forthcoming event produced by her organization. With simple matter-of-factness you promptly replied that you'd like it to reference your love of parkour and shopping. Sabrina felt that would register as odd or vapid given it would be emblazoned on a poster advertising a high-brow cultural affair. She asked that you think of a replacement for shopping, explaining that it would be preferable to say something more meaningful or substantial about who you are—like how much you love graphic novels, speaking Spanish, drawing profiles, and climbing trees. When you quickly echoed—*submitted*—to what we thought you ought to say—"Fine, say I love parkour, climbing, and hanging out with friends," you responded—we realized "shopping" is just as much a facet of who you are.

After I cleared the table, I went to your bedroom and found

you lying on your bed, quietly looking up at the ceiling. I apologized and told you that we didn't mean to make you feel bad about your retail joys. I explained that I'd always hated shopping until I experienced it with you—and it's true.

When we make our way through various department stores, you grab outfits and shoes and necklaces with such zeal and gusto, inventing bold new looks on the spot, that I experience the fun and excitement of it all vicariously. Your enthusiasm for fashion has even inspired me to think about how I can better express myself sartorially, but my self-consciousness sets in as soon as we enter Macy's or Nordstrom. Suddenly I am a kid again, awkwardly walking through excessively perfumed department stores amid the unsettling sound of hanger heads sliding across metal clothing racks: I'm anxiously scanning my surroundings to ensure none of my peers, especially girls, see me clumsily—a bad actor delivering lines, unbelievably—partaking in their girlish fun. My mom, perceiving my discomfort, inevitably asks in her brusque way, "Who's looking? Nobody's looking," but in my angsty teenage mind, an army of eyeballs are clocking me at every corner. Even though I love sneakers and leather boots and cool jackets and oversize watches and could certainly find an outfit that better represents me than my usual slummy array of over-worn jeans, threadbare tees, and scraped-up high-tops, there's still something so vulnerable—and overexposing—about attempting to enhance my aesthetics with new getups, not just for the attention new items bring, but because there's this all-pervasive sense that they won't adequately address the fundamental ugliness of my person. I fear my inability to throw my shoulders back and confidently take my space like women who nudge and push their way through sample sales in Manhattan is discernible to my fellow shoppers. Can they see it—my shame?

It will surprise you to know this aversion to shopping is not just a quirk of mine. I've heard many women complain about shopping, even famous ones like Jodie Foster, who once told Andy Warhol in 1976, "You'd have to kill me to go shopping," and confessed to *The Rake* that beyond buying basics, she'd rather stab her own eyes than look for clothes. In 2020, a poll by True&Co. found these surprising statistics: 50 percent of women "experience anxiety while shopping"; 40 percent admit they "absolutely hate" it; 13 percent have cried in a fitting room; 61 percent fail to find outfits appropriately sized; 20 percent have felt harshly appraised for their purchases; and 43 percent abandoned the undertaking altogether and fled the store. "Shopping is a narcissistic pleasure for some young women, but for many others it generates serious emotional anguish because of its symbolic complexities and the insecurities it stirs up about the body and its parts. . . . At the end of the twentieth century, fear of fat, anxiety about body parts, and expectations of perfection in the dressing room have all coalesced to make 'I hate my body' into a powerful mantra that informs the social and spiritual life of too many American girls," writes Joan Jacobs Brumberg, a social historian and distinguished professor emerita at Cornell, in her groundbreaking book *The Body Project: An Intimate History of American Girls.* Malls are, after all, the dreaded intersection—and disconnection—between the societal dictates surrounding ideals of beauty and femininity and the real-life women who fall short, whether due to gender dysphoria and/or a desire for items in the men's section that don't properly fit (like me), a body shape that defies available options, or the disapproving glances of passersby as you check yourself out in a new set of threads. It can feel a lot like you're hobbling down a runway before Anna Wintour's unimpressed eyes.

Ironically, the night we asked you to omit "shopping" from your bio and I contemplated my disinclination toward mall-going, you summarized the latest chapter you'd read in *The War That Saved My Life* by Kimberly Brubaker Bradley, which hit on similar themes. Set in World War II, the novel follows the life story of a club-footed ten-year-old girl named Ada who's been both emotionally and physically abused by her birth mother but who eventually finds her way into a loving adoptive family. In the pages you'd read, her new mom had bought her a beautiful dress, but she doesn't want to wear it. "She doesn't feel worthy of being pretty and doesn't want that kind of attention," you said. That was a totally novel idea to you because as soon as you discovered the joys of articulating yourself through style—and experienced the social validation that comes with a pretty face attached to a cute outfit and accessories—you became progressively intent on a fashionable wardrobe.

But a compliment directed at a girl's or woman's looks is a tricky thing. It masquerades as an innocuous expression of admiration but has two faces—one smooth and one rough, one pretty and one ugly. Built into such praise is the insult you've successfully evaded and the precept that your value hinges on your ability to measure up to the beauty ideal; when you succeed at pretty, you will be admired and you feel affirmed; when you don't—and the compliment is denied or the diminishing remark delivered—you will feel terrible. The dual nature of the aesthetic compliment is perfectly captured in One Direction's harmlessly harmful song, "What Makes You Beautiful." (As a thought experiment, I urge you to imagine that it's written from the perspective of a woman to a man. If that is difficult because it seems implausible, ask yourself why.) Whenever I hear you singing the lyrics, I wish you were old enough so I could explain its false tribute. On the surface reading, the track seems like a sweet ode to a beloved, but a more complicated interpretation lies beneath. Harry Styles tells his love interest that she shouldn't be insecure because her good looks compel desiring double takes everywhere she goes, which implies that if she *weren't* turning heads, then her self-doubt *would be* warranted. He even encourages her to forgo cosmetics because she is "enough" just as she is, but the subtext implies that she should "cover up" if he didn't find her adequate.

See the snub in the compliment?

The problem with putting too much stock in what other people think—especially as it pertains to your aesthetic condition—is that your looks are always changing, and so are trends. Playing to the gaze and praise of others becomes a kind of balancing act—one you must undertake ever so carefully, funneling all your focus and energy into maintaining your beauty so you don't fall into the unflattering underworld of bland invisibility or outright ugliness.

I say all this thick with hypocrisy. As someone who has lived in that netherworld of aesthetic disparagement, I take quiet pride in your normality—your femininity, your beauty, your crushes on boys. (How much of that do you feel? How much does it reinforce and inform how you behave?) When I walk down the street with you and see admiring smiles, like the flashes on paparazzi cameras, flickering at you with reflexive approval, I think, *I may be a failed woman, but just look at my beautiful—and exceedingly normal—daughter.* In this weird—and perverse—way I feel suffused with your charms, just as I did when my mom would visit my elementary school classroom for all my peers to bear witness to the beautiful woman who made me, proving that I, too, derive from beauty. "I'm not sure how, but Sabrina and I have managed to raise the straightest, girliest girl in human history," I'll joke with feigned disappointment on my face to friends and strangers alike. Your beauty and orientation toward style and glamorizing seem to overshadow the ways in which I don't measure up—as if you're a kind of corrective to, or shield covering, my own failed femininity and uneasy lesbianism. Holding your hand, as we amble down the busy streets, I get to experience the pleasure of the attention bestowed upon you from passersby, attentions I've never received.

On three separate occasions in my adolescence, I was told I was ugly, point-blank.

At a middle school in San Diego in 1987, where I'd just moved from Los Angeles for sixth grade, I faked interest in a cute boy, Jake, to mask my same-sex desires. A straight-A student with dirty blond hair, expertly gelled, he wore a preppy wardrobe of boat shoes and polo shirts and beige chino shorts. I confided my pseudo crush to Jake's best friend, Gabe, but the "feelings" weren't mutual. On the phone after school one night, I asked Gabe if Jake was interested, and he bluntly replied: "No because you're ugly, he said." In the background, I heard Gabe's parents scold him for saying something so cruel, but all I could muster was submission: "Okay," I replied and hung up.

My "feelings," a performance, were less hurt than relieved by Jake's lack of interest, but hearing someone use that word to describe me—taking it out of the private realm of my mind—was a new kind of painful. It now felt concretely true, and the problem is, you can't hide your face, you can only endure it. It was the one shameful thing I could not conceal, unlike my sexuality.

While it solidified my ugly self-concept, it also provided a weird kind of relief to know, unequivocally, that my self-understanding was accurate—that I wasn't measuring up so I could stop trying. It was liberating in the same way it is for women of a certain age who say they relish their seniority for the invisibility it bestows upon them, the freedom it offers from the overwhelming pressures of their younger years to be and look a certain way. I, too, felt I could finally opt out, that I could find an uncommon peace outside the status quo.

Two years later, another boy's harsh assessment passed through me cold, like a hard fact. I had only been "going steady" with a quirky kid who had spiky brown hair and a freckled face and played Christian rock music on his electric guitar for a few months when he pointedly said during an argument: "You don't know how hard it is to date you when my friends keep telling me how ugly you are." Silence followed. I numbly accepted this unfair verdict.

It wasn't until I got to high school in 1990 that I really began to understand something more pervasive and systemic about the power dynamics between the sexes that was larger than my personal experience: that boys and men expect women to be well groomed and cosmeticized for their viewing pleasure and that women who don't comply (obey)—or reek of sexual disinterest in them, as I did—will be met with contempt.

Despite my gender-bending garbs—drab and oversized—with the intention to avoid sexual visibility, I nonetheless got caught in the line of vision of a fellow freshman, who taunted me at our bus stop for a series of weeks for no apparent reason other than because, he said, I was ugly.

I've seen that same sneering attitude toward me and other women in countless settings since then: walking down the street, standing on a packed bus, disembarking from a train, riding in a cab along a busy Manhattan avenue—and all over popular culture, where even someone like no-great-shakes Homer, the father on *The Simpsons,* a satirical show about the quirks and idiocies of American society, can say to Marge's twin sisters, "Go ugly up someone else's house, you penis-curling she-devils!" (His snide remark points to women's main societal function—to raise a dick.) In another episode that we watched together, "Lisa the Beauty Queen," Lisa confesses to Homer: "I'm ugly, dad." Homer affirms her beauty but also affirms that her quintessential purpose *is* to be beautiful by entering her into a beauty pageant in the hope that it will improve her self-esteem. He could have, instead, reminded her of her incredible mind or her musical aptitude—she plays the sax—or her good ethics, but when you're a female, that matters less than being perceived as pretty. In another scene, Marge offers to take her to a salon: "I'll take you to the beauty parlor and show you how lovely you can be," as if she's not lovely as she is. When they pull into the driveway after their makeovers, Homer urges Bart to gush over their new looks, which they both do by saying Lisa and Marge are unrecognizable, a poignant observation: Women must not look like themselves, must not *be* themselves, if they want to fulfill their obligation to the male gaze. In the same episode, Homer asks foul bar owner Moe Szyslak and beer buddy Barney Gumble if they've ever felt unattractive, and they respond with knee-jerk certainty, "No," which is an astute commentary on society's successful cultivation of self-love in men (even when they're utterly abhorrent) and self-loathing (and self-doubt) in women. The end result is someone like you—intent on crafting a pleasing aesthetic for all to admire—and someone like me—calcified in shame for my inability to do so—and other "weird" girls like musician Janis Ian, who memorably captured the experience of being on the sidelines of pretty in her heartrending song "At Seventeen," which she released in 1975. Ian, who came out in 1993 as a lesbian, hauntingly croons about an unattractive and misfit girl who nurses amorous crushes and fantasies at home on Friday nights, while her prettier peers ("beauty queens" with "clear-skinned smiles") enjoy Valentines and lovers and dances and dates.

My appreciation of your beauty and normality is not just that I've often felt illuminated by it like a sliver of moonlight coming into a room at midnight or that I take pleasure in the ways you make a mockery of the societal angst about parental queerness begetting queerness in children. It's that your attractiveness, inextricably linked to your successful femininity, spares you the hostilities I've endured for falling short and from knowing the pathos in Ian's "ugly girl" ballad, although you already apprehend—with surprising nuance for someone so young—the unfair psychological burdens and disadvantages of your sex:

"The boys at school roast each other all the time, but girls don't. But if a girl does it to a boy, the boys think it's so funny," you once told us at dinner.

"Yeah? What kinds of things do they say?" I asked.

"Dumb things. They just make fun of each other."

"Why do you think girls don't roast each other?"

"I think they're too sensitive, and they don't want to look bad in front of people or be made fun of."

"But boys don't care about that?"

"No, they care about how they look, too. They want muscles."

"Sure, but do you think John looks at himself in the mirror before he leaves the house in the morning?"

"God no! He still cleans his nose with his shirt collar. One day we told him to look in the mirror because his hair looked crazy, and he did and then said, 'What? I look fine.'"

"What do you think about that? That boys get to be gross and inappropriate and sloppy and silly and have their hair running, unruly, in all directions and they *still* get to look in the mirror and like who they see, while girls risk feeling bad about themselves or being disliked if they look and behave in *exactly* the same way?"

"It's not fair. I get why some girls want to 'transgender' into a boy," you said, a troubled formulation I didn't correct because I understood your point perfectly.

Chapter 8

Clean

Honestly, I, too, bristled at Poly Styrene's "Germfree Adolescents," but for different reasons. As someone who's consumed by cleanliness—yours and mine and everyone else's—and averse to the bodily musks, visible disorder and filth, as well as the health risks baked into the funk factor, I felt punched by the literal reading of the lyrics. I've always, defensively, joked about the patchouli-scented, incense-fumed, pothead hipsters and hippies—those who proudly showcase their greasy hair and B.O.-stained vintage getups—walking down Bedford Avenue in Williamsburg or through the Haight in San Francisco, eschewing regular bathing as a form of subversion or some twisted notion of cool-kid carefreeness. And yet I've longed for that kind of liberation, the freedom to forgo washing my hands or to skip a shower for a few days, to sit with delicious self-contentment in my own stink.

But it feels too much like anarchy to me, like the moon has disappeared from the sky and the earth is spinning out of control, like I am on the verge of inexorably slipping off into a frightening unknown.

—

The year I turned ten and entered puberty, my body truly became a stranger to me, and the thin illusion of my boyhood began to tear.

Fleshy hills of tissue continued to grow on my chest while waves of wiry hair sprang out in surprising places, and then—blood.

"You are a woman now!" my mom exclaimed, as I hobbled over to her with my pants down in alarmed disgust. She said it like it was a personal achievement, only I heard it as a put-down. She took me to the store to get pads and bought me a gift—I forget what—to celebrate my arrival into womanhood.

Those five words—*you are a woman now*—irreparably cracked my self-image. That liberating stage of development when little girls can easily pass for little boys and little boys can easily pass for little girls was over. I now had to face what I was, only I couldn't.

So I tried to scrub my body away.

In the shower, I'd lather up so much, the surface of my skin looked like a bubble bath. I'd suds up twice—before I shampooed and conditioned my hair, and then after. Whenever my mother forced me to skip a shower because we'd be late for something or because she didn't deem me sufficiently dirty, it felt intolerable to sit in my uncleaned skin. It was as if I were trying to wash my unwanted female body away, along with its deviant desires—to scour off the ugly like Sabella Nitti did in 1924.

Nitti, the first woman in Chicago sentenced to death by hanging for allegedly murdering her husband in 1923, despite scant evidence, was an Italian immigrant and a poor farmer who spoke little English. A brawny, masculine-looking woman, she spent most of her days toiling under the hot sun for long hours, building up dirt and grime in her nail beds and deep wrinkles in her face from sun damage. A lack of running water in her home made bathing regularly an impossibility, leaving her hair greasy and clothing stained, as she sat in front of a judge, a jury, and a group of journalists, including one who called her "a cruel, dirty, repulsive woman."

More frequently than not, women accused of murder in the Windy City were ultimately set free—either acquitted or had charges dropped—because it was unthinkable that the so-called finer sex was capable of such violence, or they persuaded the jury that they murdered in self-defense; the central difference between those who were exonerated and Nitti was their femininity and attractiveness—cleanliness being a core feature of beauty. When she got a retrial, her lawyers presented her with a well-scrubbed look: a nicely coiffed hairdo, layers of makeup, and fresh clean clothes. It worked; she was set free in 1924.

—

When you were an infant and *Yia Yia* came to visit, she insisted I didn't need to bathe you every night. "She's just a baby. She doesn't sweat or stink. She's not crawling all over the floors yet," she said, rationally, but I couldn't stop myself—you were my baby, and I would keep you nice and clean. "You're washing the skin right off her!" she laughed from the doorway of our kitchen as I immersed your body in Johnson & Johnson bubbles in the sink. Irrationally I thought, *I will wash the world off your body—I will protect you from the ugliness of filth.*

When I hover over you in the bathroom to ensure you are using a sufficient amount of hand soap and warm water to wash off the germs and various bits of school-life debris when you return home to our small, well-tended apartment, I know I'm ensuring therapy bills you will be paying long into adulthood.

The ways in which my twisted orientation toward cleanliness impacts you stared me down with cold eyes—and sobered me up momentarily—during a family vacation to the Jersey Shore when you were four. Your uncle Jamie and aunt Joanne rented a palatial house with dazzling views of the Atlantic Ocean. On the roof deck that allowed us to take in the most stunning sunsets, I remember the swirl of soft oranges, fading reds, and vibrant yellows from one beautiful August evening. With large glasses of pinot grigio and chardonnay all around, we listened to the waves crash and the seagulls *keow,* swapping stories and memories, while you and your cousins Mari and Emmy laughed and tumbled and shrieked with the unbridled joy of your uncomplicated love for one another. But all I could think about was the countdown till bedtime and the need to expunge the muck of ocean swims, sunscreen, and sand-filled hair from your body. Finally, I urged you to the bathroom. "But my cousins aren't taking a bath," you reasoned, resisting my attempts to scoop your tiny body into my arms. I could have let it go; a sane person would have. What's a day or two without showering when you're a kid? I looked over at Aunt Joanne, effortlessly beautiful in her chic clothes and chill vibe, and wished desperately that I could be as relaxed and carefree as she. She seems to come in and out of each moment of her life like a gentle breeze, all ease and composure. Instead, I fought your resistance amid an epic meltdown of tears and flailing arms. I heard Grandma Elizabeth say with concern and a pinch of reasonable scorn, "She doesn't need to take a bath. This is terrible." I felt everybody's alarmed eyes on me, daggers of judgment. I barely got you through that very short-lived bath. Slowly, sanity crept into my madness, and I was finally able to see past my anxiety, to see you, my beautiful little girl, crying. I suddenly felt like Faye Dunaway's character in her 1971 movie *Mommie Dearest*, throwing wire hangers on the floor in a frightening fit. It truly *was* terrible. Afterward, we all went back up to the deck to look at the last streaks of sunset, but I felt heavy with guilt and shame. I held you and kissed you and tried to undo what I'd just done, but I'd crushed the lighthearted spirit of the moment. Then someone, probably Grandma, suggested we take a family photo. In it, I'm holding you, but your body language is communicating to me that I am no refuge. That photo hangs on Grandma Elizabeth's wall, a constant rebuke every time I look at it.

I've learned to better manage my cleanliness compulsion since then, but still, sometimes it takes everything in me to stop myself from reaching for 90-proof alcohol to douse the tips of your dirt-lined fingertips.

In those moments, I try to remind myself: The dirt signifies that you aren't tepid or afraid of digging into this messy life. When the funk and disorganization in our apartment begins to overtake me, I try to remember that the odd stain, crack, or dent in our home represents fond memories we've created together, signs of life, of the people I love—that this existence, unlike the body of my youth, is not one I want to clean away.

—

In my gender-dissonant youth, in order to create further distance between my body and my inner sense of self, I started peeing and showering in the dark. My genitals were so incongruous with my self-perception then that looking down at them felt like a smack in the face each time.

I wanted to deny my female body—confine her to the dark, never see her again. She made me feel so much shame and self-alienation, I couldn't even bear that she produced waste.

I'd turn the bathroom sink on full blast, cut the lights, grope my way toward the toilet, pull down my pants, and sit on the open seat, hoping to mask the aural sounds of piss and shit. Sometimes the visual and auditory masking wasn't sufficient to obscure the offenses of the body I lived in, so I'd shut my eyes tight and put my hands over my ears, as if I were on a roller coaster careening off the tracks, and start babbling dribs and drabs of content from my fantasies aloud to pretend none of this was happening.

Even now, it's hard to place myself—was I boy then or just a boyish girl under the misguided belief that I'd have to morph into a boy in order to express my most tender longings and affections for girls? Did my identification with boys extend from the privileges they enjoy and the greater societal affection they receive or from the idea that I could better endear myself to my many crushes if I inhabited a male physique? Or did my facial dysmorphia, my aesthetic inadequacy, make me want to flee from the body I had since I knew I could never fulfill the expectations prescribed to it by that troubled and troubling category, "woman"?

Via Zoom, I put some of these questions to Susan Stryker, the world-renowned—and dazzlingly brilliant—trans activist and U.C. Berkeley–trained historian who wrote *Transgender History: The Roots of Today's Revolution.* Sitting amid floor-to-ceiling shelves overrun with books in her home office one early evening, I wondered aloud if there was a spectrum of transness, quietly thinking I may have resided there in my formative days, but she nixed the notion. " 'Spectrum' gives you degrees of deviance from an unstated norm," she explained. Instead, she argued, there is a "constellation" or "different configurations" of transness, whereby an individual may not feel wholly aligned with the sex they were assigned at birth as far as breasts go, so they may undergo top surgery and opt for *he/him* pronouns, or they may feel more like themselves with more facial hair and muscle mass, so they take testosterone shots and hit the gym regularly. As much as I've wanted to place my story, myself, into a discrete, tidy category or trajectory of experience, to bring clarity and understanding to who and what I was, to explain away my idiosyncrasies and deviations and diversions in the comfort of a unifying and cohesive set of identities—lesbian, queer, tomboy, writer, mother, *trans-ish*—I know that I live in a knotted cluster of incomplete and opaque truths on a quest as elusive and never-ending as Ahab's search for his white whale. We all do. I'm aware, above all, that fixed notions of self, however politically efficacious and expedient they are in helping us rally for our civil liberties, cannot contain the sum of us, that we spill out—sometimes intentionally, sometimes not—into spaces others occupy, undoing our self-understanding in the process.

Robin M. Mathy, a scholar and trans rights activist, conducts a thought experiment with her students that demonstrates the instability of our conceptions of sex: "I'll ask a student, 'What sex are you?' And they may say, 'I'm a woman,' for example. And I'll ask, 'How do you know?' And they might say, 'Because I have ovaries or breasts,' And I'll ask, 'So if you had to remove your ovaries and your breasts,' would you still be a woman?' Any kind of definition you try to give, even down to hormones, even down to chromosomes, falls apart. We do not walk up to people and determine gender by examining their chromosomes or their primary characteristics. We go off how they appear against our idea, our own mental self-image, of how someone of that gender should appear. So it's part judgment and part cognitive schema that we develop when we're very young," originating in our formative attempts to assimilate or accommodate gender norms. As Princeton English Professor Diana Fuss argues in *Essentially Speaking,* even things we take to be indisputable facts—like nature or our bodies—are always understood, and even produced discursively, through cultural meaning. That's why it's misleading to treat "sex" (i.e., male and female) as a fixed biological reality untouched by language.

During the course of our conversation, Stryker, too, challenged the facile and flimsy border between who legitimately embodies transness and who does not in her analysis of the more transphobic manifestations of feminism. Contemplating the vitriol of TERFs (trans-exclusionary radical feminists) and trans-averse lesbian separatists, she mused, "I read some of that stuff and I think, 'Oh, you are just really gender dysphoric,' and that doesn't [necessarily] mean they're not women; it means that they're just really unhappy about the state of 'woman' or of being a woman in the world. They find it profoundly disempowering. So much of the political impetus behind those versions of feminism is to redefine what it means to be a woman in a way that addresses those feelings of dysphoria. The thinking goes like this: 'I am not holding myself to *your* standards of what a woman is. We're creating a new women's community of women loving women. We're finding our own way, making our own world.' There's something that's very powerfully healing and transformative about that, but it's rooted in this need to overcome a profound sense of unhappiness about being nonconsensually *girled* and *womaned* because of a body they never picked."

Her analysis resonated with me. I've spent countless hours watching female-to-male videos depicting the process of transitioning, feeling envious of trans men who've made seamless transitions with cut physiques, nicely groomed facial hair, and testosterone-sculpted bone structures. Before I knew better, I espoused hostile—ignorant—views, burning with envy, about trans men: that they were misogynists who hated women so much, they rejected their female bodies, or that they were so homophobic, they sought to transform their bodies so as to appear straight—and enjoy male privilege—vis-à-vis female love interests. That understanding of trans men better describes *me,* however, and I continue to have a fraught relationship with my "*womaned* body" to use Stryker's phrase, an identity that was not of my choosing.

The more intense version of dysphoria I experienced as a child did not persist past age twelve. The fundamental distinction between me and trans men is that through some confluence of psychological transmutations—invisible gymnastics, the alchemy of which I am utterly unaware—I started to adapt, however dissonantly, to my femaleness, my "*womaned* body," but the memory of that battle I quietly fought for years stays with me. Sometimes it's a large shadow, sometimes a barely visible one, but it's there, a lingering feeling of disquiet.

That's why I panicked when I saw you kill the lights in the bathroom before racing onto the toilet seat. You were five. You'd just decided you no longer wanted to wear dresses or skirts—and eliminated all the color from your wardrobe—in favor of dark leggings, printed T-shirts, overalls, and jeans. You triumphantly reported being misgendered and would occasionally say in your imaginary play, "I'm a boy, okay, Mom? I'm a boy."

Were you trying to be like us, your "tomboy" moms? Or was this your first act of feminism? Were you just experimenting? Or were you depressed?

It was less than a year into the pandemic. We saw the light in your eyes, once so bright it could illuminate a baseball stadium, go faint. A self-consciousness set in. You seemed to grow into an angsty teen overnight, no longer the small kindergartener that you were supposed to be.

Your teacher called to let us know you were exhibiting signs of anxiety, putting your hands in your mouth and picking your skin. We bought you fidgets—spinners, stress balls, and squeezable figurines—popular toys in the age of Covid that gave your hands something to do.

The thought that you might be trans—that you might not hold your body in tender estimation, that you might want to hide from it or shroud it out of existence—felt unendurable. I knew I couldn't possibly carry that for you.

"Turn the lights on!" I barked.

"I like the lights off," you countered.

"It's not good for your eyes," I replied, aggressively flicking them back on.

Was fantasy your refuge, too—that place around the bend, where everything was okay?

Maybe your drab clothes, once so vibrant with patterns and colors splashed across an assortment of dresses and skirts, simply reflected the sad and tragic state of our world during the height of the Covid crisis: social isolation from family and friends, ejection from in-person school, economic instability, a preoccupation with avoiding germs, and the ever-present fear that we, and our loved ones, could die at any moment, especially with Sabrina employed as a social worker at our community hospital, where bodies in refrigerated trucks piled up by the hundreds.

During that time, the sirens of ambulances were constant, and Sunset Park, the lovely oasis steps from our apartment, was completely empty on beautiful days. It was eerie, a feeling like none other. Depression started its subtle creep, a cruel colonizer, into every region of my mind. It started like a whisper of self-doubt, a cold uncertainty, then became a slight feeling of sadness that grew with each passing day into an abyss of existential dread, a spreading sensation of meaninglessness that I felt palpably. As soon as the sun set—that time of day that feels like a memory sweet with nostalgia—I'd start to panic at the thought of tossing and turning through another sleepless night. Like a lonely orphan in a mysterious aunt's decaying Victorian that creaks and howls and feels eternally drafty, casting large shadows, angry ghosts, on the bedroom's walls and ceilings, scarier threats than embodied ones for the limitless ways in which they continually reconfigure themselves, I felt irrationally scared all the time. In that merciless arctic, I started to sense that the melancholia I felt then was a primordial sadness, one that formed with the bedrock of my being in my dis-eased youth, when my body felt like a stranger's house, inhospitable and cold, as I struggled to align—in gender, sexuality, and aesthetics—with the world's expectations.

Chapter 9

A Theoretical Life

In my childhood, I couldn't adapt to my materiality or clean away the ugly, so I learned to live in a rich fantasy life that often felt more true than reality. Sometimes fantasies say as much about us as our lived realities. Perhaps they say *more* because they are the blueprints of our longings, the worlds, the bodies, the ideals we wished we existed in rather than the lusterless ones in which we do. They are home to the unrequited loves we pine for in perfectly imagined scenarios but fail to inspire in actuality, settling, instead, for a thinner—dingier—sliver of the megawatt romances in our minds.

When you were nine, I asked you if you have fantasies and how they function in your life. "My life *is* a fantasy, so I don't have to fantasize," you said. "I think people fantasize a lot when things are bad in their life or they don't have something they want," you added, obliquely referencing a friend who'd been going through a hard time.

I agreed. That was especially true in my case, and for older generations of queer people, when it was unsafe to express or act on our same-sex affections. For many of us, fantasy, like a nurturing home in which your shortcomings never compromise your lovability in the eyes of your beloveds, was the only place we could be fully human, fully alive. Fortunately queer kids today are supported by greater societal awareness and acceptance and can easily—and furtively, if need be—access LGBTQ communities and romantic prospects across a variety of online platforms. Even while, at the moment I write this, the Supreme Court is shaking the foundation upholding all our hard-won progress, eight in ten Americans support laws that protect LGBTQ citizens, creating an atmosphere in which queer kids feel freer (depending on their families and communities, of course) to express themselves.

I summarized our social advancement after we'd read *The Stonewall Riots: Making a Stand for LGBTQ Rights,* but you noticed the potholes on the road to progress—that it's nonlinear, that it's dependent on place, culture, and community and cyclical in nature: "My friend from camp told me she has a crush on me, but I told her I don't like girls like that," you revealed, refusing to identify which friend. You added that she's now dating one of your mutual pals, but your shared friend won't hold hands with her in public or tell her best friend and family they're a couple. "So it's still not easy," you said.

Some people in the queer community, including scholars, take umbrage at the notion of LGBTQ progress, challenging us to see it as a shallow aspiration, a downward descent, a narrowing delineation of the borders between who is and is not included, who is and is not represented, who is and is not valued in our assimilationist politic. Rather than try to coerce people into the prevailing order (say, via marriage or military service), these thinkers espouse the view that marginalized communities would be better served trying to change or overthrow the existing power structures. Rather than seek validation from the dominant culture, which tends to accept more mainstream LGBTQ people (i.e., gender conforming, monogamist, well resourced, and formally educated) and ensure the disenfranchisement of *others* (gender deviants, polyamorists, anti-materialists, working class), they want to build systems that benefit the many rather than the few. They see a false equivalency between "acceptance" and "liberation."

While I'm all for keeping the vitality of queerness—in all its freaky permutations—alive and staying in that queer realm of infinite possibilities, concealing and stifling my romantic longings for so many years was quietly devastating. Being in the closet felt like enduring the daily duress of cruel parents, for whom you constantly self-censor and hide to avoid shame and punishment. It makes you a stranger to yourself, a kind of liar, someone willing to surrender one's truth or adapt to others' expectations for the illusion of acceptance and love.

In fifth grade, I tried to will away my queer lusts by deliberately cultivating a "crush" on Jesus, thinking—hoping—that if He flooded my thoughts the way girls did back then, I'd gain a foothold in heterosexuality. But all it did was create more inner strife and self-alienation. I would imagine Him from the images I'd seen at the Greek Orthodox Church we'd patronize on high holidays or the Baptist Church I'd go to on the various weekends my brother and I would sleep at our Argentine grandparents' house in North Hollywood. I'd conjure the image I'd seen innumerable times on crucifixions or stained glass windows: long dark hair parted in the middle like a hippie's, soft brown eyes, slightly parted lips surrounded by a well-manicured goatee, a kind face illuminated in a circle of celestial light. I'd ponder his face and pray hard for a hetero transformation . . . until my will faltered halfway through. Then I'd change the tape to my first infatuation, Wendy, a fourth-grade girl with a terrible bowl haircut, gentle brown eyes, and an easy laugh. I'd engage in a wide range of idiotic behaviors, ones I loathed in my peers, to elicit her full-body laughter—a chaste orgasm—humiliating myself in the way only hormones can. My desire for her showed me to myself in a way I never wanted to see. I was unmistakably, unquestionably gay, a rigid six on the Kinsey scale, and I needed to quickly learn how to contain my emotional excitement and revelatory goofiness around girls I desired.

But whatever those years took from me, they gave me things, too. They made me sensitive to social injustice, minorities, and misfits. They also gave me a vibrant imagination, where I've lived thousands of lives unknown to anyone but me: I've lived lives with surprising plot twists and turns through the old cobbled streets of Boston or Paris or London, down into the stacks of impressive library collections, where I've pored over first folios of Shakespeare's sonnets, trying to prove, queerly, that the Dark Lady *is* the Fair Youth defiled through the act of sodomy. I've walked across the campuses of the world's finest and oldest universities to hear queer talks on, say, how Mary Shelley's *Frankenstein* is a parable for the dangers of solitary pleasures, as articulated in eighteenth-century anti-masturbation tracks. I've spent meandering afternoons in the world's finest art museums, returning in the evening to a bohemian-chic apartment overlooking a storied city. I've discovered new plants in the Amazonian rainforest while living with a Brazilian botanist in a wooden straw hut. I've gone to Cape Town en route to the Knysna forests to study trees, where I fell in love with a local zoologist. All in my mind, a place reality has never matched, until Sabrina . . . until you.

Pop artist Andy Warhol, who also felt unattractive, once said: "Fantasy love is much better than reality love. Never doing it is very exciting. The most exciting attractions are between two opposites that never meet." I lived for so long in that suspended state of yearning, I had convinced myself that Warholian axiom was true. But I'd trade every unreturned affection of my lifetime for the privilege of loving—and being loved by—Sabrina. She seemed to eclipse all other loves, real or imagined, large or small. Only after falling irreparably in love did I realize how hollow and empty fantasy had been, a refuge, but a cold one, a lover too shadowy to grasp. Nonetheless, my inner life helped me endure my underspent youth, starting as early as elementary school: I had a small closet in my bedroom that, ironically—*or appropriately*—I'd sit in to will my deepest longings into being on the well-lit, opulently decorated stage of my mind: I was always a handsome boy with an inborn gentleness and understated cool, inspiring the affections of girls and the envy of boys—scaling a tall tree to save a whimpering kitten or standing up to a bully on behalf of a defenseless person.

At some point in my twenties, I was on a quest to find cultural representations of what an unlived life might look like—to give legitimacy to it—in literature or film, wondering all the while if mine counted as a life at all.

Some years ago, I learned about a sociological concept called "symbolic annihilation" from Gayle E. Pitman, a psychologist and LGBTQ children's book author, while reporting a story on the thirtieth anniversary of *Heather Has Two Mommies* by Lesléa Newman. Pitman, whose book about a joyful pride parade, *This Day in June,* has been challenged, banned, and burned in the United States, explained that symbolic annihilation is the phenomenon whereby a person suffers a kind of waking death if they can't see themselves—their communities, their stories—in the representational world. I know the fallout of cultural expungement firsthand; it's like looking in a mirror but not seeing your face. If you can't see yourself, are you there? You *feel* your existence—arms, legs, heartbeat, breath—but you're not sure you really exist. Whether you're a person of color, a person with disabilities, or a member of the LGBTQ community, that kind of cultural erasure doesn't just create a sense of loneliness and disconnection from other people; it can also foster feelings of self-loathing and shame.

That's why we wanted to be sure you saw all your identities—your queer family, your Ecuadorian roots, your Jewish heritage—reflected in the symbolic world we carefully curated for you in an array of thoughtfully chosen books and toys. We over-stacked your shelves with stories that affirmed our kind of family and read you picture books about prominent Jewish people like Ruth Bader Ginsburg, Anne Frank, and Albert Einstein, and we purchased brown Barbies, O.M.G.s, and American Girls to match your phenotype, including your especially prized Ecuadorian doll dressed in traditional attire complete with bright colors and geometric patterns.

One night, when you were four, you were lying against my chest in your twin bed as I read you *Heather Has Two Mommies*. A friend had gifted it to me as a joke to mock my homonormativity, but it turned out to be an important, and self-affirming, addition to your library. When I got to the part that read, "Heather also has two mommies," you looked up at me, wide-eyed, and said, "And *I* have two mommies!" The next year, you discovered your passion and aptitude for Spanish in your school's dual-language program, and your curiosity about your Ecuadorian roots took stronger hold. You learned about the early and ongoing struggles of Latino immigrants navigating life in America and about the discrimination that people of color, especially African Americans, face in a land built on their exploitation and enslavement. You felt a prideful kinship with these marginalized narratives, often muddling Latino and African American histories, trying to insert your story into theirs, reaching for children's books about the Civil Rights Movement or Martin Luther King Jr. and Rosa

Parks, poring over, again and again, two books a friend gave you—*Emma* and *The Emancipation of Grandpa Sandy Wills*—written by Spectrum News NY1 anchor Cheryl Wills about the challenges of tracing her African American history in this country.

As a substitute teacher, I've been overcome when walking into fifth-grade classrooms where kids are lying on the floor making LGBTQ equality signs or when watching pop cultural content with queer themes. I know I would have felt differently about myself—less alone, less stalked by a sense of inner ugliness—had positive representations like these existed when I was a child.

I wasn't just looking for—and not finding—the queer identity I embodied; I was looking for—and couldn't find—the everyday reality born of embodying a queer life, one that had to exist furtively, quietly, carefully so as not to be seen or found out. That kind of life becomes, by default, by necessity, a fantastical one, but I wanted to see, representationally, the play-by-play of an interior life that couldn't exist outside one's own mind. I wondered what it would look like in literature, the non-doing of one's being, when I came across Kazuo Ishiguro's *The Remains of the Day*. I caught glimpses of myself in Stevens, the butler, whose inability to bring his inner world—his love for the housekeeper, Miss Kenton, and his moral truths—into the outer one, putting duty to the status quo (in the form of his employer, Lord Darlington, a Nazi sympathizer) above duty to himself. It felt queerly relatable, like *The Phantom of the Opera,* the early-twentieth-century serial by French writer Gaston Leroux that Andrew Lloyd Webber, Charles Hart, and Richard Stilgoe immortalized in their 1986 musical—the longest-running show on Broadway from its opening in 1988 to its closure in 2023. When I started to tell you the story, you begged off listening because, you said, "It's too sad," and it is: A congenitally disfigured musical genius wears a mask to avoid public ridicule and shame but longs for connection and love. He grows wilder and angrier with loneliness from isolation after years of confining himself to the underworld of the Palais Garnier opera house, where he wreaks havoc on unsuspecting performers and audience members and becomes known as the Phantom of the Opera. Once confined to a cage and exhibited to the public like a novelty in a circus, he has good reason to distrust people and keeps his distance, tutoring pupils without revealing himself. Eventually, though, he falls in love with his best student, a beautiful soprano named Christine, but she falls in love with her childhood friend Raoul. One day, she pulls the Phantom's mask away to reveal his disfigured—ugly—face, but she kisses it, radically departing from her contemporaries, seeing beauty and goodness where others see ugliness and evil. I've always read it as a metaphor for queerness, "the love that dare not speak its name" (or, in this case, "show its face"). But it could just as easily be seen as a metaphor for anyone who feels so inadequate and undesirable—more often than not, that's girls and women, especially in the era of comparison-driven selfies and social media—they choose to sit it out, stay home, withdraw from public view. The Phantom decides to let Christine and Raoul leave his captivity because he got what he always wanted from her, from the world: recognition of his full humanity, that he is someone worthy of love and kindness.

I related to his desire to confine himself to the basement to avoid confronting his own ugliness or shortcomings reflected in the eyes of onlookers. Until I experienced otherwise, fantasy was a sanctuary, not just as a place to live out impossible scenarios but as a kind of corrective—re-creation—of an unjust world, as studies suggest it can function for marginalized people.

My life of longing wasn't just the result of my closeted queer youth or my incongruent aesthetics. It extended, first, from the divergent yearnings of my parents—my mother's longing for a poor, uneducated, good-looking Lebanese man whom her Greek mother stopped her from marrying, and my father's longing for her. Romantic love in our household was an experience that could only exist in one's mind. It was something, always, out of reach.

In the tumult of her crumbling relationship—her happiness—my mom met my dad at a Greek Orthodox Church in 1969 in San Diego. A deeply spiritual and intellectual man who liked posing and probing big questions, my dad found his way to my mother's church while studying world religions. For him, it was love at first sight—a bring-you-to-your-knees moment of sublime certainty: He was meant to love her, no matter what—no matter her rebuffs or declarations of love for another, or her inability to return his affections. When my mother's entire family turned against her in a united front to compel her to let the Lebanese man go, she succumbed. It's what "good girls" are expected to do—surrender themselves to others, deny themselves, shrink themselves, make themselves small and conciliatory.

She would eventually yield to my father, the safe choice, but safety can carry its own risks.

They married on Valentine's Day in 1971: "The saddest day of my life," she once called her wedding. She walked down the aisle crying like she was at a funeral rather than a happy nuptial. And it was—it is—a kind of death to disavow your truth. There is nothing, perhaps, as self-violating as making a bed with someone you don't desire. The experience of that self-transgression undoubtedly informed my mom's empathy toward the gay experience and ultimately her ability to accept me. But in my early years, I developed an aversion to my own father for being too selfish to let her go, for thinking that her paltry bits of affection were enough, for getting in the way of the real love story—for recognizing too much of myself in him, the undesirable one seeking love where there was none, in unattainable girls as outlandishly out of reach as celebrities.

Before heading to college, I dumped my massive binder of articles about Jodie Foster, whom I'd harbored a decade-long fascination with and fidelity to, in the trash and promised myself I'd start *actually* living. "Dude," my brother said at the time, "This is part of your history. Don't throw it away." But it felt shameful and pathetic that the mere idea of a woman *was* my history, and I, regretfully, didn't heed his advice, even pawning my complete collection of first- and second-series Garbage Pail Kids trading cards, which would be worth a small fortune now. I remember when Sabrina surprised me with a new box so I could relive that joyful part of my youth. You proposed we make our own version. Together we designed a half-mermaid and half-Medusa image with blood gushing out of her severed snake head. With a perverse kind of poetry—an entryway into seeing things against beauty norms—for a stretch of time, you'd often say, "That could be a Garbage Pail Kid" anytime you saw something grotesque.

Starting school at U.C. Berkeley, I wanted to begin my life anew, especially now that I was going to be living in the Bay Area, a short subway ride from the Castro, San Francisco's queer neighborhood, but I couldn't do it. I was too accustomed to fixing my gaze on someone inaccessible, which I did again, this time nursing a long-term crush on a young professor, hoping I could acquire enough knowledge and academic excellence to shape myself into a desirable, albeit unlikely, romantic prospect.

I couldn't seem to resist the pleasure—and control—such longing offered. It allowed my imagination to stage elaborate multiyear fantasies colored by fleeting glances across campus, short interactions in class, unnecessary trips to office hours, and emails with contrived research questions. But the larger truth is that I wasn't ready to be truly vulnerable with someone available to me. I consistently chose women who were straight, coupled, or utterly disinterested. Disinterest, in fact, seemed to stoke the flame higher.

At a certain point, I resigned myself to a life of perpetual longing. I decided an academic career would lend itself well to a monk-like existence, quiet and contemplative, deep within the stacks, where theories and words and ideas abound, a perfect world in which to imagine but not actually live.

Chapter 10

Life After Death

To that end, in 2000, I packed up my things, which mostly consisted of bad clothes, cheap sneakers, and too many books, and shipped them to a shoebox of an apartment in an old Victorian in Inman Square. It sat, in ruinous elegance, within walking distance of Harvard's School of Education, where I was an incoming graduate student. I went by train, which took me across the country from San Diego to Chicago to visit a friend for a week, then on to Boston, where I would live for the next two years.

You love the story of me sneaking into the sleeper section of an Amtrak train to shower but getting "arrested" and guided back to my cheap seat. Too poor for a sleeper car with its luxurious promise of a bed and bathing, I traveled east in coach class, sitting upright and unwashed for forty-eight hours, until I couldn't take my own stink anymore and tried to break into the upper echelons of the railcar, an experience that would mirror the one I would soon have in the world of academic elites: "I knew she weren't no *sleep-ah!*" an attendant snapped loudly for all to hear.

I was gently apprehended and ushered back to my seat, stewing in two days of filth amid greasy wisps of hair.

Almost immediately upon arriving in Boston, old stony New England felt more like home to me than young sunny Southern California. Its storied past with cobblestone streets and colonial-style houses felt strangely familiar, like a city I'd woken up to across a century of lifetimes. The history of the place felt like a palpable presence, a body I could actually see and touch. I heard the whispers of the apparitional Wampanoag peoples mourning the disease and destruction the European colonizers brought to them and their way of life. I saw the shadowy outlines of Pilgrims stepping off the *Mayflower* in the winter of 1620—first to Provincetown (how scandalized would those religious zealots be to learn it's now a gay mecca?) and then to Plymouth.

I could hear the panic and religious hysteria in Salem, where women like Sarah Good, Bridget Bishop, and Martha Carrier were hanged as "witches"—for no greater crime than bucking conventions.

I could even sense the revolutionary fervor that would erupt decades later: the dumping of a British shipment of tea into the Boston Harbor in 1773 to protest taxation without political representation and the shots fired at the British troops in Concord and Lexington two years later, officially beginning the American War of Independence.

I could hear—like a memory in the wind—the political squabbles and marital strife of luminaries like John and Abigail Adams, the impassioned orations of Samuel Adams, John Hancock, and Paul Revere. Even the creative musings of the region's rich literary lineage seemed to stir: Emerson elaborating the core tenets of transcendentalism in Concord; Dickinson imagining death as a polite gentleman in Amherst; Thoreau walking around the dense forest of trees near Walden Pond; and Melville in Pittsfield, composing one of the greatest American novels of all time, *Moby Dick.*

It was a state—a city—of ghosts. And I was a ghost, a phantom, standing in the shadows of a moonlit graveyard full of fabled, sometimes ugly, lives.

For all my enchantment with the city, I felt the exact opposite while walking across the lush lawns of the oldest institution of learning in the country.

Harvard, for me, *represented* the status quo, a stilted or overrun idea of greatness, a sleepy canonical way of thinking with its history of exclusions—socioeconomic, racial, gendered, sexual. Although I know its past is more complicated than my experience or knowledge, Berkeley *represented* the exact opposite—inclusivity, thrilling deviations into new pedagogies and epistemologies, a radical history of undoing and unbecoming, an amorphous mess of broken norms, a place to play and have fun and reimagine what could be. One was the mainstream within which I've always struggled to adapt and thrive; the other was liberation from—or successful resistance to—normality.

I only went to Harvard because I didn't get into Berkeley for graduate school, and I'd planned, misguidedly as it turns out—I didn't have the scholarly chops—to pursue an academic career and thought I needed a prestigious educational pedigree to get into a good PhD program.

In Cambridge, I felt like an imposter, a nerd who'd snuck into a cool-kid house party through a cracked window in a dank basement. The fact that I made it into Berkeley and Harvard, honestly, is a spectacular joke because I nearly failed out of high school with an academic record so bad some junior colleges might have resisted my enrollment. My transcript was riddled with F's, D's, and C's and a few sporadic A's in English.

In fact, I nearly didn't graduate because I failed P.E. *twice*—I know, the irony; it's like a headline from *The Onion:* "Lesbian

Fails P.E. Twice and Doesn't Graduate!" I got an F as a freshman, then as a senior. My high school had a policy that required ninth-grade students to shower after gym class, but I was a closeted lesbian full of bodily self-disgust and insecurity. I could barely handle my own nakedness in the privacy of my own bathroom, let alone a locker room teeming with other girls. I'd sneak off campus to smoke cigarettes with my skater-chic crush behind the pizza parlor across the street. Studies show that some women and girls experience anxiety disrobing in locker rooms—where their naked bodies will potentially be assessed and critiqued by others—especially if they experience some form of body dysmorphia, and honestly, who doesn't? It's such a disorienting experience: Society breeds crippling self-consciousness and aesthetic self-doubt in women and then expects us to confidently shed our garments in a space of collective nakedness. Lesbians, especially gender-nonconforming ones and trans people, often have a hard time exhibiting their nude bodies in these sometimes unwelcoming places—or even coexisting with other women in public bathrooms. One queer woman named Bente in a 2022 German study said that after coming out, a classmate urged fellow students to be "careful" because "Bente [might] jump you." My fear of a similar fate kept me ditching class or changing in the bathroom stall when I *did* show up. By the time I reached my final year of high school, my freshman-year P.E. teacher, a masculine woman whose sexuality was the subject of endless speculation, had already formed an unflattering conception of me. It was as tough as Teflon to reshape when I had her again as a senior. Even though the school had changed the showering policy by then—and I'd given it my best most days—she gave me an F *again.* It felt unjust. It felt personal.

Under her wilting gaze, I felt my ugliness in the extreme and wanted to run for cover under the nearby bleachers. I avoided her like I still do mirrors. Looking at her was to look at myself.

As a teenager, she represented the parts of me I wished I could will away. Her masculinity—hunched shoulders, downcast gaze, acne-pitted face with angular jawline, arms extended outward at the elbow as if her muscles were too big to remain flush against her body—made her an easy target for adolescent cruelties. I frequently heard cracks about her butch affect—"carpet muncher" or "she-he," they'd idiotically laugh under their breath.

To give you a fuller picture of the hostilities we, as queer people, had to endure, I want to tell you about a teacher I had in a creative writing program in downtown San Diego. One day before class started, I walked in on a conversation he was having with a student in which he told her that he thinks gays and lesbians should be rounded up and sent to their own private island far away from everybody else. I saw my classmate struggling to talk him out of his hateful—ugly—point of view. "You don't mean that," she said hopefully. "Oh yes I do," he said, nodding his head up and down vigorously. In reply, I wrote an essay in defense of homosexuals and called out his unkind remarks. He praised my work, but confessed he'd had a "bad experience with *one*" in his early youth, clearly conflating pedophiles with homosexuals, trying to justify his animus. *That* was the '90s.

I can only imagine how often my P.E. teacher must have heard mean comments about her aesthetic queerness, how they must have hurt and created a sense of unease and unbelonging. We were, in the end, a mirror to each other, a reflection, perhaps, that neither one of us wanted to see.

I found out I'd failed out of high school from my academic counselor, who had a smiling face with kind eyes framed by long black witchy hair that gave a subtle edge to her softness. I was walking with a friend to get my cap and gown, knowing I'd never *actually* attend the ceremony—I still dislike pageantry and being on display in that way—when she caught up with me and whispered, as if she were my coconspirator, "You can't graduate.

She failed you *again.* I have an idea for how to get you out of here!" When I stopped by her office, crumbling at the prospect of being forced to repeat a year at a school I hated as passionately as goth girls love black, my counselor said: "Why don't you do four hours of filing for me, and I'll let you pass with a D, but only if Coach signs off on it. Okay?" She sent me off to our fitness instructor's office to get her approval, which I wasn't sure she'd give, but she did, grudgingly: "How'd you manage *this* one?" she said as she scribbled her assenting signature across the four-by-four-inch index card I handed her. I laughed uncomfortably and said thanks. "Yeah" was all she could muster in reply, not "Good luck," not a modicum of support. Maybe I was the *her* in *herself* that she could not be kind to.

After barely graduating, I went on to a local junior college, where I excelled, and transferred to Berkeley a few years later.

But being at Harvard was pure theater of the absurd, like living in a surreal Elizabeth LeCompte production. It wasn't that I wasn't smart enough, although I did feel intellectually inadequate and ill-prepared. Rather, I'd been trained at Berkeley to swat away grand claims to truth and to dismantle universalizing narratives—and Harvard's classical liberal arts education, steeped in tradition, legacy, and the musty air of inherited privilege, seemed wholly unacquainted with the queerness I'd learned to locate in unlikely literary texts.

In one class, we broke into small groups, and I mused on the symbolism of a character who chronically stood in doorways: The space in between, I suggested, could reflect her bisexuality—the divide between her inner and outer worlds. More awkwardly, I proposed it might also represent a birth canal: a place of safety, a womb—maybe even a vagina—she refuses to leave. "Well, *you* get *all* the points for originality," a snarky student replied, as the table erupted in snickers with eyes that seemed to collectively say *What the fuck?*

Later, in a seminar on the Victorian novel taught by a gifted and incomparably kind professor, I analyzed a story about a sadistic teacher and argued that her cruelty was a plea for connection: a way to psychologically embed herself in her students' minds, to be seen, to feel less alone. The teacher responded: "Has anyone ever told you that you're perverse, Stephanie?"

Those queer readings embarrass me now for their overearnestness, and I can see why they drew sneers. But back then, I was still high on the fumes of Berkeley—and I took my professor's question as a compliment.

Compounding my status as weird was the fact that I was researching the history of attitudes toward masturbation in sex education curricula in an independent study. While it was fun kicking the school off its imperious perch by telling people I was "getting a masters in masturbation," I was truly curious about cultural perceptions of purported "antisocial" sexualities, setting out to prove a theory developed by cultural historian Thomas W. Laqueur, a professor of history at U.C. Berkeley, in a book he wrote called *Solitary Sex: A Cultural History of Masturbation.* Calling the Enlightenment-era treatise *Onania,* published in 1712, the beginning of our cultural discomfort and disgust with masturbation, he looked at anti-masturbation tracts from the eighteenth and nineteenth centuries and argued that the larger fear overriding all the surface anxieties expressed in the medical pamphlets—that solo sex was morally, spiritually, and physically dangerous and could lead to blindness, hairy palms, a deformed spine, weakness, chronic fatigue, and insanity, not to mention an afterlife in eternal hell—was the fear that people would stop depending on one another for pleasure, threatening the social order by nullifying our sexual interdependence. In my studies, I found that in sex education curricula, when masturbation is addressed in a moderately positive way, it's always cast as a momentary substitute or preparation for heterosexual sex, not as a pleasure unto itself, independent of other bodies, proving the enduring unease it generates for the reasons Laqueur outlined. People are especially weirded out by the image of a masturbating child, maybe even more so than they are by picturing teens having actual sex: The fall of Joycelyn Elders is a case in point. Elders, a pediatrician and the fifteenth surgeon general of the United States—the first African American and second woman to hold the position—was forced to resign in 1994 for saying, "I think that it is part of human sexuality, and perhaps it should be taught," when asked at a U.N. conference on AIDS if masturbation, as part of sex education, should be encouraged to help youths avoid riskier sexual behaviors. That such a measured statement led to her dismissal reveals the deep discomfort, and even panic, surrounding masturbation, particularly when discussed by women—and even more so when the woman is Black and in a position of power. It speaks to a broader cultural desire to control women's voices and bodies. How frightening, after all, is a world in which women are no longer dependent on men for pleasure or validation?

Most people fantasize about other people when they masturbate, so it poses no real threat to sociality, but I wanted to shed it of its cultural baggage and hold it up as a legitimate sexuality in and of itself. Similarly, I wondered why tenderness—a hug, a kiss, an encouraging pat on the back—had to be expressed to another person in order to be a valid expression of love. Why can't we, privately or publicly, lavish *ourselves* with such affection? It wasn't clear to me then, but it is now, from a distance of twenty-five years, that these are the musings of someone trying to disavow the need for real-life connection, someone fervently trying to elevate a way of being that makes real vulnerability—and growth—impossible.

Obviously I'm not the first woman to eschew physical contact to protect against exposure to a lover's potential scrutiny and disapproval. Studies show that women who experience bodily dissatisfaction have weaker sex drives, often avoiding intimacy altogether, while their younger counterparts, adolescent girls, suffer "sadness and loneliness" due to negative self-images. I'm honestly amazed, given the near-constant appraisal of women's looks and the self-doubt and insecurity it breeds, that more women don't feel too tender to be touched. Looking back, I can see why I wanted to circumvent the centrality of body-to-body contact.

While there aren't, as far as I know, any studies that have investigated the quirky question I posed in graduate school, part of the reason it registers as strange and might generate unpleasant feelings in onlookers may have something to do with what American social psychologist Leon Festinger called "cognitive dissonance theory." In Festinger's formulation, people experience distress and discomfort watching a member of their social group behaving in ways that contradict expectations, including shared values and beliefs—and no doubt, it's startling to see someone kissing or petting themselves.

While these lines of inquiry may have been off-putting to the ruling academic elite, I was sure that if we got at the reason they generated so much unease and disgust, they'd reveal interesting and important truths about our society and our collective ethos around sexuality.

Our hypersexualized culture, for one, has engendered a manic preoccupation with sex that props up whole industries and economies inextricably linked to the beauty standard—the cosmetics, fashion, fitness, and dieting industries, for example—making us, women and men, feel undesirable if we aren't getting laid and compelling us to trespass ourselves by hooking up with individuals we only tepidly fancy in an effort to prove our appeal to others and ourselves. As intimate conversations with various female friends have revealed to me through the years, as well as academic research, I'd argue that women are often less motivated by carnal lust in anonymous hookup culture than by *the desire to be desired.* Our self-worth is so intertwined with our ability to attract male attention and to submit to their wants and wishes. In one study, nearly 25 percent of college-age women said they engaged in hookup culture to mitigate negative feelings, such as loneliness and a sense of inadequacy, and 16 percent did so to gain social status and acceptance from partners and peers. Sociology professor and author of *American Hookup* Lisa Wade echoed that finding, telling me in an interview that it's less about sexual release—men have orgasms three times more frequently than women in those first-time hookups—or securing a romantic partnership, a foregone conclusion in the culture of casual sex at universities. It's often about being desired and homosocial bonding between women eager to compare notes and elevate their status via tales of sexual conquests. In an interview she gave to *The Longing Lab* podcast, she said: "[It] isn't about hooking up with someone you like. It's about hooking up with someone your friends are going to be impressed by. It's about status." It's also, more saliently, about being *wanted,* a topic she dedicates an entire chapter to in her revelatory text. "Men are supposed to be sexual, feeling the desire, and women are supposed to be sexy, inspiring the desire. That's why, on every American family sitcom, the woman's hot and the man is a chubby dude, right? It's because his hotness doesn't matter and her desire doesn't matter," she told me. She added that women who shun male attention and who "do absolutely nothing to appear to *want* men—[don't] do their hair, wear attractive clothes, smile at them, and laugh at men's jokes" (i.e., gender-nonconforming lesbians)—"are very threatening." Consequently, Wade says, women who work at fancy law firms, for example, who collect sizable paychecks and stand on equal professional footing with men, go to great lengths to aestheticize in wearing heels, makeup, and nice clothes with expensive hairdos. "It's a way of saying, 'You're still men to me, and I still want you to think I'm pretty, and if I want you to think I'm pretty, then you still have power.' Otherwise that would be so profoundly threatening that men couldn't tolerate the equality." (And women who abide by these unspoken rules benefit: A 2011 study out of Harvard showed that women who wear makeup in the workplace are perceived as "more attractive and competent" than women who do not.)

Men, however, who refuse sex may lose more status than women—and even inspire a kind of repulsion. A woman I once knew told me she was "creeped out" by a man in her twelve-step program who confessed his celibacy. It's infantilizing and feminizing to hear a man eschew sex; it makes him creepily child- or priest-like, a shaky clammy-hand masturbator. It's instantly dwarfing. Part of the reason lies in the fact that the whole power structure of gendered relations in our culture is dependent on men fucking and women getting fucked, literally and figuratively, and it puts the patriarchy in peril if neither gender is doing their part to uphold it. For its own survival, it must stigmatize ways of being that threaten its viability and security, including men and women who don't need each other for sexual or emotional gratification either because they depend on their own bodies and minds for such sustenance or because they depend on their own genders.

The one and only time I had a one-night stand, I did so because I was in my twenties and thought I *should* be having sex, even at random. It was not because I wanted to, especially with the woman I found, who was quite literally the opposite of my "type": a long-haired hippie with multiple piercings whose name I didn't even know. As someone who is extremely uptight and obsessed with personal hygiene, I am congenitally ill-suited to a free love ethos and struggled through the experience, although I delighted at my nosy doorman-cum-friend's cracks about my newfound sluttiness. It was the validation that someone wanted to take me to bed and someone else witnessed it—the theater of it all—that I liked, but the experience itself was a self-violation, like having sex with a man or pretending to be someone I'm not.

How often do women and girls—you—feel compelled to self-transgress in ways that make them feel ill at ease for the mere spectacle of fulfilling a social obligation or norm? The beauty imperative, interwoven with the sexual one, works similarly. It's a show, a bad performance in a poorly written play that feels original but is not and often provokes punishing feelings of shame and self-doubt, even disgust, all of which could be avoided if we'd learn to delight in our own bodies and minds, and irrespective of societal demands and manipulations.

I wish you could do that. I wish I could.

I'm constantly trying to lead you to a higher consciousness, maybe too laboriously, by disrupting all the harmful messaging that might impinge on your well-being and happiness. I exasperate you, but cracking the pretty facade of ugly things feels necessary, like it's some kind of progress, even if it feels futile—or too late.

Against wiser opinions, Sabrina and I took you to see Greta Gerwig's movie *Barbie* when you were seven. Even though it was rated PG-13, we thought we could walk you through what you didn't understand and discuss the damaging impact of traditional beauty standards on women and girls, but most of it went over your well-coiffed hair. "Pink goes with everything," we heard you quote the movie while you were playing in your bedroom that evening.

"I liked Barbie better at the beginning of the movie, when she didn't cry and the shower didn't have water that ruined her hair and her feet were the right shape for high heels and she was smiling and happy," you told us at dinner that night.

"Well that backfired," Sabrina said under her breath, getting tongue-tied as she tried to explain that Barbie is just an *idea*—a *representation*—that little girls are harmfully brainwashed into believing they must aspire to. "Only it's impossible, so girls just end up feeling bad about themselves *all* the time," she said. With exclamation points in her voice, she added: "The beautiful reality is that we *do* cry, and our feet *are* flat, and the shower water *does* mess up our hair, and we *shouldn't* be expected to be happy and smiling and perfect all the time for other people's pleasure and comfort."

"I want to be happy and smiling all the time," you countered, reasonably, as we ran this way and that, two imbeciles trying to keep this ball in the air before it landed on the fundamental point: Small children don't have the capacity for nuance and abstraction; they *can't* filter out or complicate the ideas that Barbies or L.O.L.s or O.M.G.s or Bratz dolls inculcate. They develop in tandem with the ideas they're exposed to, ideas that are so integral to their identities that when they grow into women, thinking against them threatens their very sense of self.

Barbies are the bricks with which women are built, and no one wants to collapse their own house.

We told you how much we loved the idea of Regular Barbie and Weird Barbie (Kate McKinnon) and together imagined a world in which Barbies and other dolls are so individuated that they look wholly unlike one another, helping us recognize beauty in the idiosyncratic—in the differences between us, proliferating new ways of seeing and desiring women.

But, more emphatically, I want to encourage you, the adult version of you—and every other woman—to focus less on courting approval and desire in men through various exercises in self-abnegation and much more on what *you* want: *Who do you desire? What turns you on? What is your vision?* Masturbation is a feminist form of rebellion—it's about prioritizing, actually and symbolically, your imagination, your wants, your needs. As a habit of mind, perhaps it will ladder up to actualizing your full potential, to embodying your messy humanness with self-compassion and strength. There is a reason they don't want you to enjoy your own ride, to see it as a legitimate adventure, a valid form of sex in and of itself: Male supremacy—not individual men, of course, but a system of male domination—feeds on the trivialization of your mind, the doubts plaguing your confidence, the service you provide to men by contorting yourself into uncomfortable shapes—shapes that make you a stranger to yourself—all in the hope of being wanted, of being affirmed in the eyes of others. How can I teach you to value *your* own estimation of yourself above all others? Our culture makes it extremely difficult.

Peggy Orenstein, the world-renowned expert on the unique challenges adolescent girls face in securing healthy psychologies, once wrote that girls are so consumed with how they're being perceived in any given moment that they become disconnected "from their inner experience," which creates what psychologist Mary Pipher called a "split self" in *Reviving Ophelia.* It leads to a fragmentary existence whereby one version of you, which becomes dominant, chronically plays to and seeks out the affirming gaze of others (parents, other girls, and boys), while the truest version of you—the unvarnished one that flickers with Technicolor vibrancy when no one is looking—fades into an unrecognizably dull shade or becomes so small and faint, a whisper of a person, that you can't determine what she wants anymore or know who she is.

"Ma, can you please skip this? It's too sad," you say anytime Billie Eilish's Oscar-winning song for Gerwig's *Barbie,* "What Was I Made For?," comes on. I wonder if the pathos in Eilish's haunting vocals and poignant lyrics get at a truth you're not ready for or don't yet understand. But the way it captures the end result of how our culture manufactures—*deadens*—girls is something I want you to hear, to understand. Told from the perspective of

Barbie, the song walks us through her feminist awakening with its recognition that she's not human, just an idealized representation of femininity, something societally produced and "paid for," confusing her sense of purpose and provoking an existential crisis.

What I believe she was made for—what I believe you and I and all of us were made for—is our *own* pleasure, our *own* experiences and subjectivities, our *own* value—immeasurable and not defined by others.

As much as I wanted to do my queer version of Philip Roth's *Portnoy's Complaint* there in those hallowed halls, where presidents (Franklin D. Roosevelt, Theodore Roosevelt, Barack Obama), Supreme Court justices (Ruth Bader Ginsburg, Ketanji Brown Jackson), and poets (T. S. Eliot, Robert Frost, Jean Valentine) once roamed and where professors assume, de facto, one's greatness—I remember one declaring to a packed lecture hall, "Perhaps one of you in this room will write the next great American novel"—securing the institution's students a place for all time in the upper registers of the social and political establishment with their big brains, big bank accounts, and oftentimes big beautiful faces, I was as far removed from the queer environments that affirmed the new, the freaky, the "out there" as I could get. It seemed overnight, situated within a world in which I palpably felt my unbelonging, all the riches I inherited from my queer intellectual upbringing vanished.

Even the queer faculty member with whom I'd had a brief correspondence via email while an undergraduate looked at me like I was a filthy, tattered dog toy brought into her pristine, well-organized office by an administrative assistant who left the door open. As I outlined my project, she responded, eyes dead, "That doesn't interest me." She was the kind of scholar—not uncommon in academia—who acquires knowledge like capitalists acquire money; it's a different currency but it's used the same way: to feel big and make others feel small. I bolted right out of my seat for the door. Her assistant, a kind middle-aged woman, looked embarrassed by our incongruous enthusiasm for one another and ushered me out with a gentle pat on the back.

In one shriveling fell swoop, I felt stupid, poor, and ugly. All the progress I'd made to reengineer my self-concept, at least intellectually, unraveled. The anxiety and unease I felt stalked me at all hours, even in the dead of night, when I tossed and turned, chasing sleep that wouldn't come, for days on end. Alumni as loftily situated as Cornel West to social entrepreneur Due Quach to newly minted grad Kris King have spoken out about the difficulties they've endured while living and thinking against Harvard's culture and norms and its own mythology, whether due to racial disparities, lower socioeconomic status, neurodivergence, physical disabilities, or queerness. "I learned that if you didn't fit in, it was up to you to change to adapt to Harvard," Quach wrote, arguing that "toxic stress" and a lack of belonging reopened primal wounds from childhood that she hadn't adequately worked through or healed from. Similarly, for me, the school seemed to resurface all the hostile feelings I'd harbored toward myself that had entered a soft remission at Berkeley. I wonder now if the inadequacy I felt, like a diseased organ sensitive to touch, provoked my ongoing inability to sleep, because that's when insomnia started for me. I felt constitutionally unsafe, like a house made of straw, incapable of weathering the ongoing storm without intense vigilance.

It also became clear, quickly, that I wasn't academic material—at least not at the level required to avoid the trap of unstable adjunct work or landing an assistant professorship in a small conservative town, where being openly queer could come with real risks and isolation. So I decided to return to the original plan I dreamt up on Cord Street in Downey, California, in 1986 when I was ten and earnestly planned my next step—moving to New

York City to become a writer. I finished out the rest of my graduate program, taking classes just for pleasure, my pleasure, and took a part-time job at a magazine written by teens for teens, in the hope of securing a publishing job in New York City the following year, which I did.

Unlike San Francisco, which often struck me as melancholic with its chilly morning fog billowing over the Golden Gate Bridge—a place both iconic and introspective—New York City felt electric: upbeat and full of energy. Where San Francisco exuded a slow, dreamy quality, like potheads walking through the Haight, New York pulsed with a fast, forward-moving tempo. Maybe because it's been the setting of so many movies—*Taxi Driver, Annie Hall, Serpico, The Godfather, When Harry Met Sally,* the list goes on and on—it felt familiar to me in the romantic way of American cinema. Standing in Midtown, the heartbeat of the city with its blaring horns, cursing cabbies, millions in every manner of dress walking up the avenues or down the steps into the subway's roaring belly, to shops and restaurants bustling with too many bodies, alongside peddlers and performers pushing a wide variety of tricks and treats for a buck, I was in a movie, only it was my story unfolding this time, and who knew what would happen next as I made my way through the beautiful labyrinth of bodies and buildings? Is that the thrill you feel, one of endless possibilities and elation, when we visit Times Square to see a Broadway show or walk by the Christmas tree at Rockefeller Center with your cousins in tow? When you grow up, you once told me and Sabrina, you'll take an apartment right in the middle of this delightful madness—"a place where I can see billboards blinking all night long," you said. None of it is overstimulation for you; it's an electric guitar riff in the middle of a perfect song, one you never want to end.

When we started imagining a life outside the city, maybe somewhere we could get a small patch of land, a backyard with a garden to grow some hardy sunflowers or delicate irises, maybe some carrots or baby tomatoes, with a towering beech or maple tree overhead—somewhere in the Berkshires or deep in the Catskills—you panicked, like your life was on the line. "I'm never leaving New York!" you bellowed. "Never!" Every time we come home from vacation and we're driving up 39th Street in Sunset Park, as we inch closer to our Finnish co-op, you whoop, "Brooklyn!!" like it's a version of "Hooray!," a cheer that everyone should understand. This sleepless, boisterous city you were born and raised in is so synced with your biorhythms that when we went for a late-evening walk down Commercial Street in Provincetown, Massachusetts, in April to look at the full moon and listen to the waves lapping the shoreline, you got scared. "This is creepy. There aren't any people around. It's not safe," which made us laugh, because the crime rate is far higher in a city populated with nearly 8.5 million people. "But there's people around at all hours. It's safer," you reasoned, defending your home against all reason.

But I felt as safe in the aliveness of our city as you did when I first arrived. Back then, just as it was in the fantasies of my early youth, it felt like the *only* safe place for me—a setting where I could roam freely in my anonymity. Who might I become among these tall buildings and busy gum-strewn streets? It seemed like anyone—the highly fashionable and beautiful and the socially and aesthetically awkward—had a place, a palace, here. Even the magazine and newspaper world, where I'd eventually find myself, was a warm home to the scrappy, the inappropriate, the emotionally messy, the defiant, the freaky, the gloriously malformed.

In the midst of all the hubbub—the anticipation of a new life, an exhilarating adventure about to gain unstoppable momentum—my father, clear across the country in San Diego, California, collapsed from a brain stem stroke.

My sweet dad, whose infectious childlike wonder and gentle

heart could lasso the most cynical hearts; who could speak several languages, French, Spanish, English, a smattering of Italian and Greek; who made a religion of kindness, frequently compelling him to forsake all manner of personal comforts—a shirt, a set of shoes, a coat, a plate of food—for another's pleasure or nourishment; who made me feel like Einstein, no matter how youthfully arrogant or trite or small or half-baked my thoughts were; who believed, with unshakable certainty, that this earth, these bodies, these homes we dwell in are the mere shadows of a much vaster nonmaterial dimension that we can only know by faith, was gone.

It was surreal. A body, my father's body, animated with a life infinite with magnanimity, curiosity, and joy, was there one moment and gone the very next. I was never again going to get into fiery debates with him about politics, or enthusiastically join him in his spiritual musings, or fight with him for refusing to eat healthy foods—for rejecting my passionate pleas to eliminate McDonald's and Burger King from his diet—and failing to regularly exercise, all of which could have forestalled his premature death. Nor would I ever again feel the quiet comfort of his loving presence in a room, a lighthouse, my lighthouse, illuminating the way home, to safety, to love.

To avoid feeling my grief or the strange fear that started to engulf me when I imagined his cold dead body interned six feet underground—or remembered the kiss I placed on his frozen forehead at his open-casket funeral—I kept busy, making an inordinate number of plans. I put on such an Oscar-worthy performance of my *okayness* that the talented artist I lived with, who had a subtle way of being unkind that often escaped my perception until moments after she'd withdrawn from any given conversation, said, "I can't believe how well you're handling your father's death," as if she were a close friend with whom I'd share my naked devastation. I needed to keep it buttoned up to survive, and the truth is, I couldn't access the full depth of my despair until I met Sabrina—my love for her seemed to crumble the levee embanking all the memories and feelings I couldn't fully access before I knew what it was to truly love and be loved by another. Before his funeral, when he was brain-dead in a coma and we were a week or so away from disconnecting him from the medical equipment that supported what was left of his life, I met my good friend Casey at Le Gamin Café in Chelsea. My mom had urged me back to New York City, despite my father's precarious state. She worried I'd lose my job because she didn't have the means to help me. I'd just flown back days before I met Casey. At the restaurant, I bit into the most delicious peach I'd ever tasted and realized, palpably, in my body, that my disarmingly endearing dad, who deliberated over every fruit purchase for maddening lengths of time, ever awed at the seemingly limitless array of fruits and vegetables available all season long at our mega grocery stores in America, was never again going to experience a fruit as delectable as this one. I remember the experience so vividly because it nearly compelled me out of my seat. I wanted to get up; I wanted to leave and run down the streets toward life. The moment moved through me like an electric current, jolting me into my body in a whole new way. His death, his material loss, made me want to live life with the full weight and imperfection of my body. The theoretical, the fantastical, the intellectual could no longer compete with the corporeality of a human hug. I was twenty-seven, and it felt like time was running out. An urgency, a mania, hijacked my brain, and I went on a carpe diem tear, asking out women who I knew were straight, including Amanda, a book editor I'd developed a crush on from afar. Three thousand miles away, as my dad lay dying, mere minutes from his final breath, with my mom and brother huddling around his bedside in a cold hospital room with dehumanizing fluorescent lights pouring down on the last minutes of his earthly existence amid the ominous and all-pervasive beeping of medical equipment, as doctors unhooked him from machines sustaining his body, I made my way over to a café to meet a woman I'd only imagined tête-à-tête intimacies with.

I was trying to forget, to fend off grief and the loneliness that took space in me like an impossible-to-hold weight, but looking back I now know that I was actively choosing life, however inelegantly; I was shaking off the wintry touch of my own mortality for the heat, the fire, I felt for another human being. Six months later, in that frenzied headspace where I grasped frantically in every direction to all that was life, desperate to feel its hands, grimy or clean, cruel or kind, but always warm—alive—on me, I met my first girlfriend, Meg, a quietly mighty Irish American girl who stood at a towering five feet, three inches. She had a subtle splash of freckles on her pretty face, long dark hair that turned auburn in the sunlight, and kind, smiling brown eyes. We spent nearly four years together—a fire-and-fire romance—that would have singed us to the ground if we'd stayed together.

I'm not sure I believe in a hierarchy of love—love is love in the purest sense—but what I felt for Sabrina was different: a feeling as delicate as a butterfly, but undeniably strong and insistent—a passion so deep, it felt like an ache. She swooped down into the depths of my soul, altering, indelibly, the way I felt, the way I saw, the way I moved through the world, rearranging, reshaping my life forever. Fantasy became reality; theory became practice; the best of both worlds coalesced: I was in love, and I could reach out and touch the person I adored.

Our first year together, I wore socks at all times, because I was sure my unpretty feet would be a dealbreaker—but Sabrina wore socks in solidarity with me, eventually urging my feet out of hiding with the unstated but felt promise that even if I had a third arm—or eye—she'd love it because it was a part of me. Her adoring eyes became a reflection in which I could see and feel my own beauty. I could finally face my face, not every day and not always lovingly, but her love showed me to myself in a whole new way—and then you were born, and my body became your body. We were indistinguishable from one another in those first months of life, when you needed my hands for grabbing, my legs for walking, my eyes for seeing; and my face, the face Sabrina loved and I was learning to love, too, became your face. As clinical psychologist Beatrice Beebe's pioneering work revealed in the 1980s, in order for infants to form a healthy and distinct sense of self, they must first go through a process of facial mirroring, whereby, for the first few months of life, they aren't quite sure where they end and their mother begins. Slowly, they become aware of their separateness and learn, little by little, how to register and regulate their own emotions by imitating the ones legible on their mother's face. Through mine, then, you learned empathy, the highest form of intelligence, the engine that drives all social progress and change and is the cornerstone of all meaningful connection and relationality. My face and Sabrina's face gave you your humanity, the kind of beauty that transcends our materiality and is eternal.

Chapter 11

Affirming Our Differences

—

You've taught me so much about how to inhabit my body with love and grace, albeit a rough variety and nothing I'll ever master. It's a lumbering sort of self-love, but I've felt it nonetheless through you. How could I, after all, dislike a face that you once mistook for yours, that initiated your capacity for connection and compassion?

As I moved along on my uneven journey to self-acceptance, I saw you, too, making inroads in affirming your social incongruities. When you were as young as four, we introduced you to picture books that celebrate kids and families who are different. A pile still lives on the shelf behind your bed, beat up and barely hanging together from excess use. They sit alongside an assortment of child-friendly essays on famous women whose differences informed their greatness: Ruth Bader Ginsburg, Frida Kahlo, Lorraine Hansberry, and Maya Angelou.

Sabrina and I have always told you that your difference is your superpower. It's a point of view you resisted at first, wanting to assimilate rather than stand out.

Before you found a comfortable place outside the order of things, I'd see you mimic your friends—someone takes his jacket off, so you take your jacket off; another carries her own backpack, so you ask to carry yours; another likes a particular song, so you like the same song. Developmentally, it's normal for kids to mimic or emulate each other—it's how we figure out who we are. But I wonder sometimes if the burden of absorbing our queerness, a kind of social disfigurement in the eyes of certain friends you've made, and the experience of growing up fatherless have made you extra eager to seamlessly thread into the established way of being and doing.

People cling to tradition when they feel threatened, but it's a false security, an illusion spun to compel us into existing in mindless unison; it's a form of societal control. It has its uses, but it hurts, too. The ways you surprise and defy expectations, the things that make you "unique"—my paternal grandmother's highest compliment to me when I was eight, which I wanted to wear on my head like a crown and march through the streets of my hometown for everyone to see—are the beautiful essence of who you are. Each time you smile or hold a cup or walk through the park or laugh at a joke or eat a delicious meal, it's the first and only time it's been done, because there is only one you to have ever done it in just the way you have.

We read queer family books repeatedly, like others say mantras, and talked up the power of *not* fitting in. The progress has not been linear, but in fits and starts, with steps forward and then sometimes backward, we saw you begin to lean into your difference.

On a Park Slope playground, you told a little girl you wanted to pretend the two of you were two mommies, rather than a mom and a dad as she'd proposed, because you said: "I have two mommies." You didn't see the kid's eyes widen or mouth drop because her face evinced calm nonchalance when she turned to you and said, "Cool," like it was no big deal.

You soon started outing our queer family to anyone we encountered: the taxi cab driver who had just handed me a Jehovah's Witnesses pamphlet; a random woman who was teaching us about efforts to increase the oyster population in the East River on the boardwalk near Domino Park in Williamsburg; an evangelical couple, who met on a Christian dating website, whose son you were playing with in the sandbox at our local playground. "I have two moms and a donor from Ecuador," you declared matter-of-factly, not registering the awkward silence that followed as we made our way out of the park alongside them.

You offered up this factoid to anyone who would listen, often in the form of a non sequitur, dropping it into conversation artlessly, queerly. After meeting your donor siblings—the trio of three in New Jersey—you also began sharing that bit of news with perfect strangers and friends, managing to explain things with a clarity and ease we lacked in our explanation to you: "The same man who helped make me for my mommies helped make them for their mommies," you'd said.

In stories you invented with Legos or American Girl dolls and O.M.G.s, you often cast the "weird girl"—a rotation of misfits like witches, vampires, and wolf-women—as the cool girl.

And in the fantasies you cook up, you frequently *invert* the prototypical narratives of hero and villain, like when you invented a new celestial body in our solar system inhabited by witches, which you aptly called "Planet Witchland." You explained to me that the witches are evil only because they're misunderstood and that they are the targets of hatred from the "Beautiful Royals," who destroyed their planet, forcing them to descend to Earth. The witches move to a part of town that's been abandoned by the Beautiful Royals, you explained, and are living in harmony in a nice neighborhood of their making when the Beautiful Royals tauntingly decide to move in. The witches get scared because the Beautiful Royals annihilated their former world, so they instigate a war in preemptive self-defense. The fighting gets so bad, they decide to leave Earth. They go back to Planet Witchland to rebuild their home with the aid of a Beautiful Royal boy, who falls in love with a witch girl, and the fighting continues.

Your tale had traces of a conversation we'd just had about gentrification because we'd seen residents of Sunset Park protesting Industry City, a massive shopping, eating, and event space that spans several buildings on the farthest edge of our community. It's a fun place for kids to run and climb huge outdoor sculptures, but it can empty out half your checking account in a short snap of time with its Park Avenue prices. Few can regularly afford it, but we like to go once in a while with friends for a slice of pizza or ice cream. My explanation of class and racial displacement inspired you to say, "I think everything should be free," which is perhaps a universal dream all kids share, so every want can be fulfilled at any time. "That way, everyone would be rich," you reasoned, unaware that if everyone were rich, no one would be in our capitalistic mindset.

I wondered if you felt a kinship with the witches from Planet Witchland. When we watched *Encanto,* a film about a Colombian family with magical powers—one family member is endowed with superhuman strength, another with hypnotic beauty; a third can heal with a single touch, while yet another shape-shifts—I gasped when the little boy named Antonio opens the door that introduces him to his supernatural gift, the ability to communicate with animals, and a jaguar flips him onto his back and dashes away at breakneck speed. I told you I'd be too worried to let my baby ride on a beast's back, but you argued that since his gift is the ability to communicate with wildlife—because they understand each other—they are safe with each other. Mutual understanding is indeed an antidote to mistrust, but it's an insight I wouldn't expect from someone so young. Culturally, we don't give kids a whole lot of credit—we talk down to them and avoid challenging topics we believe they can't handle—but sometimes, when I listen to you and your friends, I'm impressed by your generation's precocity. But maybe my amazement is the result of selling you short.

Nonetheless, you've always had an uncanny astuteness, capable of grappling with more tender issues, like the time when you told me your friend Maximus, a boy, loved the color pink but had to pretend he didn't in front of other boys or they'd laugh at him, and I told you he ought to tell those boys that, historically, pink was a masculine color. As a watered-down version of red, a color associated with passion and aggression and virility, it was the preferred color for boys until sometime in the middle of the twentieth century. Unimpressed, you said, "That's not the point. He should be able to like pink or any other color, and if I say that to him, it's like saying that it's only okay because it used to be a boy's color. But he should be able to like it no matter what."

I saw rebellions congregating at the edges of your thought patterns in the way you saw beauty in unexpected and overlooked places, like the bubbly water gathering in an eye-catching swirl as it struggled to make its way down the drain after your bath when you were seven. We live on the first floor of a four-story walk-up, so all the hair and thick suds from the apartments above ours jam up our bathroom pipes, which frustrates me, but it thrills you for the way it creates an arresting vision of momentum and sound. "It looks like a tornado," you'd said. Discarded wastewater—something others might see as gross—registered as worthy of wonder.

Someone once told me that it swirls down like that because of the Earth's gravitational pull and rotation. While that's not entirely true, there's something divine in knowing we live on a floating orb, spinning through space around the sun, and in thinking that its movement is felt even here, in the suds swirling down the rusty pipes of our 108-year-old Brooklyn apartment. It reminds me that our little lives are part of something inexpressibly large and awesome.

I noticed other idiosyncrasies of your mind that privileged *offbeatness* when we drove through Hillsdale, New York, a farm town with a Brooklyn vibe bordering Massachusetts. We stopped by a gay-owned business with a plethora of chic home goods interspersed with novelty items. You were a little wobbly and inexact in how you moved through space still, at age nine, so I anxiously trailed you, hoping you wouldn't break anything along the way. As you walked through their maze of many fragile things, your eyes landed on something hideous—a murky old wine bottle with an explosion of colorful hardened wax dripping down its sides. It looked like something a kid had crafted for fun, not the work of an upscale artisan. You asked if we could get it, but the suggestion alone felt like a small trauma. You said it looked like "something bad happened but something good came out of it, like a volcano that erupts rainbows," which made me want to buy it until I looked at the price tag. I suggested we make our own. I hoped your quirky perceptions suggested a kind release from dominant paradigms of thought about beauty.

Around the time of our visit to Hillsdale, you kept asking to repeatedly play Bomba Estéreo's "Soy Yo," a wonderful anthem to individuality, resilience, and empowerment. You and a friend took turns dancing to it down your pseudo catwalk in our living room. It chronicles the ups and downs of a person who goes "against the current" and gets "lost," but in their failure and lostness—in separating from the pact—they find themselves, urging listeners to dispense with the naysayers, to take their criticisms as an affirmation of self.

Watching you two sing your fabulousness into being, sashaying up and down our family room, I didn't hear these heartfelt words but kept conjuring, instead, the hubristic lyrics of L.O.L.

Surprise!'s "Fix My Crown," in which the vocalist sings about being an "icon in training" and announcing herself as "a big deal." The spectacle and bravado of those words sound like insecurity to my ear, not confidence. It sounds more like someone who deeply doubts their value or desirability, but by announcing it, bold and loud, they hope to make it so—like when people who sit in direct opposition to the aesthetic status quo—"women of size" (to use Roxane Gay's dignifying term), transwomen, gay men—post provocative selfies online, highlighting their assets with self-loving declarations, like: "Girl, I'm pure fire, burning it down!"

The fun and play *is* there, sure, but the self-glorification masks insecurity, too. Historically, noisily affirming our magnificence, even when we don't feel magnificent, has been a critical act of defiance and resistance that helped fissure, however minutely, prevailing beauty norms, like when African Americans in the 1960s refused Western notions of beauty, center-staging a "Black is beautiful" politic that amplified physical features traditionally disparaged: Afros, fuller figures, darker skin. Or when second-wave feminists in the 1970s eschewed imperatives to beautify, opting instead for hairy legs, makeup-less faces, and no bras. Or when queer people marched through the streets post-Stonewall in ill-fitting clothes, showing off ample butts and six-packs, flouting gendered expectations with men in gowns and crowns and women in suits and ties, singing, "We're here! We're queer! Get used to it!"

Maybe I'd have felt differently about myself had I had the ability to strike a defiant pose, even with quivering limbs, like you on your imaginary runway or like those 1970s queer radicals, when my brother caught me fake shaving at ten and I shrank under his perplexed gaze. Maybe faking it *is* the way to making it, like smiling when you feel downcast or laughing a little harder at a joke to catapult yourself out of ennui or sadness.

Whatever mental acrobatics you've undertaken to secure yourself, even in battle with me, you're succeeding.

After your blue phase, when you ejected all the color from your wardrobe and returned to your high-femme glory, I told you that the patterns you were wearing clashed. As someone who dresses like a fifteen-year-old boy, it's laughable, in a gut-busting way, that I gave you any style guidance at all, but I wanted you to know the rules so you could break them with intention, so you wouldn't be called out or made fun of by a more fashionable girl, but you replied with a kind of rebuke: "It doesn't matter what you wear; it matters that you're a kind person," you said as you climbed the banister against my protests and waited for me to put on my ratty Adidas high-tops so we could head across the park to school. "Besides, I'm 'Mismatch Girl,'" you said, like you were some kind of superhero—and somehow I knew you'd be okay, despite it all, even if your future teenage years momentarily chip away at your self-esteem and silence your "different voice," as developmental psychologist Carol Gilligan memorably put it. When I see you, consistently, holding your ground against my more unreasonable expectations, which I sometimes take as an affront when the remnants of my old-school parenting ethos flow forth, I feel I am doing something right in cultivating your inner strength, like when I bear witness to your little acts of resistance: Daily, I face your swing-arm lamp toward your desk, and you always, every single time, walk over and point it back toward the ceiling; or when I tell you to wash your hands, and you do so superficially in protest; or when I put items away in your room to be tidy and you pull them right back out, arranging them in the exact order you had them prior, requesting that I not touch them; or when you refused to wear a jacket on that snowy day in November I wish I could forget.

The week before you decided to gut your drawers of color and go dark, we bought you an expensive jacket of your choosing with crisscrossing lines of blue, pink, and aqua, but it was no longer "me," you said, which incensed me. Despite your objections and indefatigable struggle to wiggle free from my grasp, I stuffed your arms into it like a straitjacket, and your head slammed into my mouth, causing it to bleed. It was the first and only time I'd forced you to wear something that you opposed from some deep internal place. But then I really looked at you—at the tears teetering at the edges of your eyes—and froze.

A series of similar memories from my own youth rushed forth: My mom, always up for a shopping spree and glamorizing, casting quizzical glances at my preference for clothes in the boy's section rather than the girl's and likening my sensibilities to my unfashionable father's—the less-desirable one, the man to whom she'd walked down the aisle with hesitant feet and lukewarm affections, the safe choice she regretted.

Immediately I helped you take off the jacket. I apologized. I hugged you tightly, like I was trying to squeeze the memory of the moment out of you, and then I let you enter the frigid air in layers and layers of clothing of your choosing, but you still recall the incident, even now, four years later. When you bring it up, I flush because it was an unnecessary conflict bordering on cruel, and, looking back, there's a certain pride I take in your resistance to my will. Sabrina, a clinical social worker who studied play therapy, reminds me that *sometimes* kids who are overly polite and conciliatory are actually suffering inside. Alternatively, kids who bounce off the walls and misstep and challenge you and forget to say "thank you" because they want to get to the fun in a hurry are *oftentimes* the most well-adjusted and healthy.

By watching you own your story and embody a philosophy of defiance and self-celebration, I was inspired to do the same.

"Let's take some selfies," I said one Sunday morning after looking through my phone and realizing we had too few photos together. It catapulted you from the couch, jubilant at the opportunity for more screen time. We made a series of silly faces.

"Make an excited face!" you commanded like an overcontrolling director.

"Now make a super-surprised face!"

"Now a very, very sad face."

"Now make an ugly face," you said, scrunching and contorting your beautiful face and mouth into odd configurations, and I did, too. My exceptional ability to distort my face made you laugh.

"Now back to our pretty faces," you said, the word *pretty* landing heavier than *ugly,* burdened by all it expects.

We must have taken a hundred selfies that day and laughed enough to evaporate all the sadness in the world.

Later that night I scrolled through the photos, reliving the fun with Sabrina, even seeing the "pretty" you saw in some photos of me, with our faces smushed up against each other.

I had our "pretty" and "ugly" faces printed for the fridge.

Even though I saw you growing into a confident girl who could hold her own, I sometimes thought your experience of a close friendship coming to an end left a residue of unbelonging. I tried to mitigate that possibility as best I could.

Scootering up to your friend Emilia's apartment, the night was cool and breezy and joyful as I told you about a story I was working on for *Oprah Daily.* I had just interviewed Libryia Jones, who'd founded a travel group for single parents. Jones, herself a single mom, had pulled her twelve-year-old daughter out of school to travel the world for an entire year. During an extended stay in Prague, she made her daughter sign up to play soccer with a local team of all-white girls who didn't speak English. As her daughter made her way onto the grassy field, her teammates eyed her as if they'd never seen a Black girl before. She wanted to hide, to quit, but her mother wouldn't let her, because she wanted her daughter to know that "she belongs everywhere," and with that I said: "And *you* belong everywhere, too."

By the end of their stay in the Czech Republic, the footballers were giving her daughter high-fives and trying to pronounce her name. The story was a comfort to you; you asked me to repeat it several times—so much so that I started to wonder if you sometimes feel like you don't fit, like a painting too big, and sometimes too small, for its frame. Maybe we all do. Maybe that's the unfulfillable and inexpressible longing we universally share that musician Nick Cave talked about, the one that dogs us whether we're alone in a quiet apartment in New York City or in a loud, crowded house bustling with children and extended family. Maybe it's just a fact of being human—feeling misunderstood and lonely, like tenuously tethered astronauts floating in space.

On a trip to the Catskills the summer after graduating from second grade, you told us that you do indeed sometimes feel like the odd girl out—you're not Jewish enough, nor Latina enough, nor religious enough, and unlike your peers, you don't have a dad. But I knew those were just surface reasons why you felt adrift that July. Your sense of *not enoughness* extended from the falling-out with a friend, a girl you'd loved and adored above all others. It wracked you with bellyaches, outsized fears, and a disinclination to go to school. And yet, despite feeling alienated from your shared cohort of friends, you forged a new path with a new group of girls. You found your belonging, refusing to neatly fold back into your former peer group when mutual friends begged you to make amends. "Apologize, and we can call play together again," they said. "Apologize for what?" you replied. It would have been easier to give in, but something strong and instinctive in you resisted—because without knowing what you'd done wrong, any apology would've been hollow and a self-betrayal.

I can't know for sure, and you're too young to understand

such abstractions, but it seemed to Sabrina and me that the vulnerability you felt from love lost set you back—the part of you intent on standing out seemed more intent on blending in, especially with your clothing choices. Overnight you seemed to understand that style is a gateway to new friendships with other girls, a kind of armor against aloneness or unbelonging because, culturally, girls often connect by way of compliments and things that thrill the eye. While I've never seen any of your little boy friends compliment each other's outfits, one sure way to another girl's or woman's heart seems to be through aesthetic praise. "I love your dress," I'll hear you say to a friend's mom, and she'll dutifully reflect back the light you've just cast on her. You often compliment strangers on their earrings when we strike up conversations in parks or random stores on vacation, and at department store registers, you regularly gush to women about their long gem-encrusted nails. Almost inevitably, the kind words you've given come back to you, creating a dyad of mutual adoration that you can both comfortably nestle in with the knowledge that you've both succeeded at femininity; you've both succeeded at performing pretty.

There have been moments when I've experienced your wish to adapt to normality as a rejection of me—the queer factor in our family.

One early Saturday morning on the Outer Banks of North Carolina in a house on the beach overlooking the Atlantic Ocean—its immense floor-to-ceiling windows were so grand and opulent, it felt like we were in a movie—you and your cousins Mari and Emmy ran into our bedroom and tackled us into wakefulness. You explained to them that the three of you share blood with Sabrina but not me—"Mama Sabby just married *her,*" you said, a cold demotion that froze me, corpse-like, for an uncomfortable stretch.

They sang out, "Yay!" and hugged Sabrina.

The next day, Mari squealed as Sabrina and I came into your bedroom—strewn with clothes and stuffies and creepy-cool Shadow High dolls—because she was in the middle of changing into her bathing suit. You said: "Mama Sabby can see you naked because you are related by blood, but not *her,*" referring to me, and cousin Emmy piped in, "Yeah, you have to close your eyes." When Sabrina asked you both why, you said, "Well, Uncle Jamie can't see us naked."

"Yes, but Mama Steph is not a boy like Uncle Jamie," Sabrina said, "and she is as much related to you, as much your mother, as I am."

No, we do not share blood, and we'll never look alike, but I don't feel I'd be lying if I told anyone who asked that I was your birth mother because I can see so much of myself in you: the whiplash pace with which you fly through a task—homework, brushing teeth, or eating a meal; the way you get lost in a private reverie and become totally inaccessible to external stimuli, including my loud attempts to bring you back to the present; the way you take great pains to make sure you're spreading your love evenly, offering an equal share of Play-Doh pie to Sabrina and me. I am there, in all of it. I've spilled into your biology despite the differences in our DNA.

—

That you've held your birth mother above me at certain times is a symptom of culture.

My lesser status has been communicated to you repeatedly from infancy onward; it's culturally ingrained.

"Who carried her?" complete strangers on the playground will ask when they find out we're same-sex parents, which is another way of asking: Who's the *real* mother?

Kids at your former school, where there were very few queer families, would sometimes pelt you with questions about your family, convincing you on one occasion that Sabrina was your "actual" mom and I was like an aunt. For a moment, you seemed to believe them. That's why, when Sabrina's friend—a lovely woman whom you adore as much as she adores you—began seeking quality time with you and casting you as her family, her *niece,* it felt threatening to me: We are equally positioned biologically, and had you come from my body rather than Sabrina's, I'm fairly certain she wouldn't have felt so entitled to you—an oblique indication of my lesser status as your mother.

Others instantly nullified me by asking questions about your donor: "Who's her father? How did you find him? Is he anonymous? Has she met him?"

Some people, with their limited imaginations, don't take me for your real mother, which has made it hard for you to.

Even the law doesn't fully recognize the legitimacy of my parentage as it currently stands.

That's why I have to adopt you . . .

. . . despite the fact that I'm on your birth certificate, or that I cut the umbilical cord and severed the physical tie between you and Sabrina—or that I can, and have, given you more than blood. I've given you my love, too large to ever adequately express; perfect, although imperfectly imparted; constant, even when you can't give it in return, because I am meant to love you like a horticulturist tending her garden. The gift of having you is the love I feel for you, and it is enough.

A year went by, and with space and time, tensions around toeing the line to fit in relaxed a little, or maybe you just matured past your years after rising, phoenix-like, into a new iteration of self that could better reconcile outward demands with inward truths, because at Thanksgiving dinner at Tony's Di Napoli on the Upper East Side, near Grandma Elizabeth's place, your cousin Emmy turned to me, following the ideas you'd teed up in the Outer Banks the preceding year, and said, "You're not related to anyone here," to which I replied, "Well, not by blood, but neither is cousin Roberta."

"Why not cousin Roberta?" Emmy asked, perplexed.

"She's married to Peter, who *is* related to you by blood, but she's related to you through marriage, through history, through love, just like I am," I countered.

Sensing the hurt I might be feeling, you got up out of your seat, climbed onto my lap, threw your arms around my neck, and put your head on my shoulder, nearly toppling the turkey, stuffing, and cranberry sauce onto the floor, and said: "Are you okay, Ma?"

"Yes, sweetheart. Why wouldn't I be? I love you."

"I love you, too," you said.

"You look sad," Emmy commented. "Are you okay?" she asked, mimicking you, trying to suss out the ramifications of her remark.

"There are a lot of ways to make a family. Some people make a family through friends, rather than blood, but they're no less a family," Sabrina explained.

This time it didn't unmoor me because your gesture of love seemed to cancel out the notion that I was anything less than your mother to *you*—and ultimately, that's all that matters to me. The world is as it is, and we will always be in this knotted state that both forms and constricts us. I've only found momentary escape—brief reprieves—in learning to live vertically, beyond the stifling limits of conceptuality, where meaning is made with its inevitable hierarchies and exclusions. Only through a long depression did I glimpse the liberation ahead.

Chapter 12

Transcendence

At the height of the pandemic, when the unknowns felt cataclysmic, I was overwhelmed with anxiety. I panted rather than breathed my way through each day. I had the sensation of having to pee at all hours. I couldn't sleep.

To return to simplicity, to a kind of sublime nothingness, I had a recurring fantasy that brought me strange comfort—but would, in actuality, be shattering—and is a place I continue to return when the stuff of life overcrowds my mind: I've lost everything. I'm alone. I live in a bare-bones space in a rooming house. There is a desk, a bed, a chair, and a large window that illuminates the entire space with sunlight and looks out onto a cluster of towering trees—Norway maples, white mulberries, and purple-leaf plums. I do the same set of tasks each day, over and over again, which is a gratifying kind of tedium in my private reverie. It takes on the quality of a hymn or incantation. I make enough money to get by and spend most of my days observing rather than engaging the world. Like Hirayama (Kōji Yakusho), a toilet cleaner in the meditative German-Japanese film *Perfect Days,* I live a pared-down existence full of used books and old music cassettes, taking photographs of nature, a way of living that might look like failure or poverty to the modern mindset but is far richer.

This vision, which might be nightmarish to some, offers me relief, an unshackling from the morass of meaning that governs my life. In a world that encourages the pursuit of meaning as the only viable path to happiness, it will sound ironic when I say that our overinvestment in meaning is actually a hindrance to our happiness. After all, how encumbered are we by the endless procession of evaluative thoughts, ideas, and beliefs about ourselves, others, and society? From the macro to the micro, meaning builds up and calcifies, bricks in our being like clogged arteries, stopping the easy flow of our lives. We are tangled, submerged, and utterly lost in meaning. We constantly question and ponder all the constituent parts that comprise who we are—our genders, our sexualities, our races, our nationalities, our politics, our professions, our families, and, yes, even our appearances—as if we are containable in these linguistic inventions of mind. But we aren't.

The pressing and culminating consideration for me centered on my aesthetics because in our culture, a woman's beauty decides her access to worthiness, happiness, and even love and safety. My face, filtered and perceived through my personal history and the larger history and construction of beauty and ugliness in Western culture, made it difficult for me to be seen—and to see myself—as attractive *enough,* which generated a feeling of *not enoughness* in other, more fundamental areas of my life. The inadequacy that followed me from my formative years onward produced an inner instability, a shakiness, that gave way to the anxiety and depression that continues to trail me, although I'm learning how to outmaneuver it now. Perhaps all of us who suffer from varying degrees of angst and melancholia are, similarly, wrestling with and yearning to escape oppressive forms of significance.

You're still being molded by the culture we live in. Its hands are still shaping you like a sculptor's chisel. You want to belong—to be seen and understood, to *mean* something—so you don't yet feel the urgency to wiggle free from its grip. But you will. I write these words for that time, for when you're overcome by an existential lacking that makes inner peace elusive, for those moments—and may they be fleeting—when you feel insufficiently pretty, popular, intelligent, talented, successful, for when the mattering matters more than being and meaning sits within you like a debilitating weight.

I can't go through the dark for you—as much as I wish I could—but I can tell you that a profound radiance can emerge from it. I say that with the understanding that depression has infinite gradations and bottomless depths, and some people, tragically, reach places from which they cannot return. Mine was not like that.

I had my first depressive episode when I was nineteen. It lasted six months. It started with a panic attack—a heart beating so furiously, it landed me in the ER to rule out cardiac arrest. Panic gave way to labored breathing and an inability to catch my breath. It made me want to run out of my own body, only I couldn't, which created the horrifying sensation of being interred alive like a character in an Edgar Allan Poe story. Soon the panic and anxiety turned into depression, a deadening that manifested in the surreal sense that every action was pointless. I'd look at people going to work or students sitting in classrooms or watch my brother laughing idiotically at an episode of *Friends* and think: *Why is anyone doing anything? What is all this? What are we doing here?* It made the world an absurd and unrelatable place. But in hollowing out—and leveling—meaning, it revealed something deeper: awareness itself.

Many well-known thinkers, from Carl Jung to Rainer Maria Rilke to Søren Kierkegaard, have seen depression not just as suffering but as a potential path to personal growth or enlightenment. But I've experienced it as enlightenment itself. I've found particular truths in French feminist and psychoanalyst Julia Kristeva's *Black Sun.* She draws on Freud and French psychoanalyst Jacques Lacan to illuminate the origins of depression. As part of normal development, a baby must learn to cope with the loss of oneness with its mother by stepping into the world of language, law, and social rules, known as the symbolic order. In this new space of signs and symbols, the baby forges a new sense of identity and meaning. But when a baby can't accept that separation—something Kristeva calls "the denial of negation"—she clings to the fantasy of complete unity with her mother and resists the shared world of meaning and sociality, which is the psychic root of depression. Perhaps this explains why the ability to make sense of things begins to break down during depressive episodes.

Notably, Kristeva frames aspects of this experience as particularly feminine. In patriarchal societies, traditionally, women's labor, emotional lives, and minds are often "devalued—dismissed, belittled, or rendered invisible," Kelly Oliver, a professor of philosophy at Vanderbilt University and author of *Reading Kristeva,* told me via email. As a result, women often lack the social and symbolic support necessary to develop a stable and autonomous sense of self. This can make it difficult to integrate their identities in ways that affirm their individuality and agency, leaving them especially vulnerable to depression and feelings of inadequacy.

But I wonder, conversely, if the suffering caused by meaninglessness stems in part from a social infrastructure that places too much importance on meaning itself. Once I saw past, beyond, the wreckage of meaning and form, I experienced a more expansive state of awareness outside conceptual thinking and, along with it, a much greater ease of existence.

Reflecting on the beauty and benefit of forgoing labels—and

the meaning that arises from them—I've come to see an uncanny spirituality in queer theory, an intellectual tool that is foundational to this letter and has always resonated with me emotionally.

Queer theory's refusal to uphold binaries—male/female, masculine/feminine, heterosexual/homosexual—and thus the social injustices that extend from them, makes possible alternative ways of knowing that topple the old destructive ones. In its commitment to unknowing, to constant revision in response to the world's evolving and immediate needs, and to transcending the ways that culture cuttingly produces—limits, controls, defines, *hurts*—our experience of the bodies we inhabit, whether we're men or women, Black or white, gay or straight, trans or cisgender, able-bodied or disabled, visibly affluent or poverty-stricken, and pretty or ugly, it feels like a spiritual quest. It understands that the ideas we ascribe to our materiality often smother our humanity—and within it lies a longing to move beyond all manner of signification.

You'll feel that longing one day, too. Maybe you already do.

In that spirit, I've tried to give you wings for flight for when you're tired of trudging in the muck—like when we discovered the weightless joy of scatting.

In the world of jazz, scatting involves nonconceptual utterances that travel the length of a song with lively spontaneity. Popularized by legendary jazz musician Louis Armstrong, the trumpeter was famously recording a tune—an expensive production in the 1920s—and forgot the lyrics, so he improvised with a series of indecipherable sounds he sang in harmony with the music. While that moment may have been born a mistake, it grew into a kind of language. To some vocalists scatting was an expression of resistance to the articulable words and ideas that served to subjugate and exploit people of color. For others—like Betty Carter—it may have been a way to overthrow and rearrange the order of things: "Scat . . . defies linguistic meaning systems and, by extension, the social structures and power relations that condition them," journalist George Burrows writes in *The Independent.* Maybe because of that, it has helped float us out of unhappy mindsets many times . . .

Scatting for me can also function as a space or pause between thoughts, which German spiritual teacher Eckhart Tolle identifies as the place where "glimpses of love and joy or brief moments of deep peace are possible" because it disrupts and momentarily pauses the thinking mind. The divine gaps between one thought and the next remind me of that point in the life cycle of a conscious breath, when you reach the end of an inhale and breathing stops for a beat and you can feel your limbs tingle in anticipation of the exhale and the relaxation it brings. The places in between have always had spiritual resonances. French composer Claude Debussy espoused the view that the silent interstices within his compositions were the music itself, as did jazz musician Miles Davis, who once said: "It's not the notes you play; it's the notes you don't play."

These seeds of future awakening that I try to plant may not sprout anytime soon, as our family friend Sophie says, but, she promises, they will when the time is right.

"When she needs them, they will come," she jokes, riffing on the iconic line from the 1989 film *Field of Dreams.* Although it's a little hokey, the movie speaks to all I wish for you nonetheless: that you will trust your vision, even when it registers as pure madness to others; that you will follow through on your dreams no matter how daunting or outside the current logics of what's possible; that you will have faith in a transcendent knowing that there's more to life, to you, to your value—to all of us—than can be quantified or articulated, even by science; and that our universe, amid multiverses, infinite, lives inside you. We are, after all, stardust. For me, wind and breath—invisible but felt—have always provided an easy and immediate portal to that kind of self-transcendence.

Starting when you were five, I've tried, unsuccessfully, to introduce you to the wisdom of a conscious breath. Impishly, you've made a sport of defying my instructions to slowly breathe in through the nose and out through the mouth, gulping down air like a shot and swiftly expelling it. You've laughed your way through my command to "Om"—the first and all-encompassing sound of the universe in ancient spiritual texts. We even ventured into nature together so that I could teach you kid-friendly meditations. But you'd punctuate each moment with laughs, toppling over like a tree in a hurricane and rolling through the grass in stitches.

I knew I was getting through to you, though, during our last séance-like gathering on your cosmological rug. You were nine. Sabrina, you, and I sat, as we do, in a triangle. We lit a candle and placed it at the center of your velvet altar cloth. Before queuing up a three-minute meditation, I showed you—and you paid attention to—the anatomy of a diaphragmatic breath. When you blew out the candle, you said, theatrically, but also as if a wise spirit were speaking through you, "The darkness is also the light. The darkness is also beautiful."

Surely you didn't grasp the profound depth of those words, but I couldn't stop mulling it over. It's not just the precocity in the observation that light and dark are mutually contingent and, in that sense, thus one and the same, but, more expansively and bittersweetly, it spoke to what I'd experienced in depression: that the darkest abyss sometimes contains within it, and brings forth, the brightest illumination. Your words also got me thinking about why we close our eyes when we pray—the darkness releases us from the world of forms. And it *is* beautiful, the luminous face of darkness. I hope you'll always see beauty where others don't and tend to it in yourself and others in your gentle way because, ultimately, it's *all* beautiful. Even the things that are ugly—ugly words, ugly ideas, ugly beliefs, ugly behaviors—are necessary to the expansion of our humanity and spiritual awakening.

While I don't believe in a personal god—one who lords over us, moralizes or concerns himself with the man-made content of our lives—I do find an uncanny peace in a state of unknowing. There is something quietly transcendent in that infinite field of unmanifested possibility. I see my faith as spiritual nihilism or maybe even a contented agnosticism, a reverence for meaning that is ineffable and unknowable, but resoundingly felt. I feel a deep sense of wonder contemplating the vastness and mystery of the universe, knowing it lives in me and I live in it. I often find my anchoring by looking upward—at a blanket of stars across a clear midnight sky or the tall gusty trees in the park, especially the spaces in between the leafy boughs, where the sun pours through, light shattering the darkness, giving hope to a bleak hour.

Awe researchers like U.C. Berkeley's Dacher Keltner have shown how sweeping views of nature and the cosmos function to shrink us—make us matter *less*—and in so doing still our minds. However briefly, awe releases us from the maelstrom of meaning, the social detritus that wreaks havoc on our peace. "When . . . we are too focused on ourselves, anxiety, rumination, depression, and self-criticism can overtake us. An overactive default self can undermine the collaborative efforts and goodwill of our communities. Many of today's social ills arise out of an overactive default self, augmented by self-obsessed digital technologies. Awe, it would seem, quiets this urgent voice," Keltner writes in *Awe: The New Science of Everyday Wonder and How It Can Transform Your Life.*

He and his colleague Yang Bai conducted a study in which they asked more than a thousand participants to draw themselves in either one of two settings: Yosemite National Park or

Fisherman's Wharf, San Francisco. Those in the former group drew themselves diminutive against a majestic and sprawling scene, while those in the control group in San Francisco made themselves much larger in stature. Being confronted by the awe-inspiring tableaux of nature or the universe dwarfs us and our problems, allowing a momentary respite from thought, which in many traditions is a gateway to spirituality.

In the book of Genesis, God warns Adam and Eve not to eat from the Tree of Knowledge of Good and Evil. But when they do, they lose their ineffable unity with the divine and awaken to separation, self-consciousness, and judgment. In the *Tao Te Ching,* Lao Tzu writes: "The great image has no shape; the way conceals itself in being nameless." What is truly sacred cannot be put into words—it is the quiet ground of genuine peace and lightness.

However you're able to access the formless eternal—maybe it's a shaft of light coming through a window at dusk or a piece of music wafting through your apartment—I hope it creates space within you where meaning falls away and you're viscerally present to this moment.

I've sometimes wondered if my spiritual journey is just another way to escape my corporeal existence, to disown my body. While there may be some truth in that, I also know unequivocally that it's allowed a higher consciousness to emerge, one that recognizes that a big life, the fullest expression of one worth living, thrives on the smallest, quietest moments. It's a way of living I'm trying to impart to you day by day, and together, we're getting the hang of it. We're finding reprieve and joy in small things—walking through the park with our hands clasped at sunset, our cats' soulful eyes, Sabrina's hands on our shoulders, windy days that rustle the large knobby trees in Sunset Park, a full moon and the realization that it's the same moon we all look at everywhere and have throughout time, the same one the dinosaurs saw. We're learning to stay in these moments, to breathe them in fully—because they aren't small; they are big—they are life, our life, and I don't want us to miss it. I want us to abandon life as most people live it, to kick the old, tired metrics of success in the teeth, to turn every edict about how we *should* be and live on its head and see what new ways of being and existing might emerge. I want a new kind of queer life for us, one not *against* meaning but *above* it, where liberation and transcendence from notions of beauty and ugly lie, where I know—all of us—will find our deliverance.

Acknowledgments

—

Nothing, ever, is accomplished alone: This book owes a debt of gratitude to so many wonderful people, starting with my brilliant agents Rebecca Gradinger and Albert Lee at United Talent Agency, who continued to believe in the value of this project even when the earliest iterations of my proposal kept missing the mark. With their deep intelligence and creativity and that of their magnificent assistants, Sam Solomons, Madison Hernick, and Laurie-Maude Chernard, I was able to manifest a book I hope has a meaningful impact on those who read it. I want to give special thanks to the luminous mind of Denise Oswald, my inimitable editor, without whom this book would be a shadow of itself—and to her incomparable team at Pantheon: assistant editor Shanna Milkey, publicist Rose Cronin-Jackman, marketer Julianne Clancy, production editor Melissa Yoon, copyeditor Kayla Overbey, proofreaders Karen Thompson and Alisa Garrison, and designer Ariel Harari, who created this powerful and evocative cover. I give thanks to my SHA-mate Joshua Friedman, a masterful copyeditor, thinker, and writer, who managed my overwhelming endnotes. Despite the ever-present ethical ambiguities and challenges of writing about *anyone* as a journalist, the stakes are even higher when writing about your own family, especially your child. With that in mind, I want to express profound appreciation for the loves of my life, Sabrina and our daughter, for letting me use our lives to illuminate important truths about our society and hopefully thereby heal others who've endured similar challenges—or at least make them feel less alone. On that note, I also want to thank my mother Chrysí; my brother Andreas and his wife, Stacy; my sister-in-law Joanne, Sabrina's sister; our brother-in-law Jaime; our nieces Mari and Emmy; Grandma Elizabeth; Uncle Heinrich; cousin Roberta; cousin Peter. I'm extremely grateful for the support and cheerleading from good friends with standout thank-yous to M.E.G. (my forever and always close confidante), my gentle-hearted and supportive friend Jennifer Pearson Ritter, who pointed me to high-quality market research, my wonderfully kind and loving lawyer friends Natalie Krodel and Jennifer Lazo for their unofficial legal guidance and care—thanks for the cookies and meals and spa day! I want to extend deep gratitude and love to the friends and families anonymously represented in these pages—this could not have been written without you: E.A., L.C., D.R.C.A., A.V.C.A., J.P.R., R.R., C.M.R., S.K., R.O., T.K., F.J.K.O., G.L.L., T.B., L.T., M.E.T., A.P., N.M., J.B.M., R.L., L.W., M.A.W., S.B., A.D., M.M., J.P., A.O., R.C., J.A., M.A.C., T.A.C., and L.A.C.

The cultural context for my personal story depended on key academic texts and the wonderful minds who wrote them for whom I am deeply indebted: Naomi Baker's *Plain Ugly,* Joan Jacobs Brumberg's *The Body Project,* Judith Butler's *Gender Trouble* and *The Psychic Life of Power,* Umberto Eco's *History of Beauty* and *On Ugliness,* Renee Engeln's *Beauty Sick,* Lillian

Faderman's *Odd Girls and Twilight Lovers,* Amanda Foreman's "Why Footbinding Persisted in China for a Millenium," in the *Smithsonian,* February 2015, Michel Foucault's *Discipline and Punish* and *The Archaeology of Knowledge,* Jack Halberstam's *The Queer Art of Failure,* Gretchen E. Henderson's *Ugliness,* Cathy Park Hong's *Minor Feelings,* Eric Marcus's *Making Gay History* (the book and the podcast), Toni Morrison's *The Bluest Eye,* Peggy Orenstein's *Cinderella Ate My Daughter* and *Schoolgirls,* Nell Irvin Painter's *The History of White People* (thanks to Shirley J. Velasquez for alerting me to Painter's text and giving me the opportunity to work out several ideas rendered in these pages as my editor at *Oprah Daily*), Mary Pipher's *Reviving Ophelia*, Elaine Scarry's *On Beauty and Being Just,* Susan Schweik's *The Ugly Laws,* Elizabeth Semmelhack's *Shoes: The Meaning of Style,* Thomas J. Spiegel's "Lookism as Epistemic Injustice," in *Social Epistemology* (Vol. 37, 2023), Sherri L. Smith's *What Is the Civil Rights Movement?,* and Eckhart Tolle's *A New Earth* and *The Power of Now,* Naomi Wolf's *The Beauty Myth*—and several academic papers and articles referenced in my endnotes were invaluable in helping me make sense of my story.

I thank the following scholars who were generous with their time and knowledge: Stephanie Coontz, Carolyn Dean, Cheryl Dellasega, Renee Engeln, Lillian Faderman, Amy Gansell, Abbie Goldberg, Annamarie Jagose, Jain 108, David Konstan, Rachel P. Kreiter, John Lechte, Robin M. Mathy, Laura Miller, Ingrid Monson, Kelly Oliver, Jennifer C. Pizer, Scott L. Rogers, Alice Ruby, Elizabeth Semmelhack, Thomas J. Spiegel, Susan Stryker, Matthew C. Velasco, Lisa Wade, and Katharina Wiedlack.

To professors Carolyn Dinshaw and Sharon Marcus, formerly of U.C. Berkeley, thank you for being the first to show me how to see beauty where others see ugly.

To Mary Gaitskill and Rebecca Traister, unflinching truth tellers, incomparable talents, and deeply kind humans, thank you for endorsing my original book proposal.

Finally, I want to thank our loved ones who've passed, whom we miss every day: my father, H.A.K.; my father-in-law, M.W.; my grandmothers, H.L.R. and F.E.C.K.; and my grandfathers, A.K. and N.R.

Notes

PROLOGUE: LETTER TO MY DAUGHTER

4 **Edicts about how we should look:** Simone de Beauvoir, *The Second Sex,* trans. H. M. Parshley (Vintage Books, 1974), 301.

4 **And even if we could evade:** Judith Butler, *The Psychic Life of Power: Theories in Subjection* (Stanford University Press, 1997), 2. Citing Michel Foucault, Butler posits that we are constituted by that from which we seek liberation.

5 **"I smell a child":** Eric Geron, *Hocus Pocus Spell Book: A Guide to Spells, Potions, and Hexes for the Aspiring Salem Witch* (Disney Press, 2022), 175.

5 **From the fourteenth to the seventeenth centuries:** Jess Blumberg, "A Brief History of the Salem Witch Trials," *Smithsonian,* last updated October 24, 2022, https://www.smithsonianmag.com/.

5 **Misogyny underlay the hysteria:** Mona Chollet, *In Defense of Witches: The Legacy of the Witch Hunts and Why Women Are Still On Trial,* trans. Sophie R. Lewis (St. Martin's Press, 2022).

CHAPTER 1: BLOOD

8 **The mainstream LGBTQ movement has historically:** Stephanie Fairyington, "Choice as Strategy: Homosexuality and the Politics of Pity," *Dissent* 57, no. 1 (Winter 2010).

9 **"If there were a straight pill":** Fairyington, "Choice as Strategy."

11 **Even acting on our queer lusts:** "Update on the Status of Sodomy Laws,"

American Civil Liberties Union, accessed June 12, 2025, https://www.aclu.org/.

11 **A lower court:** Art Harris, "The Unintended Battle of Michael Hardwick," *The Washington Post,* August 20, 1986.

11 **When Hardwick's lover:** Harris, "The Unintended Battle of Michael Hardwick."

11 **As Pizer put it:** Jennifer Pizer, chief legal officer for Lambda Legal, in an email exchange with the author, June 11, 2025.

12 **Before an agreement:** Mike Schneider, "Florida Teachers Can Discuss Sexual Orientation and Gender ID Under 'Don't Say Gay' Bill Settlement," Associated Press, March 11, 2024.

12 **The state's quest:** Jo Yurcaba, "Florida School District Must Return LGBTQ Books to Libraries After Settlement," *NBC News,* September 13, 2024, https://www.nbcnews.com.

13 **Just days ago:** Nina Totenberg and Anuli Ononye, "SCOTUS: Parents Can Opt Kids Out of Classes with LGBTQ Book Characters," NPR, June 27, 2025.

14 **"According to the Word of God":** Anita Bryant, interview by Barbara Howar, *Who's Who,* CBS, April 12, 1977, posted August 7, 2014, by SuchIsLifeVideos, YouTube, https://www.youtube.com/watch?v=fABwascm12s, at 5 min., 30 sec.

14 **"God made mothers":** Bryant, interview by Howar, at 8 min., 24 sec.

14 **When the *Lawrence* decision:** Lawrence et al. v. Texas, 539 U.S. 558 (2003).

14 ***Obergefell v. Hodges:*** HRC Staff, "Four Cases That Paved the Way for Marriage Equality and a Reminder of the Work Ahead," Human Rights Campaign, June 26, 2017, https://www.hrc.org.

16 **I'd just seen the movie *Top Gun:*** Sara Hammel, "Kelly McGillis: Coming Out as a Lesbian Not Easy," *People,* May 28, 2009.

17 **"There is no agony":** Zora Neale Hurston, *Dust Tracks on a Road* (Zinc Read, 2025), 126.

17 **Writers from Joan Didion:** Joan Didion, *The White Album* (FSG Classics, 2009), 11; Flannery O'Connor, *Mystery and Manners* (Farrar, Straus and Giroux, 1970), 48; John Romano, "James Baldwin Writing and Talking," *The New York Times Book Review,* September 23, 1979.

18 **"And Jamie's eyes":** Stephanie Fairyington, "I Asked My Brother to Donate Sperm to My Wife. That Was the Easy Part," *The New Republic,* October 31, 2014, https://newrepublic.com.

19 **"LGBTQ families are helping":** Stephanie Coontz, author of *The Way We Never Were* and *For Better and Worse: The Problematic Past and Uncertain Future of Marriage,* in a discussion with the author, December 11, 2023.

20 **married people ought to behave:** Stephanie Coontz, "For a Better Marriage, Act Like a Single Person," *The New York Times,* February 10, 2018.

20 **Psychologist and host:** Anonymous, "The Day I Broke Up with My Mother," *Oprah Daily,* April 10, 2024.

21 **As they argued:** Richard Kim and Lisa Duggan, "Beyond Gay Marriage," *The Nation,* July 18, 2005.

21 **With more than twenty-seven million:** "Company Facts," https://www.ancestry.com/corporate/about-ancestry/company-facts; Celeste Biever, "23andMe Plans to Sell Its Huge Genetic Database: Could Science Benefit?" *Nature,* March 31, 2025; *Finding Your Roots,* created by Henry Louis Gates Jr., PBS, 2025.

22 **In fact, 65 percent:** Joanna E. Scheib et al., "Who Requests Their Sperm Donor's Identity? The First Ten Years of Information Releases to Adults with Open-Identity Donors," *Fertility and Sterility* 107, no. 2 (2017): 483–93.

22 **Despite being well versed:** Alice Park, "Study: Children of Lesbians May Do Better Than Their Peers," *Time,* June 7, 2010.

23 **"I love you both":** Fairyington, "I Asked My Brother to Donate Sperm to My Wife."

CHAPTER 2: HISTORY OF DIFFERENCE

26 **"What defines a man":** Carina Chocano, "The World's Newest Superhero: Bad Bunny," *GQ,* May 24, 2022.

27 **"Dads push us to take risks":** Lolita C. Baldor, "Hegseth's Views on Women in Combat, Infidelity and More—In His Own Words," Associated Press, January 14, 2025.

27 **In September 2025:** Julie Watson, Laurie Kellman, and Deepti Hajela, "Pete Hegseth Had a Lot to Say When He Summoned Military Leaders. Here Are Some Facts and Context," Associated Press, September 30, 2025.

27 **"I signed an order":** Associated Press, "Read the Full Text of Trump's Speech to a Joint Session of Congress," PBS News, March 5, 2025.

28 **"pale, round, plump face[s]":** Laura Miller, *Beauty Up: Exploring Contemporary Japanese Body Aesthetics* (University of California Press, 2006), 21.

29 **"One theory is that":** Laura Miller, Japanese Studies and history professor at the University of Missouri–St. Louis, in discussion with author via email, February 24, 2024.

29 **Chinese women:** Tiffany Marie Smith, "Footbinding: Chinese History," *Encyclopaedia Britannica,* September 13, 2025, https://www.britannica.com/.

29 **"First, [a girl's] feet":** Amanda Foreman, "Why Footbinding Persisted in China for a Millennium," *Smithsonian,* February 2015.

30 **Originally worn:** Jessica Pearce Rotondi, "The History of the Bra: From Corsets to Spandex," History.com, September 30, 2024.

31 **Like bound feet:** Alexis Aberman, "Childhood Corsetry: The Development of Unnatural Body Standards from a Young Age," Cornell Fashion & Textile Collection, May 5, 2022, https://blogs.cornell.edu/cornellcostume/.

31 ***Vogue* once called:** Liam Hess, "The Story Behind Madonna's Iconic Jean Paul Gaultier Cone Bra," *Vogue,* April 18, 2020.

33 **Appropriately enough:** *Merriam-Webster Dictionary,* "dude," https://www.merriam-webster.com/.

33 **As James Baldwin once said:** John Romano, "James Baldwin Writing and Talking," *The New York Times Book Review,* September 23, 1979.

33 **With restraint but perceptible censure:** Christian Louboutin, *Pumps,* 2007, leather, plastic (vinyl), Metropolitan Museum of Art, object number 2012.121a, b, https://www.metmuseum.org/art/collection/search/146206.

34 **In tenth-century Persia:** Elizabeth Semmelhack, *Shoes: The Meaning of Style* (Reaktion Books, 2017), 161–9.

34 **As they gained in popularity:** Avery Trufelman, *99% Invisible,* podcast, "Feet of Engineering," June 17, 2014; William Kremer, "Why Did Men Stop Wearing High Heels?" *BBC News,* January 25, 2013.

34 **"Everyone knows":** *Origin of Everything,* season 1, episode 30, "When Men Wore High Heels," PBS Digital Studios, May 8, 2018.

35 **In some instances, the palettes:** Riley Black, "Makeup in Ancient Egypt," Natural History Museum of Utah, June 30, 2021.

35 **As shown in:** Gay Robins, "Hair and the Construction of Identity in Ancient Egypt, c. 1480–1350 B.C.," *Journal of the American Research Center in Egypt* 36 (1999): 55–69, https://www.jstor.org/stable/40000202.

35 **Similar to the ancient Greeks:** Amy Gansell, "Images and Conceptions of Ideal Feminine Beauty in Neo-Assyrian Royal Contexts, c. 883–627 BCE," in *Critical Approaches to Ancient Near Eastern Art,* ed. Brian A. Brown and Marian H. Feldman (De Gruyter, 2014), 391–420; Amy Gansell, "Ancient Attraction: Goddesses as Exemplars for the Beauty and Power of Neo-Assyrian Queens," lecture, University of Oslo, October 9, 2020, https://www.youtube.com/watch?v=yL28ONxIpzo.

39 **We ditched the book:** Roxane Gay, *Hunger: A Memoir of (My) Body* (Harper, 2017), 255, Kindle.

40 **a "divine quality,":** Amy Gansell, art history professor who specializes in the ancient Near East at St. John's University, in discussion with author, February 20, 2024.

CHAPTER 3: THE INVENTION OF BEAUTY—AND UGLY

43 **"In the course of time":** Umberto Eco, ed., *History of Beauty,* trans. Alastair McEwen (Rizzoli, 2005), 94.

43 **As Michel Foucault observed:** Michel Foucault, *The Archaeology of Knowledge,* trans. A. M. Sheridan Smith (Pantheon Books, 1972), 6.

45 **They believed it represented:** Gerald Bostock, "The Sacred Tetraktys: The Number Symbolism of the Pythagoreans," Academia.edu, 2–6, accessed September 28, 2025.

45 **Following the Pythagorean meditation:** Eco, *History of Beauty,* 64.

45 **While early Pythagoreans believed that opposites:** Eco, *History of Beauty,* 72.

49 **The Greek word *kalokagathía:*** Umberto Eco, ed., *On Ugliness,* trans. Alastair McEwen (Rizzoli, 2011), 23.

49 **Roughly translated, *kalós:*** Marija-Ana Dürrigl, "Kalokagathia—Beauty Is More Than Just External Appearance," *Journal of Cosmetic Dermatology* 1, no. 4 (2002): 208–10.

49 **Although the late:** David Konstan, the late Classics professor at New York University, in discussion with the author, February 7, 2024.

49 **"Mental character":** Elizabeth C. Evans, "Physiognomics in the Roman Empire," *The Classical Journal* 45, no. 6 (1950): 277–82.

50 **A few years ago, Thomas J. Spiegel:** Thomas J. Spiegel, "Lookism as Epistemic Injustice," *Social Epistemology* 37, no. 1 (2023): 47–61.

50 **As cultural critic Peggy Orenstein:** Peggy Orenstein, *Cinderella Ate My Daughter: Dispatches from the Front Lines of the New Girlie-Girl Culture* (HarperCollins, 2011), 167.

51 **One recent study:** Antonio Olivera La Rosa, Javier Villacampa, Guido Corradi, and Gordon P. D. Ingram, "The Creepy, the Bad and the Ugly: Exploring Perceptions of Moral Character and Social Desirability in Uncanny Faces," *Current Psychology* 42, no. 1 (February 2021): 1146–56.

52 **One reason it's challenging:** Hassan Aleem, Maria Pombo, Ivan Correa, and Norberto M. Grzywacz, "Is Beauty in the Eye of the Beholder or an Objective Truth? A Neuroscientific Answer," in *Mobile Brain-Body Imaging and the Neuroscience of Art, Innovation and Creativity,* ed. Jose L. Contreras-Vidal et al. (Springer, 2019), 101–10.

53 **Due, in part, to hundreds of years:** Toby Chen et al., "Occidentalisation of Beauty Standards: Eurocentrism in Asia," *Across the Spectrum of Socioeconomics* 1, no. 2 (2020).

53 **Similarly, a study:** Ngozi Akinro and Lindani Mbunyuza-Memani, "Black Is Not Beautiful: Persistent Messages and the Globalization of 'White' Beauty in African Women's Magazines," *Journal of International and Intercultural Communication* 12, no. 4 (2019): 308–24.

53 **a wider range:** Rebecca F. Lazuka, Madeline R. Wick, Pamela K. Keel, and Jennifer A. Harriger, "Are We There Yet? Progress in Depicting Diverse Images of Beauty in Instagram's Body Positivity Movement," *Body Image* 34 (September 2020): 85–93.

53 **You'd think social media:** Pilar Aparicio-Martinez et al., "Social Media, Thin-Ideal, Body Dissatisfaction and Disordered Eating Attitudes: An Exploratory Analysis," *International Journal of Environmental Research and Public Health* 16, no. 21 (2019).

53 **Many images:** Giulia Fioravanti, Sara Bocci Benucci, Giulia Ceragioli, and

Silvia Casale, "How the Exposure to Beauty Ideals on Social Networking Sites Influences Body Image: A Systematic Review of Experimental Studies," *Adolescent Research Review* 7 (2022): 419–58.

53 **"There are tons of studies":** Renee Engeln, a professor of psychology at Northwestern University and author of *Beauty Sick,* via email in May 9, 2025.

54 **"The main problem":** Spiegel, "Lookism as Epistemic Injustice," 47–61.

56 **"What we can see":** Nell Irvin Painter, *The History of White People* (W. W. Norton & Company, 2010), 30, Kindle.

56 **People from the "fertile lowlands":** Painter, *The History of White People,* 23.

57 **"They not only wanted":** Leah Donnella, "Is Beauty in the Eyes of the Colonizer?" *Code Switch,* NPR, February 6, 2019.

58 **"Adults, older girls":** Toni Morrison, *The Bluest Eye* (Vintage International, 2007), 20.

58 **"It had occurred to Pecola":** Morrison, *The Bluest Eye,* 46.

58 **"the term 'Caucasian'":** Painter, *The History of White People,* 10.

59 **"science of race":** Painter, *The History of White People,* 61.

59 **gives "pride of place":** Painter, *The History of White People,* 62.

60 **"their thick lips":** François Bernier, "A New Division of the Earth," *History Workshop Journal,* no. 51 (2001): 247–50.

60 **"truly white":** Painter, *The History of White People,* 62.

60 **"little stunted creatures":** Painter, *The History of White People,* 62.

60 **"'The handsomest women of the world":** Painter, *The History of White People,* 63.

60 **"complete savages":** Painter, *The History of White People,* 64.

61 **"The blood of *Georgia*":** Painter, *The History of White People,* 65.

61 **Painter wryly points out:** Painter, *The History of White People,* 65.

61 **"the aura of physical attractiveness":** Painter, *The History of White People,* 66.

62 **"The sort of beauty":** Painter, *The History of White People,* 67.

62 **"an offense against beauty":** Painter, *The History of White People,* 84.

63 **"Racial self-hatred":** Cathy Park Hong, *Minor Feelings: An Asian American Reckoning* (One World, 2021), 9–10.

63 **"It would apply":** Painter, *The History of White People,* 86.

64 **"The 'English face'":** Painter, *The History of White People,* 211–12.

65 **"weak in body and spirit":** Painter, *The History of White People,* 116.

65 **Ideas like Emerson's:** Michelle L. Price, "White House Denounces Trump's 'Bad Genes' Comment," Associated Press, October 7, 2024; Marc Levy, "ICE Deported 3 Children Who Are U.S. Citizens, Their Families' Lawyers Say," Associated Press, April 27, 2025; Adam Liptak, "Trump Asks Supreme Court to Let Him Send Migrants to South Sudan," *The New York Times,* May 27, 2025.

66 **"suspiciously stereotypical":** Painter, *The History of White People,* 236.

66 **"The . . . lineaments":** Samuel Morton, *Crania Aegyptiaca* (J. Penington, 1844), 3.

66 **"all smaller skulls":** Painter, *The History of White People,* 237.

66 **Although Morton's:** "500 Years of Antisemitic Propaganda: The Katz-Ehrenthal Collection," United States Holocaust Memorial Museum, https://www.ushmm.org; Naomi Zeveloff, "How the All-American Nose Job Got a Makeover," *The Forward,* October 11, 2015.

67 **"[They are] large":** Beth Preminger, "The 'Jewish Nose' and Plastic Surgery: Origins and Implications," *JAMA* 286, no. 17, November 7, 2001.

68 **A statistician named Alice Lee:** Leila McNeill, "The Statistician Who Debunked Sexist Myths About Skull Size and Intelligence," *Smithsonian,* January 14, 2019.

68 **"Aristotle proposed a law":** Gretchen E. Henderson, *Ugliness: A Cultural History* (Reaktion Books, 2015), 29–30.

68 **Even kids with cleft palates:** S. Bhattacharya, V. Khanna, and R. Kohli, "Cleft Lip: The Historical Perspective," *Indian Journal of Plastic Surgery* 42, Suppl. (October 2009): S4–S8.

69 ***Kakos* connoted:** Henderson, *Ugliness: A Cultural History*, 29.

69 **"Greek culture produced":** Umberto Eco, ed., *On Ugliness,* trans. Alastair McEwen (Rizzoli, 2011), 23.

69 **Similar ideas underlie:** Susan M. Schweik, *The Ugly Laws: Disability in Public* (New York University Press, 2009), vii, Kindle.

71 **"Unsightliness":** Schweik, *The Ugly Laws,* 16.

71 **"Does she not seem":** Umberto Eco, ed., *The History of Beauty,* trans. Alastair McEwen (Rizzoli, 2005), 217.

71 **In Naomi Baker's *Plain Ugly:*** Naomi Baker, *Plain Ugly: The Unattractive Body in Early Modern Culture* (Manchester University Press, 2015), 98–99.

72 **"In the later-nineteenth-century United States":** Schweik, *The Ugly Laws,* 86.

72 **Schweik goes on:** Schweik, *The Ugly Laws,* 159.

72 **"This class is composed of":** Susan M. Schweik, *The Ugly Laws: Disability in Public* (New York: NYU Press, 2009), 159.

73 **"things must be suited":** Eco, *The History of Beauty,* 88.

74 **"ugly things are part of":** Eco, *The History of Beauty,* 85.

74 **"monstrous men and animals":** Eco, *The History of Beauty,* 139.

74 **"belong to the providential order":** Eco, *The History of Beauty,* 145.

74 **We looked at all of them:** Eco, *The History of Beauty,* 139–41.

75 **"a bias toward formlessness":** Eco, *The History of Beauty,* 281.

75 **"a dying lady":** Eco, *The History of Beauty,* 288.

75 **"While yet a boy":** Eco, *The History of Beauty,* 288.

75 **"Beware; for I am fearless":** Mary Shelley, *Frankenstein: The 1818 Text* (Penguin Classics, 2018), 163.

75 **"There is something at work":** Shelley, *Frankenstein,* 241.
75 **"goes far beyond":** Eco, *The History of Beauty,* 294.
75 **"appreciated precisely":** Eco, *The History of Beauty,* 285.
75 **"Yes, my Léa":** Eco, *On Ugliness,* 307.
76 **"not to exclude contradictions":** Eco, *The History of Beauty,* 299.
76 **"the most disturbing aspects":** Eco, *The History of Beauty,* 330.
76 **"Ugliness was no longer":** Eco, *The History of Beauty,* 321.
77 **"accused of witchcraft":** Eco, *On Ugliness,* 212.
77 **"Attributions of beauty":** Eco, *On Ugliness,* 12.
77 **"lent them such charisma":** Eco, *On Ugliness,* 12.
80 **As a young therapist:** Renee Engeln, *Beauty Sick: How the Cultural Obsession with Appearance Hurts Girls and Women* (Harper, 2017), 39.
80 **"There are many women":** Engeln, *Beauty Sick,* 40.

CHAPTER 4: "LEZ ALERT!"

85 **"classification of 'ugly'":** Gretchen E. Henderson, *Ugliness: A Cultural History* (Reaktion Books, 2015), 46.
85 **Tracing the etymology:** Henderson, *Ugliness,* 29.
85 **"practices of investigation":** Henderson, *Ugliness,* 54.
85 **"matter out of place," a phrase:** Henderson, *Ugliness,* 12–13.
86 **Like Julia Pastrana:** Henderson, *Ugliness,* 26, 56.
87 **"same-sex relationships were far more preferable":** Lillian Faderman, *Odd Girls and Twilight Lovers: A History of Lesbian Life in Twentieth-Century America* (Columbia University Press, 1991), 16.
87 **"I am not domestic":** Faderman, *Odd Girls and Twilight Lovers,* 12.
87 **By the end of the century:** Faderman, *Odd Girls and Twilight Lovers,* 12.
88 **"unfit for . . . traditional roles":** Faderman, *Odd Girls and Twilight Lovers,* 13.
88 **"the lower orders of society":** Faderman, *Odd Girls,* 14.
89 **But some men, of course:** Elizabeth Cady Stanton, "Seneca Falls Keynote Address," delivered July 19, 1848, Seneca Falls, NY, https://susanbanthonyhouse.org/.
90 **One called them "'unsexed women'":** Naomi Wolf, *The Beauty Myth* (Harper Perennial, 2002), 68.
90 **Although there was a brief moment:** Faderman, *Odd Girls,* 62–63, 137.
92 **"midwives":** Faderman, *Odd Girls,* 60.
92 **But the phrase *female invert*:** Faderman, *Odd Girls,* 2.
92 **"inside out or upside down":** *Merriam-Webster Dictionary,* "invert," https://www.merriam-webster.com/.
92 **psychological males:** Faderman, *Odd Girls and Twilight Lovers,* 41.
92 **Although sex researchers:** Faderman, *Odd Girls and Twilight Lovers,* 48.
93 **Although Freud's theory:** Faderman, *Odd Girls and Twilight Lovers,* 130–31.

93 **"a time when authority":** Faderman, *Odd Girls and Twilight Lovers,* 131.

93 **"'lack emotional stability'":** Faderman, *Odd Girls and Twilight Lovers,* 142.

93 **"The United States was gripped":** *The Lavender Scare,* directed by Josh Howard (Full Exposure Films, 2017).

94 **A report put out by the State Department:** John D'Emilio and Estelle B. Freedman, *Intimate Matters: A History of Sexuality in America* (University of Chicago Press, 1988), 293.

94 **One victim, Frank Kameny:** Eric Marcus, *Making Gay History: The Half-Century Fight for Lesbian and Gay Equal Rights* (Perennial, 2002), 80.

94 **"I had no source of income":** Eric Marcus, host, *Making Gay History,* podcast, "Episode 5: Frank Kameny," Season 1.

94 **His bold appeals:** Judith Adkins, "'These People Are Frightened to Death': Congressional Investigations and the Lavender Scare," *Prologue Magazine* 48, no. 2 (Summer 2016).

95 **"They say they have evidence":** *The Lavender Scare,* dir. Howard.

95 **To be invited to Mattachine:** Lillian Faderman and Stuart Timmons, *Gay L.A.: A History of Sexual Outlaws, Power Politics, and Lipstick Lesbians* (Basic Books, 2006), 113–14.

95 **People who displayed their sexuality:** Duncan Osborne, "Cops in Middle of Early Gay Internecine Jockeying," *Gay City News,* August 16, 2018; Caleb Crain, "Frank Kameny's Orderly, Square Gay-Rights Activism," *The New Yorker,* June 22, 2020.

97 **"A Black group":** Sherri L. Smith, *What Is the Civil Rights Movement?* (Penguin Workshop, 2020), 34.

97 **Montgomery bus activist Aurelia Browder:** Smith, *What Is the Civil Rights Movement?,* 35.

98 **Taking cues:** Jo Yurcaba, "Different Fight, 'Same Goal': How the Black Freedom Movement Inspired Early Gay Activists," NBC News, February 28, 2021.

99 **"we were sick":** Marcus, "Episode 5: Frank Kameny."

99 **Because homosexual acts:** "1969: The Stonewall Uprising," LGBTQIA+ Studies: A Resource Guide, Library of Congress, https://guides.loc.gov/lgbtq-studies/.

99 **Officers could arrest:** Brynn Holland, "How the Mob Helped Establish NYC's Gay Bar Scene," History.com, June 22, 2017.

99 **Although there had been uprisings:** "1969: The Stonewall Uprising," Library of Congress.

99 **"an idea whose time had come":** Faderman, *Odd Girls and Twilight Lovers,* 195.

100 **"Although violent protest":** Faderman, *Odd Girls,* 195.

101 **"vestiges of the 'female slave mentality'":** Faderman, *Odd Girls,* 230.

101 **"declassed, unslick image":** Faderman, *Odd Girls,* 222.

101 **"represented artificial and destructive categories":** Faderman, *Odd Girls,* 222.

102 **"the lesbian was the same":** Faderman, *Odd Girls,* 202.

102 **" 'lesbian' has always been":** Faderman, *Odd Girls,* 205.

102 **"nonracist, nonageist":** Faderman, *Odd Girls,* 216.

102 **"return society to":** Faderman, *Odd Girls,* 227.

102 **"minor baby boom":** Faderman, *Odd Girls,* 291

102 **"clean and sober":** Faderman, *Odd Girls,* 281.

102 **feminism was out of fashion:** Sara M. Evans, "Feminism in the 1980s: Surviving the Backlash," in *Living in the Eighties,* eds. Gil Troy and Vincent J. Cannato (Oxford University Press, 2009), 85–97.

103 **"man-hating dykes":** Christina Scharff, " 'Unfeminine, Man-hating and Lesbian': Situating Stereotypes of Feminists in the Heterosexual Matrix," in *Repudiating Feminism: Young Women in a Neoliberal World* (Routledge, 2012).

103 **butch-femme dyad:** Lillian Faderman, "The Return of Butch and Femme: A Phenomenon in Lesbian Sexuality of the 1980s and 1990s," *Journal of the History of Sexuality* 2, no. 4 (April 1992): 578–96.

CHAPTER 5: DADDY

106 **I struggle to wipe away:** Stephanie Fairyington, "My Personal Struggle with Trans Acceptance," *Elle,* April 29, 2014.

106 **"Wait, so you're her mom":** Stephanie Fairyington, "I Asked My Brother to Donate Sperm to My Wife. That Was the Easy Part," *The New Republic,* October 31, 2014.

106 **At the height of Sabrina's:** Stephanie Fairyington, "Is Sexual Jealousy an Inevitable Part of Relationships?" CNN, December, 28, 2016.

106 **And yet, ironically:** Lee Edelman, *No Future: Queer Theory and the Death Drive* (Duke University Press, 2004).

108 **When I landed on your donor's profile:** Fairyington, "I Asked My Brother to Donate Sperm to My Wife."

114 **It killed me a little:** *The Parent Trap,* directed by Nancy Meyers (Walt Disney Pictures, 1998), screenplay by Nancy Meyers, Charles Shyer, and David Swift, based on *Das doppelte Lottchen* by Erich Kästner.

115 **twenty-nine percent:** Jamie Ballard, "What Americans Think about Gay Couples and Adoption," YouGov, June 26, 2018, https://today.yougov.com/society/articles/21068-most-americans-support-gay-couples-adopting-childr (accessed November 10, 2025).

116 **Aren't we all built:** Fairyington, "Is Sexual Jealousy an Inevitable Part of Relationships?"

116 **"I think that most people":** Krista Tippett, host, *On Being with Krista Tippett,* podcast, "Nick Cave—Loss, Yearning, Transcendence," November 22, 2023.

116 **The ancient Greeks knew this feeling:** Plato, *The Symposium,* trans. and ed. Christopher Gill (Penguin Classics, 2003), 22.

CHAPTER 6: PERCEPTIONS

119 **"Beauty prompts":** Elaine Scarry, *On Beauty and Being Just* (Princeton University Press, 2001), 4.

119 **"It is impossible to conceive":** Scarry, *On Beauty and Being Just,* 9.

120 **"If I had another face":** Glenn W. LaFantasie, "The Changing Face of Abraham Lincoln," *Salon,* May 29, 2011.

120 **"so awful ugly":** Stefan Lorant, "His Photographs Conceal the Real Lincoln; Lincoln's Photographs," *The New York Times Magazine,* February 13, 1949.

120 **"Lincoln is the leanest":** Brad Meltzer and Josh Mensch, "Trump, Stop Comparing Yourself to Lincoln," CNN, May 7, 2020.

120 **"horrible lantern jaws":** "Art: A Happy Mr. Lincoln," *Time,* February 14, 1955.

120 **"Well, for land sake":** Susan Bell, "Grotesque Yet Beloved: The Fascination with Abraham Lincoln's Body," USC Dornsife, February 13, 2015, https://dornsife.usc.edu/.

127 **Women don't seem to want:** Stephanie Fairyington, "Dad Accused of Inappropriate Behavior with His Son Said It Never Would Have Happened if He Were a Woman—and He's Right," *Elle,* August 16, 2017.

130 **"There are lots of different ways":** Todd Parr, *The Family Book* (Megan Tingley Books, 2003).

130 **"Each family is special":** Lesléa Newman, *Heather Has Two Mommies,* illus. Laura Cornell (Candlewick Press, 2015), 25.

133 **We stumbled through other things:** Stephanie Fairyington, "A Lesson in Queer Parenting That's Good for Any Family," *The Boston Globe,* December 20, 2020.

136 **"the way we never were in the visions":** Stephanie Coontz, *The Way We Never Were: American Families and the Nostalgia Trap,* 2nd ed. (New York: Basic Books, 2016).

CHAPTER 7: WEIRD GIRLS RULE

137 **"Is an era without ugliness":** Gretchen E. Henderson, *Ugliness: A Cultural History* (Reaktion Books, 2015), 181.

137 **"Ugliness is unpredictable":** Henderson, *Ugliness,* 10.

137 **Some people, like Isadora's mother:** Erica Jong, *Fear of Flying: 50th Anniversary Edition* (Berkley, 2023), 202.

140 **"anti-racist white, working-class":** "Transgender Pioneer and *Stone Butch Blues* Author Leslie Feinberg Has Died," *The Advocate,* November 17, 2014.

142 **"You don't get to live":** Renee Engeln, professor of psychology at North-

western University and author of *Beauty Sick,* in discussion with author, March 1, 2024.

142 **Singer-songwriter Elton John:** Cliff Jahr, "Elton John Comes Out As Bisexual in *Rolling Stone*'s 1976 Cover Story," *Rolling Stone,* October 7, 1976; Joshua Kanter, "The Long and Winding Yellow Brick Road: Three Must-Read Elton John Biographies," *Rolling Stone,* November 18, 2019.

142 **country singer k.d. lang:** Jacob Ogles, "k.d. lang Says Coming Out Denied Her a Chance to Remain Mysterious," *The Advocate,* July 12, 2019.

142 **rock star Melissa Etheridge:** Charna Flam, "Melissa Etheridge Shares She Used to Chat with Other Musicians About Being Gay Before They Came Out," *People,* February 3, 2024.

142 **the year after that, *Friends:*** *Friends,* season 1, episode 1, "The Pilot," written by David Crane and Marta Kauffman, directed by James Burrows, aired September 22, 1994, on NBC.

142 **Enrique "Rickie" Vasquez came out:** *My So-Called Life,* season 1, episode 15, "So-Called Angels," written by Winnie Holzman and Jason Katims, directed by Scott Winant, aired December 22, 1994, on ABC.

145 **"Disobedience, in the eyes of anyone":** Oscar Wilde, *The Soul of Man Under Socialism* (Arthur L. Humphreys, 1912), 10–11.

145 **"no attractive accomplishments":** Charlotte Brontë, *Villette* (Andrew Melrose, 1906), 147.

145 **"the three happiest years":** Brontë, *Villette,* 505.

146 **"There is more ado":** Michel de Montaigne, *Essays of Michel de Montaigne,* vol. 1, trans. Charles Cotton, ed. William Carew Hazlitt (1877; eBooks@Adelaide, 2010).

146 **A century later:** Giambattista Vico, *The New Science of Giambattista Vico,* trans. Thomas Goddard Bergin and Max Harold Fisch (Cornell University Press, 1948).

146 **German philosopher Friedrich Nietzsche:** Friedrich Nietzsche, *The Will to Power,* trans. Walter Kaufmann and R. J. Hollingdale, ed. Walter Kaufmann (Vintage Books, 1968), 267.

146 **He challenged the very notion:** Friedrich Nietzsche, *Thus Spoke Zarathustra: A Book For All Time,* trans. Adrian Del Caro, eds. Adrian Del Caro and Robert Pippin (Cambridge University Press, 2006), 156.

147 **Around the same time:** Ferdinand de Saussure, *Course in General Linguistics,* ed. Charles Bally and Albert Sechehaye, in collab.with Albert Reidlinger, trans. Wade Baskin (Philosophical Library, 1959), 78.

147 **By the twentieth century:** Émile Durkheim, *The Rules of Sociological Method,* ed. Steven Lukes, trans. W. D. Halls (The Free Press, 1982), 101.

148 **"I felt alien my whole life":** Amy Raphael, "The Life and Deaths of Patti Smith," *The Guardian,* November 1, 2008.

149 **"She couldn't sing":** Altrockchick, "Patti Smith–Horses–Classic Music Review," Altrockchick.com, September 8, 2014.

149 **"I'm not hung up":** Kate Branch, "Why Patti Smith Is a Beauty Icon, from Her Choppy Bob to Her Bedhead," *Vogue,* September 14, 2017.

149 **"I was aware that being a female":** Patti Smith, "Patti Smith Explains It All," interview by *Harper's Bazaar,* February 17, 2023, https://www.facebook.com/HarpersBazaar/videos/patti-smith-explains-it-all/346935802672196l/.

149 **Honoring her own creative direction:** *Rolling Stone,* "The 500 Greatest Albums of All Time," *Rolling Stone,* December 31, 2023.

150 **After the duo's TV ministry:** Ingrid Vasquez, "Husband of Jessica Hahn, Secretary in Jim and Tammy Faye Bakker Scandal, Files for Divorce," *People,* last updated July 13, 2023; Peter Applebome, "Bakker Is Convicted on All Counts: First Felon Among TV Evangelists," *The New York Times,* October 6, 1989; Jacques Peterson, "Jim and Tammy Faye Bakker's Son Reveals a Side of the Infamous Televangelists That You've NEVER Seen Before—As He Lifts the Lid on His Late Mother's Scandalous Legacy and His 'Complicated' Relationship with His Ailing Father," *Daily Mail,* March 3, 2024.

151 **"Tammy Faye Bakker had taken her makeup off":** Paul Krassner, "A Funny Thing Happened . . . ," *Los Angeles Times,* June 26, 1988.

151 **"Honey, I am going to my grave":** Tammy Faye Messner, interview by Larry King, "The Best Interviews with Jim Bakker and Tammy Faye Bakker," *Larry King Weekend,* CNN, June 24, 2001.

151 **After all, she ignored:** Associated Press, "Tammy Faye Messner, PTL Queen, Dies of Cancer," *Los Angeles Daily News,* updated August 29, 2017.

152 **She obviously wasn't just trying:** "Fauxnique's Life in Drag," *SF/Arts,* https://www.sfarts.org/story/fauxniques-life-in-drag-3qNMGQmyclRBkoCN8SIGxc.

153 **40 percent of school-age girls:** Renee Engeln, *Beauty Sick* (HarperCollins, 2017), 3,6. Kindle; Nadia Micali, Maria G. Martini, Jennifer J. Thomas, et al., "Lifetime and 12-Month Prevalence of Eating Disorders Amongst Women in Mid-Life: A Population-Based Study of Diagnoses and Risk Factors," *BMC Medicine* 15, no. 12 (2017); Michelle Kim Leff, M.D., M.B.A., Jocelyn Sudds-Allen, M.P.H., and Laura K. Grubb, M.D., M.P.H., "Breaking the Silence: What Everyone Should Know About Eating Disorders," Substance Abuse and Mental Health Services Administration (SAMHSA) Blog, February 27, 2025, accessed November 22, 2025, https://url.us.m.mimecastprotect.com/s/97AbC1w9qVhp2gkXotLfOFVEytt?domain=samhsa.gov https://www.samhsa.gov/blog/breaking-silence-what-everyone-should-know-about-eating-disorders.

154 **Unless men are socialized:** Parija Kavilanz, "The 'Sephora Kid' Trend Shows Tweens Are Psyched About Skincare. But Their Overzealous Approach Is Raising Concerns," CNN, March 12, 2024; C. Rosen and J. Gross, "Prevalence of Weight Reducing and Weight Gaining in Adolescent Girls and Boys," *Health Psychology* 6, no. 2 (1987): 131–47, https://doi

.org/10.1037//0278-6133.6.2.131; D. Neumark-Sztainer and P. J. Hannan, "Weight-Related Behaviors among Adolescent Girls and Boys: Results from a National Survey," *Archives of Pediatrics & Adolescent Medicine* 154, no. 6 (June 2000): 569–77, https://doi.org/10.1001/archpedi.154.6.569.

155 **In a 1999 study:** Richard S. Strauss, "Self-reported Weight Status and Dieting in a Cross-sectional Sample of Young Adolescents: National Health and Nutrition Examination Survey III," *Archives of Pediatrics & Adolescent Medicine* 153, no. 7 (July 1999): 741–47; Jamie Ducharme, "More U.S. Teenagers Are Trying to Lose Weight Than in Years Past. That May Be Reason for Concern," *Time*, July 17, 2019.

155 **Some of these young dieters:** Stuart B. Murray, Eva Pila, Scott Griffiths, and Daniel Le Grange, "When Illness Severity and Research Dollars Do Not Align: Are We Overlooking Eating Disorders?" *World Psychiatry* 16, no. 3 (September 2017): 321; American Society of Plastic Surgeons, *2024 ASPS Procedural Statistics Release*, 31–32.

156 **And here's what's really grave:** Susan Brownmiller, *Against Our Will: Men, Women, and Rape* (New York: Simon & Schuster, 1975); Laura Mulvey, "'Visual Pleasure and Narrative Cinema,'" in *Feminist Film Theory: A Reader* (Edinburgh: Edinburgh University Press, 1999), 58–69, https://doi.org/10.1515/9781474473224-009; Martha C. Nussbaum, "Objectification," in *Sex and Social Justice* (New York: Oxford University Press, 1999), 213–39.

156 **Even when you perform:** L.O.L. Surprise!, "Fix My Crown," track 7 on *Fierce*, Magic Star/Masterworks, 2021

157 **L.O.L. dolls:** Parija Kavilanz, "He Left the Slums of Iran as a Teen. Now He Runs One of America's Biggest Toy Companies," CNN Business, last updated November 21, 2018.

157 **"The master's tools":** Audre Lorde, *Sister Outsider: Essays and Speeches* (Crossing Press, 2007), 112.

157 **"While women, too":** Susan Sontag, Notes on 'Camp' (Picador, 2019), 6–8.

158 **In the United States alone:** Research and Markets, *United States Weight Loss Market Status & Forecast Report 2024: $90 Billion Industry Growth Driven by Explosive Sales of GLP-1 Prescription Drugs*, GlobeNewswire, May 31, 2024, via *Yahoo Finance;* IBISWorld, "Beauty, Cosmetics & Fragrance Stores in the US–Market Size (2005–2031)," IBISWorld.com, updated October 2025; Mintel, "US Adult Clothing Market Report 2024," Mintel.com, accessed October 4, 2025; "New 2022 Data from the Aesthetic Society Reveals a Surge in Nonsurgical Procedures Contributing to a 14% Overall Increase in Aesthetic Procedures," Aesthetic Society, August 14, 2023; IBISWorld, "Gym, Health & Fitness Clubs in the US–Market Size (2005–2031)," IBISWorld.com, updated May 2025, accessed October 4, 2025.

158 **"It's really a great tactic":** Robin M. Mathy, a trans researcher and activist, in discussion with the author, June 14, 2024.

158 **Defined in the fifth edition:** Substance Abuse and Mental Health Services Administration, "DSM-5 Changes: Implications for Child Serious Emotional Disturbance" (SAMHSA, 2016), table 23.

159 **When I consider:** Dan J. Stein, Andrea C. Palk, and Kenneth S. Kendler, "What Is a Mental Disorder? An Exemplar-Focused Approach," *Psychological Medicine* 51, no. 6 (April 12, 2021): 894–901.

159 **"experience their bodies":** Engeln, *Beauty Sick,* 30.

159 **She also points out:** Engeln, *Beauty Sick,* 6.

159 **"Woman" as "part":** Gen. 2:21–24.

160 **"discourse we never chose":** Judith Butler, *The Psychic Life of Power: Theories in Subjection* (Stanford University Press, 1997), 2.

162 **she was "too ugly":** Barbra Streisand, interview by Mike Wallace, *60 Minutes,* CBS, November 24, 1991, https://www.youtube.com/watch?v=Xw5dQBZavUw.

162 **"odd, skinny":** Streisand, *60 Minutes.*

162 **"The truth is that":** Barbra Streisand, interview by Barbara Walters, *20/20,* ABC, November 19, 1993, posted by John Flanagan, June 25, 2020, https://www.youtube.com/watch?v=5jWk9h5EJi4.

162 **"Why would I take off my bump?":** Barbra Streisand, interview by Gayle King, *CBS News Sunday Morning,* November 3, 2023.

163 **"Who knew what it":** Barbra Streisand, *My Name Is Barbra* (Viking, 2023), 57.

163 ***Wake me up:*** *Wham!,* directed by Chris Smith (Netflix, 2023).

164 **"What kinds of reward":** Jack Halberstam, *The Queer Art of Failure* (Duke University Press, 2011), Kindle, 131.

165 **"Some people think":** "Oh Bondage Up Yours!" X-Ray Spex, written by and featuring Poly Styrene, Virgin, released as a single in 1977.

165 **"subverted her voice":** *The Punk Years,* directed by Fay Gibson and Veerinder Mann.

165 **"I wanted to be different":** Poly Styrene, interview by John Clarkson, "X Ray Spex," *Pennyblackmusic,* July 24, 2005, https://pennyblackmusic.co.uk/.

166 **"I did cover myself up":** Poly Styrene, "Fighting Her Corner: An Interview With Poly Styrene," interview by Zoë Howe, *The Quietus,* March 21, 2011, https://thequietus.com/.

166 **"There are a lot more girls":** Poly Styrene, "Poly Styrene Interview: One of the Last Interviews with the Punk Icon," interview by Alex Hopley, *Flux,* 2011, https://www.fluxmagazine.com/.

166 **She got the idea:** *Poly Styrene: I Am a Cliché,* directed by Celeste Bell and Paul Sng (Modern Films, 2021).

166 **"deodorant":** Poly Styrene, "Germfree Adolescents," on *Germfree Adolescents,* X-Ray Spex, 1978, EMI International, LP.

169 **"You'd have to kill me":** Stephen Wood, "Life Through a Lens: Jodie Foster for Issue 92," *The Rake,* February 2024.

169 **a poll by True&Co.:** Chris Marino, "A New Poll Says Most Women Experience Anxiety While Shopping," *iHeart,* October 8, 2020.

170 **He even encourages her:** "What Makes You Beautiful," on *Up All Night,* One Direction, 2011, Syco Music/Columbia Records.

173 **"Go ugly up":** *The Simpsons,* season 21, episode 21, "Moe Letter Blues," written by Stephanie Gillis, directed by Matthew Nastuk, aired May 9, 2010, on Fox.

173 **"I'm ugly, dad":** *The Simpsons,* season 4, episode 4, "Lisa the Beauty Queen," written by Jeff Martin, directed by Mark Kirkland, aired October 15, 1992, on Fox.

174 **Ian, who came out:** Joe Lynch, "Janis Ian Opens Up About Losing Her Voice, Industry Frustrations & Agreeing to Make a Documentary," *Billboard,* April 3, 2025.

174 **"beauty queens":** Janis Ian, "At Seventeen," on *Between the Lines,* Columbia Records, 1975.

CHAPTER 8: CLEAN

178 **"a cruel, dirty, repulsive woman":** Emilie Le Beau Lucchesi, *Ugly Prey: An Innocent Woman and the Death Sentence That Scandalized Jazz Age Chicago* (Chicago Review Press, 2017), 22.

181 **" 'Spectrum' gives you degrees":** Susan Stryker, trans activist, scholar, and author of *Transgender History,* in discussion with author, January 2, 2024.

182 **"I'll ask a student":** Robin M. Mathy, in discussion with the author, June 14, 2024.

183 **"I read some of that":** Susan Stryker, in discussion with author, January 2, 2024.

CHAPTER 9: A THEORETICAL LIFE

187 **Even while:** Ariane de Vogue and Devan Cole, "Supreme Court Limits LGBTQ Protections with Ruling in Favor of Christian Web Designer," CNN, July 1, 2023; Ian Millhiser, "Did the Supreme Court Just Overrule One of Its Most Important LGBTQ Rights Decisions?" *Vox,* August 19, 2024; Andrew Chung, "US Supreme Court Leans Toward Parents Who Object to Elementary School LGBT Storybooks," Reuters, April 22, 2025.

187 **eight in ten Americans:** HRC Staff, "ICYMI: New Data Shows Support for LGBTQ+ Rights Reaches Highest Rates Ever Recorded," Human Rights Campaign, March 27, 2023, https://www.hrc.org/.

187 **Some people in the queer community:** Lee Edelman, *No Future: Queer Theory and the Death Drive* (Duke University Press, 2004); Heather Love,

Feeling Backward: Loss and the Politics of Queer History (Harvard University Press, 2007); Jack Halberstam, *The Queer Art of Failure* (Duke University Press, 2011).

189 **who also felt unattractive:** Cristina Rouvalis, "My Perfect, Imperfect Body," *Carnegie Magazine,* Fall 2016.

189 **"Fantasy love":** Andy Warhol, *The Philosophy of Andy Warhol (From A to B and Back Again)* (A Harvest Book/Harcourt, Inc., 1975), 44.

190 **a sociological concept:** Stephanie Fairyington, "'Heather Has Two Mommies' Is Still Relevant 30 Years Later," *The New York Times,* April 17, 2020, originally published in *NYT Parenting,* June 26, 2019.

190 **Pitman, whose book:** Ashley Holstrom, "ALA Announces 2018's Top 11 Banned Books," *Book Riot,* April 10, 2019, https://bookriot.com/2018-top-11-banned-books/.

191 **"Heather also has":** Lesléa Newman, *Heather Has Two Mommies,* illus. Laura Cornell (Candlewick Press, 2015), 4.

192 **It felt queerly relatable:** Kase Wickman, "The Poetic Tragedy of Andrew Lloyd Webber's Last Moments with His Son," *Vanity Fair,* April 19, 2023.

193 **"the love that dare not":** Lord Alfred Douglas, "Two Loves," Poets.org, accessed September 25, 2025, https://poets.org/poem/two-loves.

193 **But it could just as easily be seen:** Eleanor Cummins, "Bodies Are Canceled," *Wired,* October 10, 2021.

193 **Until I experienced otherwise:** Jean Hunleth, "Zambian Children's Imaginal Caring: On Fantasy, Play, and Anticipation in an Epidemic," *Cultural Anthropology* 34, no. 2 (2019); Justyna Deszcz-Tryhubczak, "Reading About Solidarity and Collective Action: Social Minds in Radical Fantasy Fiction," *Children's Literature in Education* 51 (2020): 144–59.

CHAPTER 10: LIFE AFTER DEATH

200 **Studies show that some women:** Marianne Clark, "Whose Eyes?: Women's Experiences of Changing in a Public Change Room," *Phenomenology and Practice* 5, no. 2 (2011): 57–72.

200 **Lesbians, especially gender-nonconforming ones:** Shannon S. C. Herrick and Lindsay R. Duncan, "Locker-Room Experiences Among LGBTQ+ Adults," *Journal of Sport and Exercise Psychology* 42, no. 3 (May 2020), 227–39: Ellen D. B. Riggle, "Experiences of a Gender Non-Conforming Lesbian in the 'Ladies' (Rest)room," *Journal of Lesbian Studies* 22, no. 4 (2018): 482–95.

200 **One queer woman named Bente:** Johannes Müller and Nicola Böhlke, "'I Somehow Had the Feeling That I Did Not Belong There': Experiences of Gay and Lesbian Recreational Athletes in German Sports Clubs," *International Journal of the Sociology of Leisure* 5 (2022): 337–57.

204 **"I think that it is part":** Peter Wood, "Higher Sex Ed," National Association of Scholars, August 30, 2011.

204 **Similarly, I wondered:** Stephanie Fairyington, "What It Felt Like to Show Myself Physical Affection for a Week," *Oprah Daily,* January 12, 2022.

204 **Obviously I'm not the first:** Kendall Poovey, David C. de Jong, and Kasey Morey, "The Roles of Body Image, Sexual Motives, and Distraction in Women's Sexual Pleasure," *Archives of Sexual Behavior* 51, no. 3 (2022): 1577–89; Cherie L. La Rocque and Jan Cioe, "An Evaluation of the Relationship Between Body Image and Sexual Avoidance," *The Journal of Sex Research* 48, no. 4 (2011): 397–408; Renata Forste, Marina Potter, and Lance Erickson, "Sad and Lonely: Body Dissatisfaction Among Adolescent Girls," *International Journal of Adolescent Medicine and Health* 31, no. 2 (June 21, 2017).

205 **"cognitive dissonance theory":** Leon Festinger, *A Theory of Cognitive Dissonance* (Stanford University Press, 1957).

206 **In one study, nearly 25 percent:** Shannon R. Kenney, Vandana Thadani, Tehniat Ghaidarov, and Joseph W. LaBrie, "First-Year College Women's Motivations for Hooking Up: A Mixed-Methods Examination of Normative Peer Perceptions and Personal Hookup Participation," *International Journal of Sexual Health* 25, no. 3 (July 2013): 212–24.

206 **Sociology professor and author:** Lisa Wade, sociology professor and author of *American Hookup,* in discussion with author, May 22, 2024.

206 **In an interview she gave:** "Sociology Professor Lisa Wade on the Rules of Hookup Culture," *The Longing Lab* (podcast), season 2, episode 17, October 31, 2023, Apple Podcasts.

207 **(And women who abide):** Michelle Denise L. Ferreol, "Study: Cosmetics Significantly Influence Perceptions," *The Harvard Crimson,* October 7, 2011, https://www.thecrimson.com/article/2011/10/7/study-makeup-cosmetics-participants/.

208 **"Pink goes with everything":** Lizzo, "Pink," from *Barbie: The Album,* produced by Mark Ronson and Andrew Wyatt, Atlantic Records, 2023.

210 **"from their inner experience":** Peggy Orenstein, *Cinderella Ate My Daughter: Dispatches from the Front Lines of the New Girlie-Girl Culture* (HarperCollins, 2011), 166.

210 **psychologist Mary Pipher:** Mary Pipher, *Reviving Ophelia: Saving the Selves of Adolescent Girls* (Riverhead Books, 2019), 8.

211 **"paid for":** "What Was I Made For?" performed by Billie Eilish, written and produced by Billie Eilish and Finneas O'Connell, from *Barbie: The Album,* Atlantic Records, 2023.

212 **Alumni as loftily situated:** Eric Levenson and Gregory Lemos, "Cornel West Resigns from Harvard After Tenure Dispute and Accuses University of 'Spiritual Rot,'" CNN, last updated July 13, 2021; Kris King, "Belonging at Harvard: Moving Beyond Acceptance," *The Harvard Crimson,* May 23, 2024.

212 **"I learned that if you didn't fit in":** Due Quach, "Poor and Traumatized at Harvard," Medium, January 3, 2016.

214 **nearly 8.5 million people:** United States Census Bureau, "QuickFacts: New York City, New York," accessed June 11, 2025, https://www.census.gov/.

CHAPTER 11: AFFIRMING OUR DIFFERENCES

224 **Around the time of our visit:** Bomba Estéreo, "Soy Yo," track 4 on *Amanecer,* Sony Music Latin, 2015.

224 **Watching you two:** L.O.L. Surprise!, "Fix My Crown," track 7 on *Fierce,* Magic Star/Masterworks, 2021.

225 **Historically, noisily:** "Black Is Beautiful: The Emergence of Black Culture and Identity in the 1960s and '70s," National Museum of African American History & Culture, accessed June 12, 2025, https://nmaahc.si.edu/.

226 **"different voice":** Carol Gilligan, *In a Different Voice: Psychological Theory and Women's Development* (Harvard University Press, 1982).

228 **I had just interviewed Libryia Jones:** Stephanie Fairyington, "Why One Woman Launched a Company to Help Single Moms Travel," *Oprah Daily,* November 4, 2022.

CHAPTER 12: TRANSCENDENCE

235 **In a world that encourages:** Stephanie Fairyington, "Find Your Lightness of Being by Learning to Care a Little Less About Everything," *Oprah Daily,* April 15, 2022.

237 **"the denial of negation":** Perry Meisel, "Sadness Starts Early," *The New York Times,* February 25, 1990.

237 **"devalued—dismissed, belittled":** Kelly Oliver, philosophy professor and author of *Reading Kristeva,* in discussion with author, June 9, 2025, and September 6, 2025.

239 **"Scat . . . defies":** George Burrows, "How Scat Singing Became an Expressive Language in Its Own Right," *The Independent,* November 1, 2018.

239 **"glimpses of love":** Eckhart Tolle, *The Power of Now: A Guide to Spiritual Enlightenment* (New World Library, 1999), 29.

239 **"It's not the notes you play":** Corinna da Fonseca-Wollheim, "How the Silence Makes the Music," *The New York Times,* October 2, 2019.

241 **"When . . . we are too focused":** Dacher Keltner, *Awe: The New Science of Everyday Wonder and How It Can Transform Your Life* (New York: Penguin Press, 2023), 33.

242 **In the book of Genesis:** Gen. 2:17.

242 **"The great image":** Lao Tzu, *Tao Te Ching,* trans. D. C. Lau (Penguin Books, 1963), 48.

ABOUT THE AUTHOR

Stephanie Fairyington is a journalist who writes on gender, sexuality, family, and parenting. A former contributing writer for *The Advocate* and former senior staff writer at Arianna Huffington's *Thrive Global,* her work has appeared in *The New York Times, The Boston Globe,* and *The Atlantic,* among others. She lives in Brooklyn with her spouse and daughter.

A NOTE ON THE TYPE

This book was set in a typeface named Bulmer. This distinguished letter is a replica of a type long famous in the history of English printing that was designed and cut by William Martin in about 1790 for William Bulmer of the Shakespeare Press. In design, it is all but a modern face, with vertical stress, sharp differentiation between the thick and thin strokes, and nearly flat serifs. The decorative italic shows the influence of Baskerville, as Martin was a pupil of John Baskerville's.

Composed by North Market Street Graphics,
Lancaster, Pennsylvania

Designed by Casey Hampton